STOCKHOLM

STOCKHOLM

A CULTURAL HISTORY

Tony Griffiths

OXFORD
UNIVERSITY PRESS

2009

OXFORD
UNIVERSITY PRESS

Oxford University Press, Inc., publishes works that further
Oxford University's objective of excellence
in research, scholarship, and education.

Oxford New York
Auckland Cape Town Dar es Salaam Hong Kong Karachi
Kuala Lumpur Madrid Melbourne Mexico City Nairobi
New Delhi Shanghai Taipei Toronto

With offices in
Argentina Austria Brazil Chile Czech Republic France Greece
Guatemala Hungary Italy Japan Poland Portugal Singapore
South Korea Switzerland Thailand Turkey Ukraine Vietnam

Published by Oxford University Press, Inc.
198 Madison Avenue, New York, New York 10016

www.oup.com

Oxford is a registered trademark of Oxford University Press

Co-published in Great Britain by Signal Books

Library of Congress Cataloging-in-Publication Data
Griffiths, Tony, 1940—
Stockholm: a cultural history / Tony Griffiths.
     p. cm.—(Cityscapes)
Includes bibliographical references and index.
ISBN 978-0-19-538637-0; 978-0-19-538638-7 (pbk.)
1. Stockholm (Sweden)—History.   2. Stockholm (Sweden)—Social
life and customs.   I. Title.
DL976.3.G75   2009
948.7'3—dc22   2009030105

Illustrations: dreamstime.com: xviii, 57, 120, 136, 156, 164, 174, 190, 192, 206, 214;
istockphoto.com: i, viii, xii, 2, 8, 13, 60; wikipedia: 15, 132, 203, 208; ikea-gropu.ikea.com:
71; systembolaget.se: 122, 126

9 8 7 6 5 4 3 2 1

Printed in the United States of America
on acid-free paper

Contents

Preface and Acknowledgements

By the beginning of the twenty-first century Stockholmers were proud enough to boast that they no longer lived in a small remote, isolated country on the fringes of Europe but were entitled to call their city the Capital of Scandinavia. Not everybody was convinced. Ingmar Bergman described Stockholm as not a city at all: "it is ridiculous to think of itself as a city. It is simply a rather large village set in the middle of some forest and some lakes. You wonder what it thinks it's doing there, looking so important." Stockholm City remains at variance with Ingmar Bergman and gives away a seventy-page booklet proclaiming "Stockholm—the Capital of Scandinavia". This publication does not sit well with the natural reticence of Swedes. Its back cover contains a paragraph explaining the perspective:

> There are many reasons why Stockholm is the natural capital of Scandinavia. One is that Stockholm is positioned at the heart of the region, and enjoys the benefits of a world-class transport infrastructure. Another is that it is the largest city in the largest country in Scandinavia. It is also where you find the most multi-national companies, the largest stock market and, not least, the most visitors. People come to Stockholm for the food, the design and the music. Stockholm also enjoys the highest densities of galleries and museums in the world, and every year the eyes of the world are on Stockholm when the Nobel Prizes are awarded. Welcome to Stockholm—the Capital of Scandinavia.

To get visitors interested, the City of Stockholm created a bright yellow and green format on the front of the booklet, eighty per cent of which was taken up by three anorexic Swedish girls in funny hats, wearing off the shoulder camisoles trimmed with pink silk rip cords. The girls' various expressions of shock, amusement and beaming contentment leaves the visitor in no doubt that a good time will be had by all. Linking the girls to the possibilities of shopping, nightlife, museums, galleries, recreation and special events is a white stick-on badge with the slogan "Stockholm. The capital of Scandinavia", surmounted by the unique and ubiquitous three pointed simple crown of the Swedish sovereign.

The Swedish crown is not a much-loved symbol in Scandinavia, which is after all primarily a geographic term for the peninsula stretching through Denmark to North Cape. The Finns are not Scandinavian by race or inclination, and the citizens of Helsinki are as annoyed as their cousins in Oslo, Copenhagen and Reykjavik at Stockholm using Silvio Berlusconi's media techniques to promote a questionable image.

This book nevertheless describes progress. Stockholm has grown from a Viking landing stage in the ninth century to be the capital of one of the world's most civilized nations. The city has nurtured such monarchs as Gustav Vasa, Queen Christina and the Bernadottes. Swedish sovereigns have been European strongmen and have personified successful adaptation to social change. The city has housed outstanding intellectuals, brilliant inventors and philanthropic business geniuses. It was home to the political perfection of a society organized under the umbrella of social democracy, and a pantheon of its citizens are household names everywhere, although not always recognized as Swedish. Modesty as well as achievement is still to be found among the city's birch groves, granite rocks, lakes, islands and copper domes.

☞

I should like to thank my publishers Michael J. Dwyer and James Ferguson for commissioning this book and for keeping an eye on me, even when I was once crossing the causeway from South Uist to visit Eriskay. It was very agreeable to work with Ruth Harris on this book. For encouraging my interest in Swedish culture, I am grateful to a group who would never say mine is bigger than yours: Ulf Beijbom, Amanda Bettesworth, Richard Blandy, Margaret Bowden, Suzanne Champonnois, Brian Chatterton, Lyn Chatterton, Ian Chubb, Robert Dessaix, Vesna Drapac, Karin Ehnblom-Palmquist, Pam Griffiths, Debra Hackett, Geoff Harcourt, Bo Heinebäck, Kent Johansson, Inge Jonsson, Sune Jungar, Olavi Koivukangas, Baiba Metuzale Kangere, Alexsander Loit, Bosse Lundberg, Lille-Maj Lundberg, Richard Maggs, John Martin, Jane Mitta, Mark Proctor, Chris Rann, Liz Raymond, Åsa Ringbom, Håkan Ringbom, David Seaton, Doris Stockmann and Hugh Stretton, none of whom are in any way endorsing what follows.

Introduction

Touring the Terrain

Riddarholm

I had an apartment in Vasagatan, in the shadow of the *systembolaget*, premises belonging to the state alcohol monopoly. Vasagatan is named after the most famous royal dynasty in Sweden, and naturally the street is appropriately located at the centre of things. From Vasagatan the Vasa Bridge connects downtown Stockholm with the island on which the city began, Gamla Stan. Completed in 1878, the Vasa Bridge lines up with Stora Nygatan, literally the big new street, but new a very long time ago. Touring Stockholm's terrain, ignore Gamla Stan for the moment and turn right instead at the end of the Vasa Bridge towards Riddarholm, the Knight's Harbour.

I can imagine Yinka Shonibare, nominated for the 2004 Turner Prize, doing this, wandering around Stockholm's landscape, as part of his investigation into the relationship between power and class, colonialism and European technology. As imperialists went, the Swedes were small beer. There was a Swedish East India Company founded by a Gothenburg merchant, Niklas Sahlgren. Its earliest ship, *Friedericus Rex Sueciae*, sailed for China with a Scot on board, Colin Campbell, who was the King of Sweden's first *de facto* ambassador to China. The SEIC was profitable for only a couple of decades, and was put out of business by the English and the Dutch, not lasting long enough to take part in the scramble for Africa.

Shonibare probably walked across the Vasa Bridge and crossed the even smaller bridge to Riddarholm. Riddarholm is a tiny island indeed, but as the headquarters of Sweden's ruling class for three or four hundred years it is very important. In 1773 the Swedish nobility erected a statue of Gustav Vasa to celebrate the 250th anniversary of the day that the young noble entered Stockholm after a triumphant war to deliver his country from the Danish yoke.

Riddarholm is a place with mixed messages mirroring the ebb and flow of aristocratic fortunes. The island has one site marking the spot where three other nobles, Count Brahe and Barons Horn and Wrangle, were brought to the scaffold. They were executed on 13 July 1756, charged with conspiring to undermine the constitution. Marshal Axel von Fersen

Modern installation in front of the Riddarhuset

was lynched on more or less the same spot on 10 June 1810, by a mob who believed that he had poisoned and killed the Swedish crown prince.

Yinka Shonibare was born in London, grew up in Nigeria, studied art at Goldsmiths College and, in the reverse direction to Karen Blixen, stamped his image on African-Nordic intercourse. While *Out of Africa* changed the image of Danish-African colonialism, Shonibare opened up Stockholm to an audience which might not have been reached without his fame and insight. Shonibare's daring interpretations of the decline and fall of the French aristocracy during the French Revolution had shocked visitors to London's Tate Gallery. He created puzzling mannequins of decapitated aristocrats and headless European pro-consuls re-drawing the map of Africa with subdivisions of their new colonial empires, neatly placed behind artificially contrived borders.

When he moved north for a brief time to take his talent to Stockholm, Shonibare might have called his unforgettable interpretation of Swedish identity in the Vasa and Gustavian era *Out of Nigeria*. One of tens of thousands of visitors to the Swedish capital, Shonibare was unusually and obsessively interested in European high culture. He had a particular fascination with the doomed ruling class whose self-centred and frivolous existence was to be literally cut off at the neck.

Shonibare describes himself as post-colonial hybrid. He first became famous for his recreation of an eighteenth-century European painting by Jean-Honoré Fragonard. Clothed with Dutch wax-printed cotton textile, a life-size headless mannequin sitting on a swing suspended from a tree branch was purchased by the Tate Gallery in 2002. Shonibare followed this up with surreal tableaux of groups of beheaded aristocrats. His ranges of expression developed further in Stockholm. In a short film beginning with a shot of the winter landscape of Stockholm harbour, Shonibare explained how Sweden's capital and its icons drew out from his imagination a unique response in film and mixed media.

Shonibare focused his mind on Gustav III, who had almost single-handedly transformed Stockholm into a capital city reflecting an impressive and distinct national culture. It became home to the arts with a National Theatre, an Opera House and the Swedish Academy modelled on the French original. As T. K. Derry put it in *The New Cambridge Modern History*, the king himself adorned prose dramas that outlived their author, and a galaxy of talent adorned his court. For the generation before the

French Revolution, in Derry's catty words, "Stockholm, although over-shadowed by St. Petersburg, was still the centre of what was probably the foremost second-class power of Europe."

Walking in the tracks of the Swedish enlightened class, Shonibare would have learnt that their palace and club, the Knight's House or Riddarhuset took 39 years to complete. Simon and Jean de la Vallée, Heinrich Wilhelm and Jost Vingboons built it in the Dutch baroque style. It was finished in 1641. Riddarhus Square was the town centre until the 1850s. The spire of the Riddarholm Church signalled far and wide the importance of those who worshipped there. Conspicuous with a 290-foot cast-iron spire, the church was once the home of Stockholm's Franciscans, but since Gustav Adolf's time has been the burial place of Swedish kings. In one room on the ground floor are the portraits of all the Swedish marshals from 1627 to 1865, except for Count Lejonhufvud, who was blamed for the failures of a war in Finland and beheaded in 1743.

The Riddarhuset is far from an elephant's graveyard. Sculptures on its roof symbolize knightly virtues: nobility, intelligence, persistence, bravery, honour, prudence and strength. The display of wealth and power conveyed by the blinding glare of 2,330 copper shields on its walls is awe-inspiring. On the copper are painted the coats-of-arms of all Swedish nobles who have been members of the House of Nobility, one of the four houses of the old Swedish parliament. If books do furnish a room, blazing heraldic arms furnish a palace. When the 700 remaining nobles meet at the Riddarhuset for their regular commemorations in the twenty-first century they see not piles of tusks but the glittering icons of their vestigial privilege. In a city not lacking grand spaces for ceremonies the academies of science and literature choose to celebrate their milestone anniversaries there. The burnished and glittering coats-of-arms of the counts and barons are found on the west wall on either side of the bust of King Gustav II Adolph, and those of the gentry are displayed on the remaining three walls. The coats-of-arms are arranged in numerical order according to the year of introduction, the last recipient of royal patronage being the Swedish explorer Sven Hedin, in 1902.

Well dressed Stockholmers crowded fifty deep outside the Riddarhuset in December 1865 to cheer the nobility for voting away their power. A lengthy process of constitutional reform, triggered by the 1848 revolutions in Europe, was steered through in the thorough bureaucratic tradition of Swedish administrators by Louis de Geer. In 1886 reform acts changed the constitution so that the Swedish parliament only had two houses. The nobility and the clergy were no longer forces to be reckoned with. In 1970 the constitution was altered again to the present system in which Sweden has a parliament with one chamber only. Carl XVI Gustav was the first king to reign, but not rule, from 1973 under the new constitution. A change in the succession clauses in 1979 also gave royal women the same hereditary rights to the crown as men, thus Princess Victoria, not her younger brother Prince Carl Philip, will be the present king's successor.

Gustav Vasa cemented the nobility in a pre-eminent position in Swedish society. He devised the system under which the aristocracy was divided into three classes: counts and barons, descendants of councillors and holders of noble patents. Each family had one vote, cast by its head. In return for their influence the nobles were expected to take the lion's share of administration in war and peace. Beneath them in the hierarchy were the clergy, some members of the middle class, and tax-paying peasants. Monster town palaces and imposing country estates were lasting fruits of their labours. My favourite is Hasselby Castle, but more accessible is Carl Gustaf Wrangel's home on Riddarholm, which now houses the Supreme Court. Wrangel's Palace, as it is now called, was built on Birger Jarl's Torg for the nobleman Lars Sparre in 1629. Carl Gustaf Wrangel, commander in chief during the Thirty Years War, took it as reward for his military victories. It was the largest Stockholm palace in private hands.

Apart from a changing minority conspiring against the king and being executed for it, the nobles were generally bursting with positive energy and transformed Sweden into the major power in their region. By 1645 Sweden controlled the Baltic and had taken territory from Norway and Denmark to serve as buffer zones. Russians, Poles and German-speaking expansionists fled before them, and the French and the English considered the area to too hard to contemplate attacking. Yet by the end of the Napoleonic era Sweden's might was all but gone. Sweden lost Finland to Russia in 1809 and the compensation prize of union with Norway did little to boost Stockholm's imperialist spirit.

The Finnish-Norwegian foreign policy disaster coincided with a major crisis about who was to become the next Swedish king, and whether the Vasa dynasty and its successors remained fit to reign in Stockholm. A junior army officer, Baron C. E. Mörner (whose family still attends the Riddarhuset when appropriate) stepped into the role of diplomat-king-maker, travelling to Paris and securing one of Napoleon's marshals to end one dynasty and found another. Mörner and the ruling class chose Jean-Baptiste Bernadotte, but they had to appoint him at a special parliament held at Örebro (Stockholm was considered too dangerous). The fragility of public order had been all too clear when a mob killed Axel von Fersen while he was conducting the funeral of a Gustavian prince outside the Riddarhuset. The regiments called to line the funeral route had done nothing to protect the marshal from the crowd. Bernadotte rewarded Sweden for its confidence in making him crown prince and heir to the last Vasa. He took the name Carl XIV John, and founded the longest lasting of the Napoleonic dynasties after he was crowned King of Sweden and Norway in 1818.

From the Riddarhuset head for Stortorget, the Big Square, the real seat of political power, which in the last resort sometimes amounted to mob rule. Stortorget was Stockholm's major public meeting place. Photogenic old houses stand out from their gables to the street. For two hundred years Sweden's stock exchange, built in 1778, stood on the north side of the square. The floor of the stock exchange stopped trading in 1990 when expansion and technical advances demanded a more convenient site for the brokers. Above the ghosts of the investment community remain the academicians. The Swedish Academy holds its ceremonial gatherings on the upper floors of the old bourse, a tradition begun by Gustav III in 1786. I gave a plenary speech to a meeting there, called to celebrate the achievement of freedom by Latvia, Estonia and Lithuania from the former Soviet Union, and the view out of the windows, where most of my audience gazed, is stunning. Johan Wedelstam designed the porches which are a feature of the layout. On the west side of the square is the red painted Schantzska house at no. 20, where the limestone figures of Roman soldiers have always been described as remarkable. The Seyfridska house looks unchanged since it was finished in 1650 and Grilska house is much photographed because of its beauty. The cafés and restaurants in the vaulted cellars of some of the buildings round the square are greatly enjoyed by academicians and travellers alike.

While the nobility tried to rule Sweden from the Riddarhuset, their nominal chiefs, the Kings of Sweden, could keep an eye on them a twenty minute walk away in the Royal Palace on Gamla Stan. Fortifications have stood on the site of the Royal Palace since Viking times. The most imposing was the Three Crowns Castle. A thousand years later its massive defensive fortifications can still be seen in the new palace which replaced it after the old one burned to the ground. Between the thirteenth and seventeenth centuries the Three Crowns Castle became ever bigger. So-called because the king of the castle was also the King of Denmark and Norway and thus had three crowns to choose from, it was destroyed by one of the many fires Stockholm has experienced over the years. By the time the castle folk fled it had been transformed into a Renaissance palace. Its grand scale was dwarfed by the new castle, built to designs which made it bigger than Versailles and made Buckingham Palace by comparison a wood shed. From a modern point of view it was not homely, and the present king shifted his wife and children to Drottingnholm. No longer is the palace on Gamla Stan a private residence: 608 rooms are too many for a quiet family life. While the king is not often there to glance out of the window at the changing of the guard at midday in the palace courtyard, this ceremony is said to be Stockholm's most popular tourist event. It is certainly colorful. The guardsmen look as if their uniforms have been designed by a Japanese milliner with advice from Bismarck. Kitted out in spiked Prussian helmets and wearing white gloves, they cannot be missed in their bright blue uniforms.

SKEPPSHOLMEN

Leaving the diverting guards' band behind you, cross out of Gamla Stan and make you way to Skeppsholmen Island by crossing the Srömbron Bridge to Kungsträdgården. Kungsträdgården was once a rival to Villandry, a private vegetable and flower garden where the king could stroll alone and pick carrots; now it is a restful public oasis on the edge of a working city. Dominating the area on Södra Blasieholmshamnen is the unmistakable high profile of the Grand Hotel. The Grand Hotel is a child of the palace, where courtiers still daydream about restaurant food while eyeing the hotel across the water, Norrström, as they go about their royal duties. After all, one of them, Oscar II's French chef, Régis Cadier, founded the hotel in 1874. Thirty years later Baedeker declared that the Grand Hotel was the best hotel in Stockholm. "English is spoken," said Baedeker, "it has a fine view of the busy quays and harbour." A cat may look at a queen, es-

Changing of the guard, the Royal Palace

pecially from "a comfortable and well managed house ranking with the best hotels in Europe". Among the guests who gazed at the Swedish flag flying from the castle spire are the Nobel Prize winners, put up there since 1901. Grazing as well as gazing: the Nobel banquet was there until 1929, when it was moved to the city hall.

Resist the temptation to snoop inside for a while, and follow Shonibare's footsteps across the iron bridge onto Skeppsholmen, ship's harbour, the site of the Swedish Naval Arsenal for centuries. Now it is home to many of Stockholm's museums. Stockholm has a museum for everything. All are patronized by Swedes throughout the year and they are not static summer tourist attractions. Conservation, sensitive display and remembrance are important to many Stockholmers who appreciate living in a city undisturbed by war—the natural enemy of museums and galleries. There is a Maritime Museum, a State Museum, a telecommunications museum, a dance museum, an ethnographical museum and an architecture museum. There is also a Jewish museum. For those curious about the history of alcohol consumption there is the Spirithistoriska Museet. There is a museum for stamp collectors and one for those interested in post offices. There is a medical museum and a children's museum. The bloodthirsty and the bellicose can visit a museum in the Royal Palace on Gamla Stan and see an alarming collection of weapons and learn how Swedish armour evolved. A technical museum displays the telephone Ericsson made for Tsar Nicholas II in 1903. The current Royal Palace is almost all museums. Whatever your interest, it will be covered by an excellent coterie of conservators, attendants, sponsors and donors—and writers of guidebooks. In Stockholm these are invariably written by experts, reflecting the importance Stockholmers attach to an accurate depiction of their city's past. The main contributor to DK's *Eyewitness Stockholm*, for example, is Kaj Sandell, a skilled writer of business histories who has worked as a key journalist on Sweden's biggest daily newspaper, *Dagans Nyheter*, and been head of information for Scania trucks and buses.

On his trip to Stockholm, Shonibare was most interested in two museums, the Vasa Museum and the Museum of Modern Art, which had commissioned his work and provided him with inspiration. The Museum of Modern Art is avant-garde in an avant-garde town. A Stockholm jury chose Rafael Moneo to design the museum in 1998, the year Stockholm was designated the cultural capital of Europe. When you have had a look at the Museum of Modern Art, which exhibits work by Miró, Magritte, Kandinsky, Picasso and Matisse, as well as Shonibare, leave Skeppsholmen and head to another island, Djurgården. You get there aboard one of the exhibits from the Tram Museum, Tram 7E, which is bedecked with Swedish flags and painted bright blue and yellow; it will take you across the Djurgårdsbron to Djurgården.

DJURGÅRDEN

Djurgården was once a royal deer park, and is enticing in winter or summer. It stands on its own island, two miles long and about three-quarters of a mile wide, with delightful walks and cross-country skiing tracks through oak and pine woods. The park was laid out by Gustav III and Charles XIV John. The plush villas sheltering by the water's edge are places of work and relaxation. The Italian Embassy has the best spot. Dotted around the landscape are the private summer villas for the super wealthy such as exist everywhere in Europe. But Djurgården has never been truly exclusive. At a bus-stop now called Manilla there was once an asylum for the deaf, blind and dumb. At the turn of the twentieth century, a small

peninsula called Frisens Park was especially popular on summer Sunday afternoons, "with singing and dancing, but no spirits".

Djurgården tram's first stop is the Nordiska Museet. It has a grand
entrance up three small flights of stairs, each one more inviting as you step
up. It is a classic Edwardian museum in it organization, with a million
and a half exhibits, including sixteen paintings by Strindberg on the fourth
floor. The Nordiska Museet was at first largely financed by Oscar Dickson,
"a man of Scottish extraction", as Gosta Berg put it in *Scots in Sweden*.
The Scots are all but gone now, but Gustav Adolf had a Scottish body-
guard, as well as 34 Scots colonels and 50 lieutenant-colonels in his
command. Sixty castles had Scottish governors who ruled towns in con-
quered provinces of Germany. The Scots stood out in Stockholm, piping,
drinking whisky and sword dancing. A woodcut in 1555 showed them
doing this without kilts. They were often seen in the law courts, charging
their wives with adultery, although more often in the Riddarhuset, where
as nobles they hung their shields. Andreas Keith was Baron of Forsholm
and Finsta, Hans Stuart had an estate at Hedenlunda and was raised to the
nobility in 1579. His grandson, Carl Magnus Stuart, was military tutor of
Charles XII.

Scots came to make money as well as fight. In 1572 Swedes allowed
"foreign cavalrymen, German, Scots" to settle. The Scots disguised their
identity at first, but it became so fashionable to be Scottish that Swedes
faked Scottish ancestry for the cachet. Jacob MacDougall was the com-
mandant of Frankfurt and after generations and name changes Gustaf
Duwall became governor of Darlarna. James King became Baron of
Sanshult, while David Drummond was buried in Riddarholm Church—
at least his head was. The rest of his body was left where he fell fighting for
Sweden, "to facilitate transport." Scots joined the civil service. Dr. Jakob
Robertson was physician to Queen Christina. The list is endless, and as
Berg concluded: "With none of the small nations of Europe, outside
Scandinavia, has Sweden maintained such intimate connections through
the years as with Scotland. Only France can compete with Sweden as to
the number of enterprising Scots who have immigrated into the country."

My advice is to ignore the bridal crowns and dolls' houses and table
settings, and when you have looked at Strindberg's paintings head for
Rosendal Slott, Waldemarsudde and the Thielska Gallery. Ernest Thiel
was a banker who lost his fortune when banking ceased to be profitable

during the First World War. He moved from an apartment on Strandvägen to Djurgården when his major interest, collecting art, outgrew the space in his house. Ferdinand Boberg, a leading architect, drew up the designs for the villa, which is as focused and restful as the Nordiska Museet is overwhelming. Thiel was born to be a donor, not a banker. Anders Zorn, Edvard Munch, August Strindberg and Carl Larsson were members of his coterie. He bought their work, and in 1924 the state purchased Thiel's villa and its art contents. The Thielska Gallery is about as far as you go from the Djurgårdesbron without entering the Baltic, and the trip to the end of the island is an excursion into a long past world of well-spent wealth, privilege and bohemian pleasures.

From the Thielska Gallery retrace your steps to Waldemarsudde, the home of a modern prince, Prince Eugen. Ferdinand Boberg drew up the plans for his home as well. As royals are, Prince Eugen was schooled as an army officer, but he preferred the paintbrush and the palette to the baton. In fact, so good was his work that his monumental paintings hang in the Opera House, the Dramatic Theatre and the Town Hall. In Waldemarsudde itself hangs a collection of 2,000 paintings but it is as memorable for its sensitive waterfront siting and the impact of Boberg's design. The yellow walls and the copper roof reflect the tranquility of the area, and the guest apartments remain as they were when Prince Eugen died in 1947.

In an earlier generation, Frederick Blom built Rosendal Slott in the 1820s. It is a prefabricated kit home, one of the first ever. Sweden is now a major exporter of kit homes, and they withstand winter weather well, but Rosendal was only built as a summer retreat for an aristocrat missing France, and its survival is remarkable. It has been open to the public as a museum since 1913. After Rosendal, on the way out of Djurgården, leave the best for last and call in at the Vasamuseet to see the remains of what was the world's biggest ship in 1628. Before the exhumation of the *Vasa* (see Chapter Nine), Djurgården's main tourist attraction was Skansen, the world's first open-air museum.

SKANSEN: ROMANTIC NATIONALISM

Djurgården became more popular than ever when it was transformed into the home of the Swedish expression of romantic nationalism in the 1890s by the construction of Skansen. Dr. Artur Hazelius was the guiding spirit behind this transformation. He designed a 75-acre site and moved to it farm houses and their outbuildings from other parts of the Swedish countryside. Barns, dairies, piggeries, hay stores and anything that could be carted away as representative were cannibalized and rebuilt to celebrate national identity. Hazelius focused on the harsh landscape from the key province of Dalarna in his attempt to transcend internal regional boundaries with the overarching intention of promoting harmony in a society that was rapidly changing. Dalarna stretched from the Norwegian border to about seventy miles from Stockholm. From the time Gustav Vasa was popularized as "the Swedish William Tell from the canton of Dalarna" the province and all who lived or had contact with it were idealized and romanticized. In her novel *In Dalarna*, Frederika Bremer (1801-65) wrote that in appearance, dress and temperament the people of Dalarna in the nineteenth century remained as they were in Vasa's day.

> Works and prayer have preserved their health and industriousness. They bow their heads at the doors of their cottages, but have never yet bowed them to the yoke of the oppressor, Historic events have hallowed this ground—the native soil of Swedish freedom.

The myth-making may have been overdone, but there is no doubt that the environment was beautiful and challenging. The mountains were a skier's paradise, and Lake Siljan has always been a magnet. Naturally Swedish artists in all fields were drawn to the province. Anders Zorn moved to Mora in 1896, Carl Larsson to Sundborn in 1901 and Hugo Alfvén imitated Grieg and Sibelius by expressing national identity through rewritten folk music. His *Swedish Rhapsody* (1903) was as important to the Swedes' view of where their national roots lay as *Finlandia* was to the Finns, or the *Holberg Suite* to the Norwegians.

If Stockholmers could not make regular contact with Dalarna, they could always go to Skansen. There was a Lapp camp, with winter and summer housing. The house of a Dalarna mine-owner was reconstructed. A shrine called Swedenborg's Pavilion contained relics of Emmanuel Swedenborg's life as a mystic and philosopher. Visitors could see reindeer, lynx, sea eagles, wolves, elks and otters. When homage to the founder was called for, Hazelius' grave could easily be located about 300 yards south of the polar bears and the brown bears, kept in separate cages for obvious reasons. The impression of height was provided by a 250-foot tower from where one could see the whole of Stockholm with the city's spires and domes conspicuous, and even the bays of the Baltic could be spotted.

When bored by the fauna, visitors found a place for music and dancing, a theatre, circus, a music hall, and a good spot for drinking at a restaurant which designed a particular style of roast potatoes, Hasselback. The original zoo keepers were dressed in Swedish uniforms from the time of Charles XII. The keepers in uniform are gone, and it is now unfashionable to cage birds and animals, but pheasants and hares can still be spotted, especially in the winter, when they stand out against the snow and the deciduous trees have lost their cover.

The tradition of promoting and displaying Swedish design skill and artistic talent has not stopped. There have been problems liberating Swedish pictorial artists from the reputation for being like the Norwegians, painters of boots and uniforms, or being the practitioners of peasant art. Swedes are well aware that they have not produced an Axel Gallen-Kallela or an Edvard Munch. There is something about being a subject people which brings out the best in painters. The Northern Masters of the nineteenth century are not very masterful, but the watercolours by the most famous modern Swedish painters, Karl Larsson and Anders Zorn, merit gallery space anywhere. Generally speaking, however, even at their best in art and architecture Swedes have been overshadowed by Danes and Finns. Swedes know this, and to their credit have always used imported foreigners to inspire the locals.

In January 2007 Sweden's largest morning newspaper, *Dagens Nyheter*, proclaimed that Swedish design was in a very healthy state, even among the best in the world. It based the claim on a verdict by an international design jury. The jury analyzed why the Swedish design scene had become more vibrant in the twenty-first century: a new generation of young craftspeople, prominent among them Uglycute and Zandra Ahl, had advocated an abrasive, less perfectionist and more human attitude to design. By this the innovators meant that the way forward was to jettison the motto that form had to be dictated by function. Exclusivity was out. Nevertheless Swedes remained compelled to search for what they called "democratic design". They meant that along with the other obvious purposes of their constructions and representations—profit, innovation and style—the purchaser or viewer would experience not only the pleasure of contact with creativity, but also learn something useful about themselves and their society.

While admiring the functionalism and simplicity of part artistic inventiveness, and not abandoning feminism as a wellspring of new ideas, Stockholmers look for emotional and human values in both their bijou and workaday creations. No one has forgotten that in a long Swedish tradition most artistic ingenuity has been spent on devising useful articles for every day for every one contained in the social democratic safety net. Designers accordingly tried to provide beautiful things for humdrum use. Swedes came up with a Power Awareness Cord, which measured electricity consumption by glowing at variable strengths. Electrolux devised the ErgoRapido vacuum cleaner, which their marketers hoped would be "so likeable" that users would want to keep it in view when not in use. Despite the efforts of the ministry of culture and the ministry of industry, art still remains subsumed by craft. The best work of Swedish architects readily finds world markets. Nevertheless, the best intellectual property of Stockholm can be seen in residential housing and cultural centres in places ranging from Japan to Uruguay. Architects Thomas Sandell, Thomas Eriksson and the firm CKR (an anagram of the surnames Claesson, Koivisto, Rune) have done more than simply dump pure blonde furniture. Other modernists working in the traditional fields of their international superiority, silver and ceramics, created bowls and jugs which conveyed "dissonance"—which was in.

The Swedish Institute promotes the excellence of Swedish design world wide. The best high-profile locations in each country that their products reach are hunted out to increase market share and showcase innovation. Swedish hearts are moved by injury, age and disability, so the technical perfection of furniture for these groups is unmatched. The work of such design laboratories as Syntes Studio, who produced the mobile phone O2 Cocoon, shows their experimental as well as functional supremacy.

While not desperate for stimulus, the Swedes with their inborn curiosity about foreign experiences have often turned to outside leaders in innovation for their High Art exhibitions, and there was a moment when Yinka Shonibare was the most original mind that could be found. His lingering impact rivals a lobster that turns out to be a telephone. *Un Ballo in Maschera*, as it is titled, is another of his works commissioned by the

Moderna Museet in Stockholm, which was looking for an unconventional medium. They ended up with a High Definition Digital Video produced in harmony with the brilliant technicians at Swedish Television. Running for 32 riveting minutes, it bears more resemblance to Ingmar Bergman's *Persona* than to the real historical events, or Verdi's opera. So what? It is art. The rococo setting is one hundred per cent accurate and the misty blues of washed out eighteenth-century court backgrounds are as evocative as the dream like quality created by the formal dancing of the city's nobility. There is no dialogue and, as in a dream, sequence is meaningless. Events occur at random and repeatedly, the most disturbing image being the moment before the regicide when assassin and victim look each other in the eye with their masked and disfigured female faces. Shonibare will not be the last to use creative artifice to tackle the assassination of King Gustav III, but further innovation along these lines by other creative artists will be difficult. Shonibare's interpretation had no music, just the thump-thump-thump of the dancers' feet on the floor boards as they executed *Giselle*-like ballet poses in a remorseless test of audience concentration and patience. What did it mean? What were Indonesian batik materials doing in eighteenth-century Stockholm? Why were all the dancers female?

Art, Östermalm and IKEA

Stockholmers have moved on from the days when a decent representation of a bear at Skansen passed as art. The city's embrace of Shonibare is part of a continuing pattern of looking out for innovation to trigger cultural change. An obsessive drive in the direction of design excellence and a community determination to make an impact on the world of art did not stop quarantined on Skeppsholmen and Djuargården. In a century or so the major innovative activity shifted as the successful trendsetters, the truly trendy, shifted their creative energies to the Strandvägen, Östermalm and Nobelgatan areas. Baedeker wrote approving of Östermalm in its 8th edition of 1903, noting that the district had "sprung up" in the 1880s with numerous lofty dwelling houses whose granite facades produce a very handsome effect. The Östermalm building boom reached its apex when Oscar II opened Östermalmshallen in 1888. Constructed as a brick building around an iron shell by the architects Gustav Clason and Kaspar Sahlin, Östermalmshallen was a covered market with all the best aspects of a Mediterranean open market built in. It quickly developed into a high-class delicatessen and gourmet snack café for shoppers year round. They were spoilt for choice and willing to pay. Right next to Östermalmshallen was a nineteenth-century swimming complex, far advanced for its time, having a gymnasium attached. This burned down in 1985, and was replaced by a huge shopping mall in which the architects cleverly reproduced and conserved the Jugendstil granite and copper elements of the original.

In Rörstrandsgatan, a Gothic revival building, known, like its contemporary in Florence, as the English Church, catered to the spiritual needs of English businessmen and travellers from 1860. The Rev. E. W. Shepherd, M.A., conducted services there at 11 a.m. and 6 p.m. SS Peter and Sigfrid was relocated in 1913 to a more appropriate part of the city, closer to Strandvägen and nearby Nobelgatan. Strandvägen housed Svensk Tenn, Stockholm's oldest shop for interior decorators and high-end furniture designed by the names in the business. Ingrid Bergman loved it. While in Edwardian times Stockholm's ten wealthiest citizens lived in Strandvägen, the growing diplomatic community was drawn to Nobelgatan. The first foreign diplomat to build a house there was the British ambassador, who moved into Noblegatan 7.

A free bus from Östermalm underground entrance near the new shopping complex runs every hour from ten in the morning to seven at night; such is the demand, to IKEA at Kungens Kurva. The world of design and commerce moved on to IKEA's biggest superstore. In the monster showroom modern Stockholmers can offset the humdrum life of modern apartment living, which for most still means two rooms and a kitchen, by shopping for furniture upgrades and eating. IKEA's has cult status within the city both for visitors and inhabitants alike. The superstore opened in 1963 and since then it has attracted crowds of customers. IKEA claims it is super smart every day and Stockholmers, wishing that super smartness can attach to them, approach IKEA from all directions of the compass.

IKEA knows the way to the customer's heart is through the stomach, and in its restaurant it duly provides plates of pasta with "ecological" tomato sauce, chicken with basil, chicken with quinces, cutlets with Béarnaise sauce, a children's menu with a glass of milk. On the cafeteria shelves are cheesecake and three size servings of meatballs with lingonberry jam, boiled potatoes and brown gravy. This is called Meatballs Midday and is the centrepiece of IKEA gastronomy, designed to give four hearty eaters 800 grams of potatoes and one kilogram of meatballs to stop stomach rumbles while they wander entrapped in the maze of enticing potential purchases. Only on six days every year—Christmas Eve, Christmas Day, New Year's Eve, New Year's Day, Midsummer Eve and Midsummer Day—can IKEA addicts forget planning alterations to their apartments, assembling new furniture and revamping their lifestyle. So dominant and socially necessary has IKEA become in Stockholm that IKEA now offers IKEA BUSINESS, described as "a new global concept" and targeting businessmen and women, allowing them to arrange conferences at IKEA so that they never have to take a complete break from daydreaming about alterations to their domestic circumstances.

As they drive back home from Kungens Kurva with a truck full of furniture, Stockholmers are encouraged to think well of themselves by the state. They are not living in bankrupt Reykjavik. While putting together their bedside tables they can comfort themselves with the thought that they will not have to be bailed out by the World Bank during global economic crises.

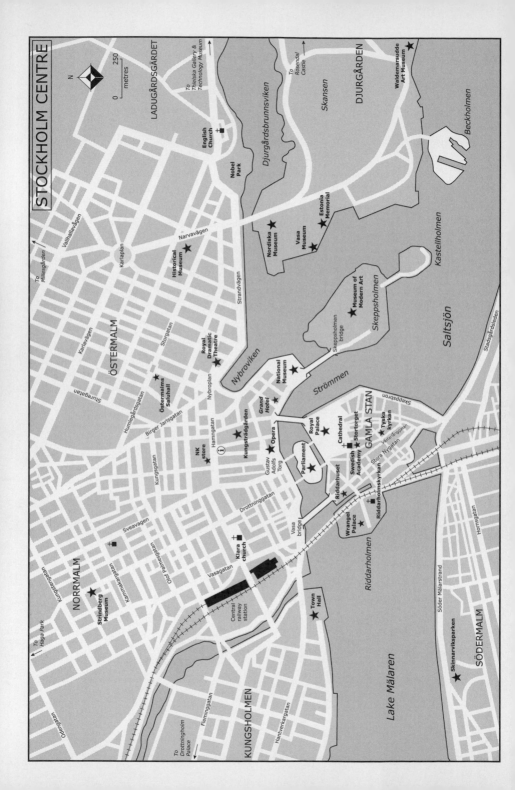

Chapter One

A Beautiful, Hungry Landscape
Approaching Stockholm

Follow the Vikings

The best way to get to Stockholm is to follow the Viking trail through the skerries on one of the ferries that sail from Finland. This will give you an experience shared by August Strindberg, who fell in love with the islands between Finland and Sweden, a love he was to retain all his life. The landscape between Finland and Sweden is harsh, with rugged stone islets and pine forests scattered over great stormy bays, backed in the distance by an ocean that even now takes over half a day to cross in the Viking or the Silja Line ferries.

An extensive archipelago stretches from one side of the Baltic to the other, from Åbo to Stockholm and in the past, in severe winters, it was often possible to ski from Finland to Stockholm. Global warming is putting an end to this adventure. Strindberg loved the simple people without locks on their doors and often re-lived, as he put it, the first archipelago memories of his youth, of sitting alone in a fisherman's hut, recalling the "beautiful, hungry landscape, the bad coffee..." For a picture of the Åland Islands in winter and their place in Swedish hearts you cannot do better than read Henning Mankell's *Depths* (2006). The hero of this novel, Lars Tobiasson-Svartman, explores among the small rocks and skerries at the edge of the open sea, paying Finnish seamen in aquavit to help him escape from Stockholm and his wife.

Although the new bridge from Denmark makes it possible to drive all the way to Sweden, the easiest and most usual way to get to Stockholm is to fly. If you fly into Arlanda you will land so far from the city centre that you might wonder if you are even in Sweden. But on descent your aircraft will provide stunning views of Swedish farms—red wooden buildings set on lakes in forests of birch and pine, scattered like a herd of cows across painted pastoral landscapes. There is no chance that the touchdown will disturb light sleepers in the metropolis. Pay the train or cab charge and you

can be where the Göta Canal boat lands you, at Skeppsbrokajen in Stockholm harbour, in less than an hour.

If you are rich enough you can follow Graham Greene's example and travel on the Göta Canal from Gothenburg on Sweden's west coast to Stockholm's Old Town and during the trip recall that the canal system took about three hundred years to perfect. The current schedule of four days takes you from Gothenburg to Trollhättan, then across a bit of Lake Vänern before darting down to Lake Vättern. You then sail up Lake Vättern to Motala before turning east to zigzag to Stockholm through Söderkoping, Trosa and Södertalje.

But my recommendation remains, nevertheless, to approach Stockholm by the Baltic Sea, travelling west from Finland, Sweden's first colony. Birger Jarl, King of Sweden, launched a crusade to Finland to complete the Swedish conquest of the country which had begun in 800 AD with Viking raids and settlement in the Åland Islands. In Kvarnbo, near Saltvik in those islands, all are now welcome in summer to a market reconstructed near Viking burial sites. Children toss knives, men and women get drunk and bake bread, just like they always did.

Before Stockholm was known by that name, Swedish and Finnish Vikings from Åland were familiar with the area. They tied up their boats on the leafy granite shore line where Stockholm now stands while getting to and from the Baltic to the Swedish hinterland via Swedish lakes and rivers.

Viking is often said to be derived from *Vik*, Norse for creek. The archaeologists Pearson, Sharples and Symonds in South Uist have another view, which could be true. They claim that evidence proves Norwegian Vikings settled in the Western Isles of Scotland and that the people of Uist are essentially the direct descendants of the Vikings. Julia Richards' *Blood of the Vikings* TV series reported a large scale DNA sampling which demonstrated that today's Hebrideans share a particular gene with contemporary Norwegians. Pearson, Sharples and Symonds argued that the word Vik, normally taken to mean bay or inlet, refers to trading emporia, that the Vikings were "pirates or emporia people" and essentially outcast fugitives or rebels of the Scandinavian world. This view is disputed by those who see them as simple farmers, looking to settle down abroad.

The Swedish Vikings, whether as progenitors of Stockholm's great department store Nordiska Kompaniet, or pirates, rowed and sailed in what was then contemporary state-of-the-art technology. Viking boats could reach twelve knots under sail. Swedish Vikings swapped furs and amber for silver and gold, reaching the towns of Novgorod and Kiev on the River Volga and travelling by river to Constantinople. "If you can't trade it, steal it" was a rule of thumb. The Vikings brought their wages in the form of bought or burgled booty back to their wives. Recent research has found that Swedish female Vikings were man managers in every sense. They calculated the risks and set the key performance indicators—such as how much torture was exactly required to reveal a hidden hoard.

Insofar as national stereotypes existed, Stockholm's Swedish Vikings were more entrepreneurial in spirit than their Norwegian and Danish cousins who were, in the first millennium, much more bloodthirsty and fierce. The Danes and Norwegians who paddled out of their Viks happily spent their days shoving priests down wells, whereas the Swedish group, while understanding the value of the sword, was driven by profit, not blood lust. Swedish Vikings announced their business plan on rune stones in much the same way as their twenty-first-century descendants put strategy on the www. "I want to find gold in foreign lands," said one representative of an early Viking Chamber of Commerce, "and feed my enemies to the eagles."

In Stockholms Län on the island of Björkö Vikings established a sort of first-millennium IKEA at Birka in the eighth century. Birka claims to be the first town in Scandinavia. It was certainly the region's most extensive Viking marketplace. Now the excavated town of Birka, some twenty miles west of Stockholm, is a World Heritage site. Viking bones are in black earth grave-fields and some of their trading stock still remains in a museum. Asgar, the first Christian missionary, arrived at Birka in 830 and was confronted by loot from Irish churches. Through Birka passed ecclesiastic booty from Ireland, and stunning treasures from many other places. The trip on Lake Mälaren to Björkö from central Stockholm takes less than half a day. The Vikings used to do it a thousand years ago in about the same time.

SWEDES AND FINNS

Stockholm was founded as a stop-gap measure to interdict Finnish raiders. Although they did not call it forward defence or a war on terror, it made sense for Birger Jarl to occupy the Finnish coastline and stop Finnish raids at their source. Over centuries of occupation the Swedes changed their Finnish focus from pillage and tribute to takeover. The initial Swedish motive was religious: to end Finnish paganism. In 1153 Nicholas Breakspear, an English-born cardinal legate of the pope, arrived and set to work in Sweden. Breakspear was later elected Pope Hadrian IV. Tradition has it that another English missionary, who had for two years been Bishop of Uppsala, led a bungled crusade to Finland. While on the march Bishop Henry stole fodder from a farm. In response the Finnish yeoman Lalli killed Bishop Henry with an axe. Henry was canonized and 20 January became his saint's day. Other Swedish bishops followed St. Henry to Finland and their knights established a ring of defensive castles to keep out the Russians. The most important of these was in Åbo, which became the Swedish administrative capital of Finland and in 1154 was logged as such on an Arabian atlas, where it was described as an important eastern trading post.

The lords of the castles ruled Finland in the name of Sweden until 1397. Then, as Jutikkala and Pirinen put it in their *History of Finland*: "Fate intervened with a cruel stroke: the last male heir to the Swedish throne died. Only his mother, Margaret, Queen of Denmark and Norway, survived." Queen Margaret amalgamated the crowns of Sweden, Norway and Denmark in 1397 under the Union of Kalmar but only agreed to be recognized as the sovereign ruler of Sweden if she kept Finland as a prize. Not that it mattered to the Finn in his sauna if he was governed from Copenhagen or Stockholm.

Whether in Viking times or now, leaving Åbo for Stockholm by ferry takes you past about 6,500 islands studded as in the Aegean. The Skärgård streams like the Milky Way. When the Finnish islands are on the beam, the Swedish skerries are almost on the horizon. Some islands are just rocks with a summer holiday cottage on them, others substantial hideaways for film directors and captains of industry. En route to Stockholm, you leave Nådendal, Pargas, Nagu, Korpo and Houtskär in your wake to reach the open water and head for the Swedophone Åland Islands of Brändö, Kökar, Vördö, Föglö and Lumparland for a brief stop in Mariehamn. From Mariehamn it is about five hours to Stockholm.

Until the beginning of the nineteenth century successive Swedish kings built up the power base of the richest minority in the world, the Swedish-speaking Finns. It was Swedish-speaking Finns who governed a country largely inhabited by wild and primitive people Tacitus called "Fenni", who were not Indo-European and whose language was—and remains—unintelligible to almost everybody. By the late eighteenth century Swedish kings and castle rulers could come and go to Finland in an atmosphere of weary indigenous acceptance. The Stockholm nobility sailed their yachts and picnicked on the islands of their Finnish subjects, with the same sauciness as the Anglo-Irish in Connaught. Gustav Vasa regularly used to hunt on Kastelholm. When the Swedes retreated over the ice in 1809 and lost Finland to Russia during the Napoleonic wars, the Russians turned Finland into a playground for the ruling Tsars who became Grand Dukes of Finland until the Russian Revolution.

Travellers feel they have reached the sheltered waters of the western world on the coast of Sweden at Kapellskär. The coffee is still bad, but in winter there is a grand silence in the beautiful, hungry landscape. The boat sails on past national parks to Furusund, Vaxholm and Lidingö before reaching Stockholm itself, splashed across fourteen islands and barring entrance to the inland waterways of Lake Mälaren, navigable for hundreds of miles into the heart of Sweden. The swirling of the waters around the lock, Slussen, where the lake's fresh water meets the salt water of the Baltic, is both magnetic and hypnotic. The battles between Swedish, Estonian and Finnish Vikings that took place at this point of contact are long over, replaced by optimistic city fishermen looking for the estuarine fish that are always found where fresh and salt water meet.

Birger Jarl founded Stockholm, more or less where the Royal Palace now stands, on the islands of Staden, Helgeandsholmen and Riddarholm. How the town island, the Holy Harbour and the Knight's Harbour came to be sited precisely where they are now was, legend has it, left to chance. A log was thrown into the tidal flow in Lake Mälaren. The current carried it toward the open seas of the Baltic at 59° north latitude. Where it washed up on the shore was thought to be auspicious, and so Stockholm, literally "log harbour", was born. This accepted story is as probable as that of Romulus and Remus, but who knows, it is pleasing and seems appropriate, if not likely.

Walking down the gangplank on arrival, modern travellers have to pick their way through drunken teenagers lying on the floor, while those youths who can still walk stumble and clutch at the sober passengers. During the eleven-hour trip from Åbo to Stockholm, the Finnish and

Swedish young ignore the *smörgåsbord* and fill themselves with alcohol. The Viking Line has done its best to reduce the brain damage by imposing a strict minimum age of twenty on Saturdays, all public holidays, the 8 a.m. Stockholm to Åbo departure time and the 2.35 p.m. Mariehamn-Stockholm run. Travelling with parents or written evidence of valid reasons for making the trip, such as study, visiting relatives or work, is acceptable. Evidently the shipping directors have not seen the 1998 movie *Fucking Åmal* in which compliant parents provide limitless alcohol for their teenage children to guzzle at parties.

VENICE OF SCANDINAVIA

Stockholm was accurately described in Baedeker's 1903 *Norway and Sweden*, which declared that no comparison of Stockholm with Venice or Geneva could convey an accurate idea of the picturesque beauty of the place. At the beginning of the twentieth century Baedeker stressed of Stockholm that "its most striking peculiarity consists of the immediate proximity of primeval rock, practically unaffected by the hand of man, with a flourishing seat of modern culture." Usually cities (said Baedeker) wholly transformed the ground on which they stood and most of their surrounding districts. Stockholm made a virtue of wrestling with its environment without destroying it, noted the guidebook, and the bare granite rock often sprouted through the middle of houses.

The name "Stockholm" first appeared in a document dated 1252. The earliest archaeological sites also date from around that time. Stockholm grew fast as a trading station. Even in the thirteenth century regular commerce between Sweden and the German Hanseatic ports was conducted through Stockholm, which for its first hundred years was confined within the defensive walls of Gamla Stan, where the German language was heard almost as often as Swedish. From the turn of the fourteenth century, the village boundary moved north of Stadsholm to the mainland, Norrmalm, and colonized the larger island of Södermalm in the south.

Metal exports made Stockholm a target for entrepreneurs from its beginning. German immigrants were first to exploit Sweden's natural resources. In time, the Swedes revoked ordinances determining that at least half of the town council had to be German, effectively relegating the Germans to little more than an influential minority. German footprints remain in Gamla Stan's Tyskabrinken and Stockholm's most beautiful church, Tyska Kyrkan, the German Church at Svartmangatan. Consecrated in 1570, Tyska Kyrkan was enlarged to its current size between 1638 and 1642. The stained glass windows, the gallery paintings and the gold painted altar are offset by the ebony and alabaster pulpit. The Royal Gallery (1672), built for German members of the Royal Household, like the church, is visited constantly. Tyska Kyrkan has a congregation of about two thousand.

By the Vasa era Stockholm's strategic and economic importance was so much greater than its earlier upstart rival Uppsala that the court moved to Gamla Stan and—most important for this book—Stockholm became the national capital of Sweden, if not of Scandinavia. From the time the Vasas moved in, the city's rulers were careful to ensure that their castle's environment was systematically organized and as attractive as possible for all Stockholmers. As early as 1636 Stockholm had a city planning office, and master plan after master plan followed, just as they do today.

The late sixteenth-century city

In the seventeenth century Swedish noblemen built Florentine-style rows of imposing stone town houses in Gamla Stan and on the southern bank of Norrmalm. The middle-class merchants constructed warehouses and go-downs, and the bureaucratic elite housed themselves in stone mansions in the shadow of the Castle of the Three Crowns, as it was called, reminding all of the union of Sweden, Denmark and Norway under Queen Margaret. A northern architectural renaissance was accelerated by a fire that destroyed most of the town's wooden buildings in 1625.

Klas Fleming was appointed the first city overseer in 1634. He masterminded the demolition of everything in the way of his vision of a Stockholm reconstructed into rectangular lots. Many of the old walls and fortifications of Gamla Stan became builders' rubble. Fleming's plan lasted for a couple of hundred years and the city's boundaries remained much the same.

Stockholm remained a small town, in European terms, until the nineteenth century. In 1710 a plague killed about 20,000 (36 per cent) of the population. Poverty and disease encouraged many Swedes to migrate to the United States but industrialization changed the city's social structure. The population leapt from 86,000 in 1840 to 300,000 in 1900. A total of 460,000 lived in Stockholm in 1940 and there are about 900,000 Stockholmers today. In the nineteenth century epidemic sickness was a part of life in Stockholm. Alfred Nobel and August Strindberg grew up in a city as well known as Calcutta for cholera. In the twentieth century Greta Garbo, as a teenage towel girl, lathered the chins of tubercular clients in her Södermalm barber's chair. There is still, of course, sickness in Stockholm. Despite the expertise and knowledge of Swedish pharmaceutical companies and doctors, drug addiction and AIDS are likely to remain problems of public health.

Over the last two hundred years, sparsely settled, detached housing areas, often with large gardens behind, have been largely replaced by apartment blocks of five storeys in streets and four storeys in courtyards, mimicking the architecturally brutal façades of the earlier nobles' stone buildings. In 1886 Albert Lindhagen drew up plans to imitate Paris and Vienna in Stockholm. Broad tree-lined boulevards were never created, although small inappropriate developments along these lines were made in Karlaplan. In 1871 the central railway station opened in Vasagatan and horse-drawn trams moved around Stockholm from 1877. Kungsgatan was bulldozed through Norrmalm in 1911 and became established as the main thoroughfare to the city's office centres.

Stockholm was well placed to exploit and develop telecommunications from the time of the invention of the electric signal telegraph. In 1853 the first line was set up between Stockholm and Uppsala. A year later Sweden established underground telegraph communication with Europe outside the Scandinavian peninsula via a submarine cable. The telegraph revenue was enormous. Running on pole lines alongside the railways, telegraph demand grew so much that a "telegraph net" was invented. Such was its popularity that "telegram rooms" had to be set up. By 1902 the telegraph industry employed about a thousand men, summer and winter, to keep messages flowing: customers paid for 2,556,323 in that year alone.

Telephone usage began on a small scale in 1883. The Swedish utilization of the telephone received its last—but certainly not final—burst of entrepreneurial activity when it embraced and for a time took over and drove forward the world mobile phone industry a century later. Naturally, Stockholm was the hub of the country's telephone system. The first General Telephone Company serviced all subscribers within a 45-mile radius of Stortorget and began with a fifty-year concession to erect telephone lines along the public highways and across ground belonging to the state. Almost from the beginning, the Stockholm telephone companies used underground conduits where they could and combined patriotism and practicality by always using Swedish-made instruments and furniture. Stockholm's underground telephone net was immune to damage from winter snowstorms which otherwise would have brought down large clusters of wires and aerial cables. Low fees and charges were possible because L. M. Ericsson manufactured an unrivalled telephone system. This was an automatic switch apparatus, invented and first used by H. T. Cedergren, which allowed as many as five subscribers in the same neighbourhood to use one line to the exchange. Stockholm soon carried not only the greatest number of telephones in proportion to its population of any city in the world, but by 1904 its absolute number of telephones was level with that of New York and below only the major European metropolis of Berlin. Callers to Stockholm from Riksgränsen in the Arctic Circle near the Norwegian borders, Umeå on the coast of the Gulf of Bothnia, Gothenburg, Malmö, Gotland and Örebro were all irritated by the Stockholm voice and telephone manner. They thought residents of the capital to be haughty, stand-offish and aloof with a marked tone of superiority in the way they said *noll åtta*, the 08 designation of the Stockholm exchange. The number 08, pronounced Knoll Otter, reminded elderly English-speakers of Tarka (if one deleted the webbed feet certain Stockholmers indeed could be described as fur-wearing rather than fur-bearing carnivorous mammals feeding chiefly on fish).

URBAN UTOPIAS

When Stockholm City took responsibility for municipal planning in 1904 there was a swift change of focus. By the 1960s most Europeans visiting Stockholm went home thinking they lived in hovels compared with the Swedes, and to a large degree they did. In the early twentieth century the city fathers began buying land outside Stockholm's existing boundaries: forests, farms and eventually whole rural districts. The land was bought after free negotiation and incorporated into the city, which planned for eventualities twenty years ahead. Between 1913 and 1916 two single acquisitions increased the size of Stockholm from thirteen to forty-four square miles. Forty years later the national parliament made it even easier for Stockholm to appropriate land to house its citizens. The ensuing buying spree saw the city increase in size to seventy-one square miles, in which garden suburbs linked by the underground train system were designed to house clusters of neighbourhood units large enough to justify generous spending on them. Thanks to the skill and systematic approach of the town's dogged bureaucrats, Stockholm escaped the worst effects of industrialization and the chaotic development that destroyed other fine European cities.

In a BBC documentary Alan Whicker, was among the first to analyze the Swedish genius for town planning and to demonstrate how far advanced of the rest of the world 1960s Stockholm was as far as innovative solutions to urban living were concerned. A generation later Stockholm is still miles ahead, as the cluster of happy families in Hammarby Sjöstad and Gåshaga Brygga now illustrates. Located in the south central inner city of Stockholm, Hammarby took its name from Hammarby Manor, which was demolished in 1945. The old manor was surrounded by farming land with fields of tobacco plants and cabbage patches. Typically, small farmers would pay a toll to enter a local market and, as Westman Torsten recalled in *Det nya Stockholm* (2001), would sell everything they had stored in their barns and earth cellars: Swedish turnips, potatoes and salted Baltic herring, fresh eggs, and newly slaughtered pigs and calves together with hares and other game. The market also provided hay and oats for all the horses in town.

In 1844 Lars Hierta, who founded the national newspaper *Aftonbladet*, set up candle and weaving factories. These were among Stockholm's largest workplaces for some time. These were followed by a clothing factory making army uniforms, the Luma light bulb factory and even in 1928 a General Motors assembly plant, with technology imported from the United States. Old timers, as they do, recalled that life then was idyllic for the Stockholm working class. Picnics, berry and mushroom picking on the lake shore, boating and bathing in summer, skating and skiing in winter, a pavilion, a farm and an artists' collective all contributed to Carl Larsson-style scenes of unusual urban content. There were windmills on the surrounding hills and places to dance and drink beer.

By the 1990s the Arcadian past was largely over but Hammarby, as prime waterfront land, was ripe for development in a different Stockholm, conscious of the need for security from muggers in the streets and looking for mixed-use residential areas. The opportunity came in 2004 when Stockholm put in a bid for the Olympic Games. The bid failed but the Olympic Village concept did not die with it. Arish Adi Dastur, having grown up in Bombay and worked as a consultant for the World Bank, describes in an intelligent and evocative investigation how Hammarby became Stockholm's showcase of lower-class (by Nordic criteria) urban sustainability. When he visited the area, trying to understand what it was that made Stockholm work so well, he spent much time walking around Hammarby Sjöstad to get a feel for the area and, like many US visitors, he liked it. It was very accessible by public transportation and close to the city centre. There was a central tramway running more than a mile through the area and the tracks were flanked by commercial establishments on either side. At Fredriksdal a factory combined a heat and power plant and marked the beginning of the main arterial street, the generators providing energy to central Stockholm. Dastur noticed that it was impossible to tell the difference between public and private housing, something he had intended to try and notice. To him, most of the housing looked impressive, and was built with large balconies, big windows and small interconnecting parks. When night fell, according to a trendy Swedish custom, commercial establishments lit tiny oil lamps and placed them on the footpaths by their entrances. At night the residents turned on decorative lights in their balconies and lit candles in their windows. Walking along the picturesque waterfront, Dastur saw families with strollers, people sitting by the water, running and biking, and commented: "The scale at which things are built is very human and immediate." Dastur pointed out how sensible it was for the old light bulb factory to have been renovated to host

Hammarby Sjöstad

offices, and for a small hilly park to be built around it and concluded that domestic happiness could be engineered by skilled social democrats and their architects.

CITY OF SEA, GRANITE AND COPPER

Stockholm is not just a pleasant spot to live in domestic comfort. Throughout history, as Jan Morris elegantly put it, "a streak of the heroic ran through Swedish society." Stockholm became the capital of a country which was the homeland of the Vikings, the bravoes of medieval Europe, whose trading settlements extended as far as the Eastern Mediterranean, who reconnoitred Greenland and North America, and whose occupation of Normandy (Norseman's land) led to the conquest of England.

The story of Stockholm is not, like one of Jan Morris' favourite cities, Trieste, the story of nowhere. It is the story of somewhere. Stockholm was, from its inception, home to a fighting aristocracy, although it is true, as Morris observed, that in recent times the Scandinavians have been among the least aggressive of European countries, devoting themselves chiefly to social progress and enrichment. Sweden still practises neutrality better than any other country. Its efficient military strength is only used in support of United Nations objectives to preserve peace and stability abroad.

Ever-present sea, granite and copper provide a dramatic physical background. If Paris is the "City of Light", Stockholm is the "City of Copper". So much of the ore was buried under Swedish soil—there were mountains of it in the north—that for a long time most of Stockholm's roofing drainpipes were made of copper. The utilitarian glamour of verdigris copper drainpipes, never rusting, always gushing, was a symbol of the unfair generosity of mother nature and the slippery ease with which Stockholmers utilized their patrimony—although it could never be said of Stockholmers that they gush like their drainpipes.

The blue of Stockholm Harbour and the copper of the town's central ancient rooflines are offset by the granite of the city's bedrock. The predictable stability of each Stockholm footfall, the strength of nature's donation of mineral stability to the built environment, has over a millennium put more than a touch of granite into the Stockholm psyche. A certain inflexibility based on strength is part of the Stockholmer mindset. Copper has complex applications: it can be beaten, changed in texture, painted and is malleable.

One of the most agreeable features of Stockholm is that the rich are not neglected. As the ferries cruise from Finland to Stockholm's inner harbour, they pass Gåshaga Brygga, a residential development adjacent to Millesgården on the island of Lidingö. The architect Thomas Sandell has realized a brilliant concept of forty elegant two- and three-storey villas; one could call it a Grand Design. The houses are sometimes cantilevered across the Baltic and provide minimalist interiors to live out the pressured life of privileged modern Stockholm families, supplied with cold and heat resistant windows, private yacht moorings and views from their terraces. Of course, the secure siting of the exclusive complex ensures that you will not see the rich in repose. In common with architectural best practice throughout the twenty-first century, the interior set-up of modern housing protects the privacy of modern man. Blank curtain walls shield them from the street while behind the opaque entrances is the chic world of the products of the designer store Svensk Tenn.

Open for all Stockholmers to enjoy is Millesgården, built on a site on Lidingö by the sculptor Carl Milles. Millesgården is a work of art in its own right: terraces, sculptures, columns and a view across the waters of

Millesgården

Värtan to the rocky heights of Hersund, usually described in Swedish as "immense". Carl Milles was born Carl Wilhelm Andersson in 1875 near Uppsala. After prizes and rudimentary study in Stockholm, he was drawn to Paris like many other talented Swedish down-and-outs. He stayed longer than most, keeping himself alive by jobbing work as a cabinet maker and haunting his inspiration, Auguste Rodin. In 1906 his sculpture commissions brought him back to Stockholm and he began to erect buildings on a site on Lidingö, cannibalizing as time went by a marble portal that once belonged to the Hotel Rydberg and a massive sandstone column originating from the former Stockholm opera house erected by Gustav III. Inside Millesgården are originals and replicas of work to be found elsewhere in Sweden. Most representative is the *Dancing Girls* (1917) in black bronze on the upper terrace. Milles' life changed when in 1929 he visited the United States and was inspired by the New World. In 1931 Cranbrook Academy of Art in Michigan appointed him resident sculptor. By 1935 Yale University had bestowed an honorary degree and the following year Milles turned Millesgården into a foundation and donated it to the Swedish people. He and his wife Olga became American citizens in 1945. The American Academy offered him a studio in Rome in 1951 where he lived, returning to Sweden for the summer holidays in a routine followed by many Stockholmers.

VASASTAN: HIP VIBE OR SIBERIA?

While the thoroughfare of Vasagatan is not home to the urban poor, it lacks the serenity of Gåshaga Brygga. Phaidon's *Wallpaper City Guide* to Stockholm now singles out the district of Vasastan along with Östermalm, Skeppsholmen, Norrmalm, Södermalm, Gamla Stan, Kungsholmen and Djurgården as the city's most enticing and satisfying offerings. Perhaps the promise to provide an informative insider's checklist to one of the world's most intoxicating cities might have been put differently but it is true that Vasagatan is emerging from its dark past—Stockholm is permissive as well as intoxicating and much is allowed in Stockholm which would not be elsewhere. As in Oslo, the high cost of alcohol means that a night out involves sitting on a drink or two. Stockholm's young have an almost complete aversion to recreational drugs. As one ambassador sagely noted, Swedish lawmakers have stringent policies on AIDS and shut down bath houses very early in the epidemic; political correctness ensured that such issues were dealt with factually and without moral overtones, making them more addressable than in comparable societies. But wander out of Vasagatan and Östermalm, Södermalm or Gamla Stan after dark and you will walk past regular evidence of window breaking, car theft and burglary. While not on the scale of many other capitals, the morning after the night before often shows evidence of opportunist criminals in Stockholm.

However, crime in general has been accepted as a social problem to be shared by all. Individual criminals are not stigmatized as in the Anglo-Saxon world. Instead, government ministers struggle to provide education and a more-or-less full employment system to complement the welfare state, thus lifting the burden of crime from the shoulders of the criminal and placing it at the doorstep of all the city burghers. Trying to white out the concept of individual responsibility for criminal action and lay it on the parquet floorboards of society rather than the perpetrator was a nice idea that has not always worked. The very few twenty-first-century addicts, thieves and non-conformists, like their Viking predecessors, simply have yet to be convinced that crime does not pay.

While it was very special to live in Vasastan with all of its historical associations, things were often rough there on Friday nights before it became what Phaidon now describes as a "friendly residential area with a hip vibe". The bull's-eye for Stockholm's criminals, Vasastan was the heart of active commerce when Sweden was a great power and the street itself was heavy with the weight of the name of Vasa. Vasagatan stopped being a track through the woods and became a street, a *gatan*, more or less at the same time as Stockholm replaced Uppsala as Sweden's capital city. Unlike most of medieval Stockholm, Vasagatan was paved. It was the most important part of the basic town planning grid in the growing metropolis that emerged from the forest. Although Vasastan was outside the old town—Gamla Stan where Stockholm's written history began—it remained one of the most important parts of town until the Napoleonic era, when it slumped.

When I lived in Vasastan, it was experiencing decline and had gone down in the world. Certainly, I could step out of my front door and scoot down into T-Centralen, the main underground station. So if a central location was the criterion, I was privileged indeed. But seedy Vasastan was not glitzy Östermalm, which I discovered much later. While I worked at the Vitterhets Academi I lived near Valhallagatan, the Beverly Hills of

Stockholm. When I was required to identify myself, as I had to do frequently, and presented my ID card and gave my Vasastan address to the custodians of the many protocols Stockholmers have to master to live comfortably in the town, I often detected a quickly suppressed shrug of sympathy. Not pity. Sympathy, for no-one living in Stockholm was so destitute that they merited pity. Nevertheless, by the time the Swedish prime minister was killed just around the corner from my flat, Vasastan had fallen to such a low level that it had become one of the least enticing and most disreputable areas of the central business district.

As far as I knew, I was the only full-time inhabitant actually living in the building: sleeping, having breakfast there and going off to work in the morning. Although I was a beacon of foreignness, a suntanned Australian in Stockholm in February, being *utländsk*, close to meaning "exotic" in common usage in Stockholm, was not, as in other capitals, an invitation to be insulted, mugged or begged from. On the contrary: be they pineapples or people, animal, vegetable or mineral, foreign things and outlandish people are treated in the first instance with courtesy, respect and genuine (if distant) interest. Even so, I slept uneasily every night. All the families had long since left the building, a huge block earmarked for redevelopment, almost next to a busy central post office and near the police headquarters that did brisk and unpleasant business every Friday night.

I had two rooms and a kitchen, so dark at night and so empty of human life that "Kafka" was the most common word used by my visitors. None would stay overnight. My wife and daughter even refused to see my apartment, which was a reverse tourist attraction, rather like the motor museum near Riga housing the limousines of the long gone Soviet heads of state. Although not actually called "the spook house" like its near neighbour which housed some of the ancient eerie offices of Stockholm University and a major Swedish bank, there was a ghostly malevolence around the empty entrance hall, staircases and caged lift-well. The building was most certainly haunted. The ghosts of the long dead never appeared to me but there was a *spöktimme*, hour of the ghosts, every night. I did not care to test myself against the lurking phantoms and apparitions. There was a clear presence of evil and when darkness fell an air that something dreadful was going to happen. Each night the wind blew in drunks and dead leaves, cigarette butts and used styrofoam food containers.

Things should have been better, and indeed they are now, as Vasastan was geographically bounded by Kungsgatan and Drottningatan, and is close to all the main profitable and mushrooming department stores. At the time of Olof Palme's murder, the upper floors of the building I lived in at Vasagatan had not been cleaned for years. But the electricity was connected, the central heating was full on (to stop the building rotting from the inside), and when Karl the odd-job man opened the door at dawn, a few shady traders working on what looked like dirty daytime business drifted in with discarded morning newspapers and the disorientated alcoholics left over from the night before who rattled around the vestibule during daylight hours. As I had seen in Leningrad, an open door in winter was an opportunity for the less fortunate members of society to get warm and meet undisturbed in a quiet place.

Vasagatan was particularly attractive to a fairly large group of the nicer sort of domesticated drug addicts. They climbed up the faded *jugendstil* staircase to the nearest "bright" windows, although "bright" is a relative term in this context. As their berserk ancestors had done a thousand years before, they turned themselves into catatonic zombies, shooting up heroin among the dust mites. The addicts and I were usually the only ones left inside the fortress-quality exterior door when night finally fell. As part of our daily comings and goings, the addicts and I said our routine good mornings and good evenings at the almost liturgical winter opening, closing and locking ceremonies of the great outside door. The heroin addicts stared at me with their glassy eyes as I passed up, bent on scholarship, to my rooms, heading roofward in the nineteenth-century but stylish lurching art nouveau-design elevator cage.

Once or twice addicts, curious or bored, knocked for diversion on my door. I pretended to be Finnish, using my most useful Finnish phrase: "500 grams of meat for the dog". The accent, if not the message, was convincing enough to be off-putting. As a further defence, I put a sign on my door, "GONE TO ICELAND", but soon learned that the addicts, despite their leopard skin fake fur coats and unconventional headgear were, in the Stockholm manner, just being neighbourly and were not interested in burglary. Their addiction was thoughtfully paid for by the state, which gave them the funds to purchase drugs without the need to mug or break windows and steal jewellery, mobile phones and electrical goods. All the addicts had to do was to visit their counsellor, who would explain the dangers of addiction and reassure the addict that their addiction was not their fault but that of society, after which the welfare state paid the addict money to buy more drugs.

Even so, Vasastan was as dangerous a street as you could find anywhere and I did not leave the flat after dark except once, on 28 February 1986, walking quickly through the dirty, slushy, melting ice the hundred yards from my front door to one of the entrances to T-Centralen, having picked up a bottle of Jacobs Creek from the *systembolaget* as my contribution to a Latvian dinner party. I had been invited to eat with a Latvian-Swedish-Australian professor, Baiba Metuzale-Kangere, and her husband Karlis in Södermalm. Baiba worked as a member of the Baltic Institute at Stockholm University's Baltic Studies Department. She was part of a project team working on one of Olof Palme's personal interests: the future democratic independence of Latvia, Estonia and Lithuania. (Curiously, Sweden's current bestselling author, Henning Mankell, used the names Baiba and Karlis as stereotypically Latvian in *The Dogs of Riga*, a detective novel in which the fictional hero Kurt Wallander solves horrific crimes in the former Soviet possession. Stockholm's Baiba and Karlis are anything but stereotypical and unfortunately Kurt Wallander exists only in print, otherwise Prime Minister Palme's murder might have been solved.)

I explained to Baiba and Karlis that I would be leaving their home early and they scoffed at my fear of walking alone on a Friday night near T-Centralen. Friday night is the most dangerous night of the week in Stockholm. Police walk around in threes or stay in their cars as drunks and drug addicts, muggers and burglars weave about town. Heavy snow had fallen and I found it difficult to keep my feet on the pavement on the way to my underground entrance to T-Centralen. I was conscious that I had been mocked by my hosts and that they thought I was a coward for wanting to leave their home in Södermalm before 10 p.m. to avoid being caught up in the random violence of a drunken Friday fracas.

Smug at preserving my own safety and conscious that I had been very frightened entering a dark, empty building, I ran a spooky gauntlet, barricaded and locked myself in and jumped into bed with Tove Jansson's *Who Will Comfort Toffle?* At 11.21 p.m. that Friday night the prime minister's blood had flooded a nearby footpath so much that when I looked at the scene of the crime the following noon there was still a three-foot-wide ice block of congealing gritty pavement debris mixed with Palme's frozen solid blood.

Chapter Two

MURKY ENDS

A HISTORY OF ASSASSINATION

GUSTAV III: MURDER AT THE MASKED BALL

When Gustav III was murdered at a masked ball he provided a dramatic opportunity for generations of creative artists. Yinka Shonibare was following in the footsteps of the most famous, Giuseppe Verdi, who first exploited the theatrical potential of an opera set in a brilliant era. Gustav III's court sparkled with diamonds; in Herman Lindqvist's words, "never had Swedish life at court been so magnificent as under Gustav III." Paradox was abundant. The king personally was enlightened and stuck to Versailles protocol when possible. He lived for weeks at Gripsholm Castle, spending twelve Christmases there, to the despair of his servants, in a summer castle with no heating. It was recorded that 1,248 candles a month were burnt to light the drawing room, stairs and corridors and that the king played the leading male role in eight performances of the Gripsholm Court Theatre. Lindqvist, who branched out from a career as a journalist by writing innovative history books, noted that a Swedish-speaking Finnish stable master played the leading male role when Gustav III pioneered infertility experiments and produced a widely circulated drawing by Carl August Ehrensvärd to illustrate his point.

A more elaborate setting for a brightly-lit murder in a luxurious setting could not have been found than on the occasion when Gustav III, King of Sweden, was shot at a masked ball in the centre of Stockholm on 16 March 1792.

Gustav III was unusual among the Swedish monarchs insofar as he was born and raised in the country he ruled. He bore the illustrious name of Vasa and, like many heads of state, sought popularity at home by war abroad. His life ended when he was assassinated by men in black masks during a performance at which he was a guest of honour. Gustav III's murder inspired Giuseppe Verdi to write *The Masked Ball*, one of his most dramatic operas and, at the same time a work that illustrates the cultural

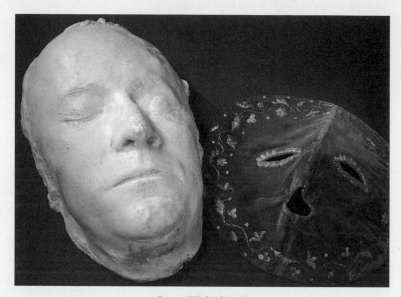

Gustav III's death mask

blindness that becomes apparent when a distant Swedish tragedy swims into the everyday artistic imagination of global creative artists. Murder during a masked ball at the opera in Stockholm was simply too irrelevant, remote, incredible and unpleasant for nineteenth-century public opinion to accept, and mainstream values forced Verdi to change the scene of the crime to a more resonant and culturally acceptable locality.

Giuseppe Verdi was a poor villager whose father was a grocer. Born in 1813 in the Italian duchy of Parma, Verdi grew to know that Italian uni-fication, like the French Revolution, would probably not be possible without the assassination of the senior members of Italy's ruling classes. Verdi was seen to be a spokesman for many Italian aspirations in a world so complex it was impossible to be consistent. The Napoleonic conquest meant that although he was born at Le Roncole near Busseto and grew up in an Italian-speaking environment, he was technically a French subject who took his values from Austrian-dominated Milan. He was quickly in hot water over the success of *Nabucco*. Many Italians identified the Jewish experience of captivity with their own national condition as the subjects of Austria. By the time he had written *Rigoletto, Il Travatore* and *La Traviata*, Verdi was an international figure who could write whatever he liked, but not set in Stockholm. To produce, in Rome, *Un Ballo in Machera* during 1859 was perfect timing. Italy was then, as always, in political ferment. A year earlier Napoleon III narrowly escaped death when he was attacked by Felice Orsini, and for obvious reasons political censorship in Europe was heavy on the subject of royal assassination. After twelve months of negotiations about the location and nature of the crime, Verdi's *Masked Ball* was gutted and transformed. The operatic possibilities were conceived initially as potentially subversive and dangerous to monarchs everywhere. Verdi had the disappointment of having to change eighteenth-century Stockholm to republican Boston, a ridiculous outcome that undermined the natural force of the production and trivialized the tragic real events at a real Stockholm masked ball.

The Gustavian era has provided Stockholm with some of its most enduring cultural legacies. The most striking is the Drottningholm Palace, which Gustav III made over and improved. Drottningholm is now included in UNESCO's World Heritage list. The castle came into Gustav III's hands in 1777. Its most notable feature then was a Chinese pavilion given as a 33rd birthday present to Queen Louisa Ulrika. The pavilion was made in Sweden and designed by Carl Frederik Adelcranz. Adelcranz was also in charge of the project to build a royal court theatre, which is Europe's oldest theatre still in active use. Drottningholm Court Theatre was reopened in the 1920s, having been closed up after Gustav III's assassination.

Gustav had a passion for Italian and French style and was a great enthusiast for the Grand Tour. On the eve of the French Revolution he headed south to Rome to educate himself, and his European study stimulated his interest in architecture. It was a visit to Italy in 1782 that led him to commission a series of pavilions in neoclassical style. The combination of design brilliance with the ostentatious and prolific use of copper is found nowhere else in the world. Today, the Chinese and Turkish pavilions in Haga Park testify to the eclectic enthusiasm of a designer-king in the era of rococo. Gustav used another architect, Frederik Magnus Piper, to build the English-style park in the Haga area, a few miles north of the city centre and just south of Ulriksdal Castle. Assassination put an end to the project to add a Versailles-inspired palace to the park, but not before Gustav had overseen the building of a copper pavilion with a hall of mirrors and a quite unbelievable "Roman battle tent". Finished in 1790 and designed by Louis-Jean Desprez, it housed all the king's horses.

PRIME MINISTER PALME: "RED OLOF"

Deeds of darkness, shadows of the night and absurd terror go hand in hand with gloomy prospects and dismal outcomes for many of Stockholm's frowning townsfolk, including Statsminister Olof Palme. "It doesn't look promising," "things look black for him," "arrest lurks just around the corner": these were phrases sufficiently common in everyday use to make most Stockholm schoolchildren initially as temperamentally pessimistic as their lexicographers. In the early twentieth century the old walls of 08 apartments were almost certainly like mine—dingy with age. If I looked out my window in the 1980s all I saw was the deadpan blank wall of the adjacent building, windowless and menacing. I lived an overshadowed life in a dark building.

The townsfolk of Vasastan more often than not had swarthy complexions (*mörkhy*) and were togged out in black clothing suitable for the wearer's obscurity. I joined them wearing black ski overalls and a black parka topped off with a luminous green skullcap pulled over my ears to avoid death by Volvo driver. (In Stockholm the system-wary Swedish drivers, sober as judges with not a drop of alcohol in their bodies, frequently kill drunken pedestrians.) My suntan faded fast but I never developed the characteristic murky depression of the majority of winter city dwellers because I spent every morning skiing for a couple of hours in Djurgården as an antidote to darkness and *ennui*.

I got up as usual at 7 a.m. on an unusual Saturday morning and moved the two steps necessary to get from one side of my flat to the other—from bed to kitchen table—switched on the radio and kept up my practice in Swedish pronunciation by mimicking the morning news reader. "Prime Minister Palme was murdered last night at T-Centralen," ran the broadcast. I repeated this carefully in my BBC Swedish and poured out my muesli. I moved on to strawberry jam on hard bread, then straight on to the coffee. "A madman killed the prime minister last night," I repeated as well as I could, thinking the weather was rather unsuitable for my ritual cross-country skiing regime from the Italian Embassy in Djurgården to Walmersudde and back. "The prime minister was shot dead at T-Centralen," I repeated as I looked for my skiing gear—Yugoslav—I could not afford Karhu, Finnish skis, although I did have a pair of Karhu sand-shoes.

As I walked to the Vasagatan bus stop I realized something was wrong. People were crying in the street. I had never seen a Stockholmer in tears and hardly ever seen a sober Swede upset, certainly not in public. When I got off at the Italian Embassy in Djurgården the regular group of pen-sioner-age ski-aholics were not heading off to commune with the squirrels and snow hares. They were clustered in groups, in lachrymose astonish-ment. Who could have shot the prime minister? Initially Stockholmers could not imagine a motive. I argued that it was most likely "assassina-tion", not "murder", but soon gave up the "a" word as I was repeatedly told—at first—how loved Prime Minister Palme was and how only a madman would murder him.

Palme took over the Swedish helm in 1969. He had served his ap-prenticeship as Tage Erlander's personal secretary between 1954 and 1963. His Latvian grandmother, and his family experience as a dispossessed Baltic-German landowner, moulded Palme into a complex mix of ruling class and underdog. As he grew older his sympathies lay with the latter. Palme's early childhood of plenty in Östermalm did not stop his life's work of championing minorities and looking after the interests of the Swedish working class. Before his election as chairman of the Social Democratic Party when Tage Erlander retired, Palme deeply offended the United States to the extent that it was rumoured he had become a CIA murder target. On 21 February 1968, almost exactly eighteen years before his assassina-tion, Palme took part in a torchlight march through the streets of Stockholm, conspicuous in a stylish fur hat, marching alongside the North Vietnamese ambassador Nguyen Tho Chan. Palme's address to the demon-strators had a note which is relevant today:

> The good of democracy can never be reached by using oppression as a means… In Vietnam thousands of American soldiers have been killed, seeing themselves as champions of the democratic ideal… It's ghastly that young men should be sacrificed unnecessarily in an unjust war.

This was not the full extent of "Red Olof's" affront to the US. He ac-tively encouraged deserters from the US military to live in Stockholm. By 1981, after the Korean passenger aircraft KAL007 had been shot down by the Soviet airforce and Russian submarines had run aground in Swedish waters, Palme had also made himself a worthwhile target for the KGB by denouncing the Soviet Union. The Soviet submarines that ran aground were from what the Russians called "whisky class", and the Stockholm press amused itself with stories about whisky on the rocks. Palme had many love affairs. Add the numerous husbands affected by his bedroom frolics to the secret service divisions of the American and Russian governments, and there was an almost infinite list of probable or possible assassins. Palme hated apartheid and was mysteriously hated by some sections of both the local Jewish and Muslim communities. The South African security police were among the first suspected of shooting him. Kurdish immigrants were closely investigated, with some being deported after the murder. Palme was also targeted for his Latvian ancestry, one deranged potential murderer thinking of killing him because when the prime minister smiled, he bared "the thick sensuous lips of Latvian women". It seemed there were few sections of the Swedish population that were not suspects.

I feared that I myself resembled an early identikit picture of the "murderer's face", emblazoned across the newspaper menu boards. Finns and Latvians, people with mental illnesses and the many local disgruntled opponents of social democracy were all treated as possible criminals. Indeed, a Finn may have been the killer. A tele-movie, devised by French, produced by Germans and paid for by a TV consortium stretching to Australia, placed a Finn at the murder scene, lurking in the doorway of the Dekorima shop with a pistol in one hand and a walkie-talkie in the other. The prime minister was even in the sights of the numerous piano accordion players in Stockholm, although folk musicians, generally speaking, were low on the list of serious suspects to be investigated despite Palme, as a young journalist, reviewing a folk music concert thus: "the misery continues tonight." He also detested folk dancers, sharing my sentiments that while the dancers appear to enjoy what they are doing, the pleasure cannot be shared by the audience. Not even the greats of Swedish literature were spared the venom of Palme's critical pen. He took a swipe at a Vilhelm Moberg play he reviewed, writing that "those who sat furthest back couldn't hear a thing, but perhaps that was an advantage."

After his death Palme was publicly exposed by his critics as having an insatiable sexual appetite, whetted by his high office. He married for the second time in 1957. Like characters from an Ibsen play, Olof and his second wife Lisbet spent their honeymoon in Rome. On returning to Stockholm, they set up their first two-bedroom flat in Rörstrandsgatan in, as Chris Mosey describes it in *Cruel Awakening* (1991), "that part of Stockholm known officially as Vasastan and unofficially as Siberia because it was considered so cold and inhospitable."

By 1986 Palme and Lisbet had moved up in the world. Their new apartment illustrated general rapid social mobility in Stockholm. Having shifted from Vasastan to Vällingby, where they lived for almost a quarter of a century, the Palmes swapped a simple terraced home for their luxurious apartment in Västerlånggatan in the old town, Gamla Stan. The apartment had been owned previously by Gunnar and Alvar Myrdal. Gunnar Myrdal won the Nobel Prize for Economics in 1974. He knew the value of a dollar as well as a crown, so when his wife Alvar described Palme's new home in Gamla Stan as a "work of art", you can be sure that it was not furnished by IKEA. What the Myrdals lacked in sensitivity to racial identity and compassion for the disabled they made up for in their keen perception of what was the best apartment in the best street in the most historic part of the city. Even the cobbles in the narrow street were, in aesthetic terms, a work of art.

It was from Västerlånggatan that Palme meandered to the cinema while I took the train past Gamla Stan on my way to dinner with my friends Baiba and Karlis in Södermalm. Olof and Lisbet stepped out of their door into the winter cold and slipped down a dimly-lit alleyway. Palme felt quite safe, as no chieftain among Swedish citizens had been murdered since Gustav III in the eighteenth century.

Mosey describes the prime minister's last night before his death:

Palme told Säpo, the Swedish security police, that he planned a quiet evening at home and had dismissed his body guards. Then, when his son Mårten phoned to suggest that Olof and Lisbet join him at the movies, Palme simply agreed and didn't bother to tell Säpo of the changed routine. He thought of Stockholm very much as "his" city. Here he had been born and grown up, and he knew it intimately. It was a safe, familiar place where he was spared the indignity of the continual security surveillance to which he was subjected elsewhere in the world. Palme was fond of boasting to other world leaders that in Stockholm he could walk the streets without fear.

Perhaps Palme should have studied Swedish history, not economics at Kenyon College, when he was expanding his intellectual horizons in an American university. Olof and Lisbet left Västerlånggatan, walked into Stora Nygatan and entered the *tunnelbana* (underground) at Gamla Stan. As I was passing in a different train in the opposite direction to Zinkendamn, Lisbet showed her monthly card and Olof paid six krona for his ticket. Olof and Lisbet passed through T-Centralen for the Haymarket, Hötorget, and got off at Rådmansgatan. They met Mårten and his girlfriend and sat down for the film at the Grand Cinema. At 11.15 p.m. they left *The Mozart Brothers* movie behind them and walked past the local *systembolaget* with its sign: "this shop is protected by an alarm system and bulletproof glass."

Urinating in nearby doorways were Stockholm's Hell's Angels, complete with studded leather jackets and Harley-Davidson motorcycles. Just before midnight in February it is always very deserted in central Stockholm. Mosey describes how:

> Lisbet and Olof walked for six minutes along Svedvägen. At 11.21 pm a killer with what looked like a Wild West revolver stole up silently in the snow and shot the Prime Minister between the shoulder blades. Palme's backbone, aorta and windpipe were destroyed and he collapsed on the footpath. Seven minutes later, a pedestrian flagged down Inspector Gösta Söderström's "polis" car on Kungsgatan. The murderer meanwhile jogged off down the pedestrian mall Tunnelgatan, and sprinted up 86 stone steps to the higher level suburban maze of Malmskillnadsgatan, to vanish forever. One newspaper reported that Söderström asked to see Lisbet Palme's ID card, and she screamed "Are you crazy? I'm Lisbet Palme. That's my Olof."

Mosey recalls that despite their formidable array of technological aids, the Swedish police were one of the most incompetent in Europe. The joke at the time was that the bad news for the assassin was that the police were after him; the good news was that they were Swedish police.

The joke has now become a very bad one. Palme's killer has never been found. The working policeman's view at that period in Stockholm's history was neatly put by a fictional detective from Ystad in Henning Mankell's *Sidetracked* (1995). Because of decades of social democratic

Mourning Prime Minister Palme

police education, which took an enlightened and progressive view of criminology, crimes were routinely left unsolved. Law enforcement had shifted from the pursuit of villains to such an extent that when Palme was murdered policemen and women thought it "was almost shameful to be a policeman." Stockholmers cared more about the fate and distress of the criminal than the city's rising crime rate. In 1792 everyone knew who assassinated Gustav III, and why. Gustav III was on the verge of leading a Thermidorian revolutionary crusade to Paris to put an end to the French Revolution. In 1986 there was no shortage of discontented nobles in Stockholm, a town paradoxically still supplied with the most blue-blooded, conservative ennobled citizens to be found in Europe.

Graham Cornwallis' *Lonely Planet Sweden* (2000) takes the official line on Palme's assassination. Although he is covered in the text, Olof Palme does not even feature in Cornwallis' index. Cornwallis thought:

> ... [the assassination] shook ordinary Swedes' confidence in their country, its institutions and its leaders. Although there have been many theories about the unsolved killing, it seems most likely that foreign intervention and destabilization lay behind this appalling act.

I think Cornwallis is wrong, yet following the Cornwallis template Becky Ohlsen touches on the crime in her later *Lonely Planet Stockholm* (2004): "Conspiracy theories abound regarding Palme's still unresolved killing. A brass plaque on the street marks the spot of the murder, at the corner of Sveavägen and Tunnelgatan."

The plaque is still usually bedecked respectfully with flowers, marking and symbolizing both the death of Palme and the fluctuating vitality of Swedish social democracy. There have been trials and investigations, but the third millennium has dawned with Stockholmers as much in the dark as they were on 28 February 1986. Stockholm has seen more blood than Macbeth and Stockholmers have stepped in blood too far.

It is unlikely that the truth will ever be known. A 2007 TV series on political assassinations, *Murder in Stockholm: Who Killed Olof Palme?*, answers the question by blaming right-wing extremist police officers. The Franco-German production interviewed eyewitnesses who put together a picture of the Stockholm police force being split between neo-Nazis and social democrats. It claimed that the extremists were admirers of Pinochet, held meetings at which German marching music was played and formed a gun club. These police, known as "the baseball gang" (a reference to their preferred weapon of law enforcement), were only ever investigated by other police, whose report gathers dust.

ANNA LINDH: KNIFED AT NK

On 10 September 2003 Palme's protégée, the Swedish foreign minister Anna Lindh, was knifed to death in front of horrified fellow shoppers in what 08s colloquially call NK, Nordiska Kompaniet. The company was founded in 1902 by Josef Sachs and looks like Paris' Galeries Lafayette with many layers of shopping floor-space exposed internally by Sweden's leading architect, Ferdinand Boberg. One of Ivar Krueger's companies constructed the building, which has an internal load-bearing structure and an external façade of granite. With the Kungsträdgården Park opposite and the circular neon sign 25 feet in diameter installed on the top of Stockholm's telephone transmission tower, NK is a landmark visible from almost anywhere. L. M. Ericsson constructed the sign, which has the NK logo in green on one side and a clock in red on the other.

Sorrow and horror, in that order, comprised the Swedish reaction to the murder. In a country known for gender equality, it was locally unremarkable that the foreign minister was a woman. Anna Lindh was young, a stereotypically Nordic blonde with blue eyes, open, intelligent, a receptive expression characteristically on her smiling face, her forehead lined with thought. She was stabbed over and over again in a department store so centrally located and so prestigious that it was as appalling to Stockholm as it would have been if a female British foreign minister had been stabbed to death in Harrods food hall. The Swedish politician lay bleeding from multiple slash wounds in front of hundreds of peak hour shoppers in the most fashionable part of the city. It took nine days for the Stockholm police to arrest their first suspect, only to release him when they found a better one.

The first response was that Lindh had been killed by an anti-European Union fanatic. The press reported that just after 4 p.m., while browsing in the ladies' department of NK, she was stabbed in the chest and stomach. Her arms were cut as she tried to save herself. Surgeons at the Karolinska Institute worked on the foreign minister for nine hours. Blood transfusion after blood transfusion failed to staunch her internal bleeding from a slashed liver. The murderer was captured on NK surveillance videos. Miljailo Mijailovic was recorded, his sleeves rolled up, striding through the store in a grey Nike hooded sweatshirt with a baseball cap covering his long hair and moving with an insane, haunted expression. Anna Lindh was in the recovery unit for hours before doctors were forced to return her for further operations, but by 5.29 a.m. she was pronounced dead, a little over twelve hours after she was struck to the floor.

Mijailovic was convicted on DNA evidence. During the trial, as during the murder, witnesses—and there were many—failed to come forward to testify as they had failed to come forward to overcome the attacker—a timid, reluctant and cowardly reaction that some might find significant. In the Pink Panther tradition of the Stockholm police, a Swede named Per-Olof Svensson had been arrested earlier for the same murder on 16 September, giving Mijailovic the hope he might run free. But on 24 September the Serbian immigrant was in jail, and after months of questioning, on 6 January 2004, Mijailovic confessed. The trial was swift; justice delayed is justice denied. The trial lasted three days, 14-17 January, and was a textbook example of how Stockholm regards crime. Whether murdering the foreign minister or stealing a mobile phone, crime is primarily seen as the responsibility of society, not the criminal. Mijailovic was sentenced to life imprisonment, but had the sentence overturned as he was suffering from mental illness at the time of the murder. He then had his life sentence reinstated after a further appeal by the crown, and finally the Swedish justice system declined his request for prisoner exchange to Serbia lest he be injured in a Serbian jail by his countrymen.

A distinguished campaigner for Euro-Sweden, Anna Lindh was born and buried in Stockholm. Like Palme, she protested against the Vietnam War and was equally opposed to the invasion of Iraq. At the time of her murder she was one of the most likely candidates to succeed Göran Persson as president of the Social Democratic Party and take over as prime minister. Her only connection with Serbia was that the prime minister, Zoran Dindic, was assassinated when he arrived to meet her, as she waited for him in a Serbian foreign ministry building during her visit to the Balkans.

Stockholm had a mini-repeat of the public funeral accorded to her mentor and inspiration Olof Palme, during which all of the citizens present in town that day (including me) stood three to five deep around the cortege route as Palme's body was taken for burial to the remorseless beat of muffled drums. Her private family funeral was preceded by a memorial service broadcast live on television and attended by the prime minister, king and queen. The whole country stopped to watch the great and the good.

Most Swedes had expected Anna Lindh to lead the Social Democrats to a fourth straight election victory in 2006, and her death severely dented the party. When she was killed Stockholmers were bewildered and few more bewildered than Prime Minister Göran Persson. Persson was not only deprived of his political crown princess, but his pain was made worse as he was physically incapacitated by a disabling agony in his hip, which needed replacement surgery. Before Lindh's death he had contemplated standing down. He was also attacked by the political opposition on major and trivial issues. Persson's response to the 2004 Asian tsunami, which left thousands of Swedish tourists and expatriates cut off and helpless in Thailand, with many of their friends drowned, was rated as so poor that his personal approval rating sank to around thirty per cent. The Stockholm daily *Expressen* mocked him with a photo of the prime minister and his "new friend". Persson was photographed stroking a ginger cat with his high-tech crutch propped beside him under the headline "Göran's Summer Fling". Ingvar Hedlund reported to *Expressen* readers that the prime minister was so confused that he did not even know the name of his cat. At first Göran, who was described as "smitten by the cat", called it Maud. One of the leaders of the opposition Centre Party was also called Maud, Maud Olofsson. The Centre Party was likely to be a popular people's choice at the next general election. In *Expressen* Maud Olofsson's photograph was superimposed with the words: "think that Persson will have me around the whole time." Hedlund finished the whole page story with black capitals: "BAPTIZE GÖRAN'S CAT. Help the Prime Minister. For Persson's sake and for the cat's sake, text your suggestion to perssonkatt@expressen.se." Persson changed his mind and called the cat Christina but the cat was out of the bag, and he lost the general election.

On 17 September 2006, twelve years of uninterrupted Social Democratic Party power in Sweden was over and the parliament inaugurated Frederik Reinfeldt as prime minister. Reinfeldt had been chosen as leader of the conservative organization, misleadingly called the Moderate Party, in 2003. He presided over a fractious coalition of the centre-right who proved to be inexperienced, incompetent and corrupt. Two ministers resigned within ten days of their appointment because of what were called "irregularities in their private finances". But Persson's party has the distinction of going down in history as the most unpopular group of Social Democrats since the introduction of universal suffrage in 1921.

Although the Social Democrats remained the largest single party, the conservatives were sure to control parliament as their coalition, Alliance for Sweden, held 178 out of 349 seats in the chamber. Yet Reinfeldt did not seem to have many ideas to pursue. Annual economic growth, at four per cent, was excellent by European standards; Swedish nationals could proudly shop with their krona rather than the generic euro; the Stockholm stock market had been rising for years; everyone was getting richer and the new prime minister could remember the name of his cat.

Chapter Three

FEARFUL LINGO

MUTUAL MISUNDERSTANDINGS

A NEW HUMAN IDEAL: DE BOTTON AND MEYER

Most visitors to Stockholm experience more light than darkness, and for centuries tourists and savants alike have travelled north without seeing a drop of blood. Many of them found Stockholm to be a city where new human ideals had been reached. Thousands of the world's most creative individuals, scholars in every imaginable field, have visited Stockholm. For their part, many Swedes reciprocated by private and fierce criticism of their visitors and the world outside and regarded the wandering intellectuals as savages. Strindberg, in a typically dismissive comment, spoke as a representative of the Stockholm snob when he complained that he could find no bookstores in Paris except pornographic ones, and that when the French were not stealing from him they were begging. Reciprocal misunderstanding has long been common.

Even so, the leading public intellectuals promoting western culture never give up trying to decipher what Stockholm has to offer. This is illustrated by the tone of some of the most perceptive recent observations about Stockholm made by the intellectual self-help guru, Alain de Botton. References to Swedish tastes and to Stockholm's architectural expression of egalitarian social values are scattered throughout his 2006 book, *The Architecture of Happiness*. De Botton knows that for five hundred years the Stockholm Town Hall decided major policy issues that determined how Swedish citizens lived in their built environment. He also senses that the relationship between the government, the people and the capital city was unique in the world insofar as it threw orthodoxy on its back and showed that it was possible to be both rich and good. In numerous cases de Botton's text is sprinkled with positive comments about Swedish innovation and Stockholm's grasp and use of beauty and utility. Fetching half-page photographs illustrate the book. One photograph is of Carl Fredrik Adelcrantz's Sturehof, an iconic manor-like residence completed near

"A grumpy old man": August Strindberg

Stockholm in 1781, which, in de Botton's words, "speaks to the sensitive today."

Yet by some perverse mechanism, while the literary possibility of investigating the nature of Sweden and Stockholm has gripped the minds of bestselling authors and they cannot leave out repeated references to the country and its people in their texts, publishers' indexers do not share this view. Alain de Botton, for instance, a cult purveyor of serious but playful manuals for living, went north and later observed how a gambrel-shaped roof can "rapidly prompt memories of a Swedish history and holidays on the archipelago south of Stockholm." (For those who do not know what a gambrel is, de Botton illustrates a nineteenth-century farmhouse.) As far as the indexers are concerned, however, a sort of snow blindness cuts deep into their work whenever it is appropriate to specifically identify and credit the sensitive Stockholmers with complex contributions to civilization. De Botton acknowledges that Sweden has managed to finesse away the traditional antithesis between luxury and simplicity. As he explains it, "the idea of luxury tended to be associated with grandeur, pomposity and arrogance, while simplicity has been equated variously with squalor, incompetence and inelegance. However, the interior of Skogaholm Manor in Sweden, decorated toward the end of the eighteenth century, triumphantly contradicts any inclination to render the pairing of these two qualities impossible."

De Botton describes how Swedish furniture is detailed in a fine rococo manner, carved with gentle, aristocratic curves and garlands of flowers. But as the eye moves towards the ground, something unusual comes into view. "Where we might expect chairs to meet a floor which resembled them in tone—made of marble perhaps or highly veneered parquetry— instead we find rough, unvarnished wooden planks, of the sort one might use in a hayloft." He concludes: "The manor house proposes a new human ideal, in which luxury would entail neither decadence nor loss of contact with the democratic truths of the soul, and in which simplicity could be synthesized with nobility and refinement."

The indexing profession's use of a Bermuda Triangle in which to consign Stockholm suggests that its practitioners felt whatever happens there is not quite real. Stockholm is absent from de Botton's index, which ranges from Bath, Colombo and Edinburgh to Oxford and Urbino. This omission highlights the difficulty Nordic identity has overall in achieving parity in the mandarin minds of southern seers. None of the references to Stockholm or Sweden is easily signalled in the book's index. Why? Ludwig Wittgenstein's plan for his family house in Vienna is indexed. To be sure, an author is not responsible for the indexer's choices, but the absence of Stockholm is revealing at a deeper level. It shows that Stockholm might as well be Wewak for all the interest it stirs among Oxbridge dons when deciding what is important in the world of ideas and what is not.

Even Michael Meyer, brilliant linguist, translator and author whose biographies of Strindberg and Ibsen are unsurpassed, thought it most instructive to see Stockholm as it related to the ancient university towns that have dominated the English-speaking cultural landscape. He wrote that Stockholm at one time grew from "a small city of about 90,000 inhabitants, roughly the size and population of modern Cambridge". He describes how in the nineteenth century new stone and brick buildings were beginning to rise, but Stockholm remained essentially a rustic town, more so than most European capitals. In the heart of the city unpaved country lanes were common. Until 1855 two pillories still stood on the present site of Birger Jarlsgatan. More attractively, writes Meyer, there were large houses with orchards, and as late as 1870 twenty-four windmills, standing on high ground, formed a characteristic feature of the city skyline.

Meyer's description of urban change is hard to better. He describes how in Ladugårdslandet hundreds of cows grazed on meagre and trampled grass. (Ladugårdslandet is still a huge open space close to Nobel Park. Stockholmers now exercise their dogs and horses, fly kites and go on fun runs on the soft, small hills that look out across the water to Djurgården.) Until the late 1840s Stockholm had no footpaths. Paved roads were usually surfaced with cobblestones, hard on the feet and ruinous to shoes, a fact frequently commented on by foreign visitors. A water reticulation system was not started until 1858 and until then everyone had to go to public pumps. There was only one municipal public bath for the entire city and that contained only twelve baths. Open sewers full of night soil ran down the sides—and sometimes the centre—of the streets and stayed there until cleansed by rain. Things became especially unpleasant when spring unfroze the three-month detritus of winter. Gas lamps were not seen until 1853, nearly forty years after they had reached London.

Meyer describes how the first twenty years of August Strindberg's life were a period of great economic and industrial growth for Stockholm.

Sweden had been a poor and backward country, half a century behind its time, but in Strindberg's day it began to enter the modern world. Cafés, hotels and museums sprang up. A contemporary of Strindberg recalled that in his youth the city contained eighty-five restaurants and over five hundred pubs. In 1860 it acquired its first daily morning paper, *Dagens Nyheter*, and its first railway connection, to Södertälje. Other lines followed to Gothenburg in 1862, Malmö in 1864 and Uppsala in 1866. Nevertheless, Meyer observes that "even as late as the 1870s Stockholm was still one of the most squalid capitals in Europe... a town of dreadfully overcrowded, cold and damp wooden hovels in narrow, dirty streets which were often nothing but muddy country lanes... for most Western Europeans an exotic and primitive place almost Siberian in character, a byword for poverty, epidemics and underdevelopment."

Meyer observed thus:

> The Strindberg shipping company owned ten small paddle steamers, which carried passengers and freight along Lake Mälaren to the neighbouring towns of Uppsala, Nyköping and Örebro. In the absence of rail connections, this was the quickest and most convenient method of travel. Stagecoaches existed but, since they also delivered mail, they took eight to twelve hours to cover the forty miles between Stockholm and Uppsala. By 1854 Carl Oscar's fleet had doubled and was serving ports as far distant as Gothenburg and Malmö; a third of the steamships plying from Stockholm sailed under the Strindberg flag (and Stockholm was reckoned at this time to have more steamships than any other city in the world).

GEORGE BERNARD SHAW: HIGH MEDIOCRITY

The Strindberg family oversupplied Stockholm with steamships and plays, but Strindberg was the first, not the last, to bemoan the fact that Swedish achievements were not taken seriously. It was partly a question of the language barrier, as Strindberg found when he met George Bernard Shaw. It was not simply that the Swedish language had three more letters than the English alphabet—å, ä and ö—but Anglo-centric minds were simply not hard-wired to comprehend the Swedish logic in their Germanic thinking. In the nineteenth century, Nordic musicians, authors, poets and dramatists were world benchmarks for imagination and technical skill. Yet

Stockholm's literary lions quickly grew bored at being disturbed and diverted from their work by authors courting them. Among the pioneers to stumble was George Bernard Shaw, one of the many Europeans drawn to make the difficult, unrewarding trip to Stockholm.

Given Shaw's experience it is not surprising that many men of letters preferred to leave their contact with Swedish literature uncontaminated by personal experience. D. H. Lawrence spoke for those who held close to ignorance and prejudice and refused intellectual engagement. Lawrence happily confined his knowledge of Stockholm to three words: "that rotten Strindberg". James Joyce preferred to take his nourishment in the stewed rabbit of the Polidor in Paris rather than eat Leksand crisp bread in the Hotel Rydberg. But even he looked wistfully up from his zinc table to pen a letter of congratulations to George Bernard Shaw in 1926: "Allow me to offer my felicitations to you on the honour you have received, and to express my satisfaction that the Nobel Prize for literature has gone once more to a distinguished fellow townsman." These three lines were the only congratulatory letter about the Nobel Prize that Shaw kept.

Despite evidence to the contrary, George Bernard Shaw considered himself an expert on the Swedish language. He told J. M. Synge's biographer, Maurice Bourgeois, that the word "playboy", as used in *Playboy of the Western World*, was difficult to translate from its original Gaelic meaning, and in European lexicography had "its exact equivalent only in Swedish". Shaw loved to travel and said he felt joy in Dubrovnik when he swam in the Adriatic. The cold waters of the Baltic were an altogether different matter.

Shaw was drawn to Stockholm, among other reasons, by his interest in Strindberg, Europe's most innovative creative writer at the time. In heading north Shaw badly misjudged the Stockholmer and his market. Not put off by their less than cheery titles, Shaw carefully studied seven of Strindberg's plays in preparation for his voyage. *The Black Glove, The Bridal Crown, The Dance of Death, The Diary of a Madman, The Father* and *Miss Julie* were all on Shaw's bedside table in his home near the Fens. While he had done his research and turned up on the author's doorstep well versed in Strindberg's work, truly described as an extravagance of voluminous creativity, Shaw's meeting with Strindberg was not what he expected. When he knocked on the front door, he was invited in for vomit, not tea for two.

It served him right. Shaw's Scandinavian excursion and adventure in literary exploration was driven by his desire to not only meet—and perhaps benefit intellectually from—a theatrical innovator, but also, more importantly, to make money from the association by getting, if he could, permission to represent Strindberg's literary interests in England. In thinking he could derive income by introducing Strindberg to London theatre audiences Shaw devised a scheme that had more than a whiff of Mel Brooks' *The Producers*. In 1910 Strindberg's work was unknown to English speakers. Certainly the theatre-going toffs of the West End had never heard of him, and, like virtually every other Englishman, Shaw could not read Swedish. He knew Strindberg's work through a German translation which, because of its mangled syntax, did not reveal the dramatic craftsmanship and poetic genius of the Swede. This rendered some of Strindberg's flightier expressions as if they were instructions for assembling a vacuum cleaner—and a Miele rather than Electrolux at that.

Despite the shortcomings of German translation Shaw felt confident enough to tell Strindberg that he "must have been inspired directly by heaven" to write *Lucky Per*, and pestered the puzzled playwright to let William Archer translate it for Sir Herbert Tree and the London Stage. Shaw also had a sneaky feeling that some of the characters and content matter in Strindberg's plays were dangerously challenging, if not actually "vile and disgusting"—the words English critics routinely used to describe the works of the Norwegian Henrik Ibsen—and as such over the heads of typical Londoners. To skip around this Shaw suggested, for example, that Strindberg delete characters such as a nurse who appears carrying strait-jackets in one of his scenes, as such confronting episodes were likely to reduce box office receipts.

By the time Shaw arrived in Stockholm, Strindberg was at the end of his career and was confirmed in his determination to harbour all his long-standing grievances and disappointments. He had collected slights from personal injury the way other boys collected stamps. He was bitter: the class war had gone nowhere in Stockholm and love had bypassed him. From the time he could distinguish between reward and punishment he savoured and almost seemed to prefer failure and resentment. It was certain that he would never win the Nobel Prize for Literature. His place was at the head of the rejection list, although on one occasion enthusiasts from the Stockholm working class marched to his flat, having taken the hat around for an anti-Nobel Prize. Strindberg received the marchers on his balcony as a grumpy old man.

Strindberg's loneliness was the opposite experience to that of his fellow countryman, Carl Larsson (1853-1919), whose watercolours of his happy family showed bourgeois Sweden at its homely best: his son Esbjörn on his skis in a backyard garden; a neighbour's brick-red wooden house glimpsed over a canary yellow fence, all the brighter for the unusual sunny reflection of deep winter snow; two dogs, Joup Joup and Kicki, snug inside a cottage decorated with orange and white checked gingham curtains; painted and decorated washstands in the dreamy Dalarna style.

Strindberg (like Adolf Hitler and Winston Churchill, not primarily known for it) could also paint a bit but his subjects never showed the neo-Gustavian soft wash interiors of Carl Larsson's *Evening Before the Journey to England*. For Strindberg there had never been any spring afternoons with dogs and children lazing about on lakeside edges, a red painted summer cottage, hidden and all but buried in birch groves, rowing boat tied to the family jetty, and a picnic spot marked out in untidy grass around a couple of seat-sized rocks. To be honest, Carl Larsson himself did not always paint happy farmers shovelling horse manure onto fields hungry for it or snub-nosed pubescents with wheaten plaited hair greeting each other, nose to nose, through picket fences. Larsson once allowed himself the private luxury of breaking his mould, painting himself as a haggard Munch-like ghost, but the innocence of children, the heroism of lasting marriage and the optimism of the young were always at the heart of his art. Larsson's subjects glowed with a calm Strindberg never felt.

Strindberg grew up near the bottom of the hierarchical class system that ruled nineteenth-century Stockholm. Like Greta Garbo, he spent his life trying to deal with the misfortune of his teenage years. Strindberg had no idea of London middle-class values and no interest in West End audiences and their interval chit chat, chocolates and champagne. Shaw sensed a momentary glimmer of the approaching entrepreneurial defeat when he arrived at the Stockholm flat, hardening himself to disappointment by congratulating himself that at least he had succeeded in "achieving the impossible" by managing to arrange a meeting with Strindberg.

In July 1908 Strindberg promptly rejected Shaw's offer to act as a go-between for proposed London productions. He pointed out that only one of his plays, *The Father*, had ever been produced in England and that was

Self Portrait with
Daughter Brita

an amateur production in 1891. Shaw ought to have known that Strindberg, who founded his own Intimate Theatre in Stockholm in 1907 to produce innovative plays, was completely out of sympathy with English public opinion. The most popular author in London in Edwardian times was J. M. Barrie. For Shaw to suggest to Strindberg that *Miss Julie* might help London theatre managers realize their dream and "find another Peter Pan" was ludicrous.

To be sure, Shaw had metaphorically dipped his toes in Lake Mälaren on a previous literary adventure and made lots of money from a very funny play about the possible annihilation of the human species. As he took the lift up to Strindberg's upper-floor corner study, Shaw bolstered his flagging confidence with the recollection that he had already tasted fame and fortune, and had written a 1905 West End hit, *Major Barbara*, with a Swedish theme. *Major Barbara*, which opened in London at the Royal Court Theatre, was about Strindberg's schoolboy chum Alfred Nobel. The plot revolved around the romance between Alfred Nobel (recast as Andrew Undershaft, "a millionaire cannon factory founder") and a pacifist lady Salvation Army officer. The real Nobel was not as lucky in love as the fictional Undershaft. Troops from the Salvation Army were thick on the ground in Stockholm doing sterling, if mostly unappreciated, work amongst the drunks. The scene at the end of the second act, where Undershaft, having purchased the whole of the Salvation Army, marches in a Salvo parade playing the trombone is considerably less confronting than the horrific events that disturbed Strindberg's Stockholm playgoers. The contents of *Peter Pan* and *Miss Julie* illustrate the huge gap between the imaginative calibre of the innovative Swedish and the Edwardian English stage productions of the time.

Strindberg's reaction to Shaw's visit was embarrassed silence and a pale smile or two. After Shaw tried to communicate in what he confessed was "a fearful lingo"—half German, half French—Strindberg, Shaw recorded, took out his watch and said, in German, "At two o'clock I am going to be sick." Never one to miss a cue, or a stage direction, Shaw fled the apartment, took the lift to the ground floor and sailed on the ferry from Stockholm to Lübeck. Cross and disgruntled, he then turned his artistic venom on the city, describing Stockholm as "a very jolly town to look at and the people very superior within certain limits of high mediocrity." He also penned a vicious retaliatory postcard to Sydney Cockerell, to the effect that all the art Swedes understood was architectural, and in the style of seventeenth- and eighteenth-century grand ducal ornament.

STRINDBERG: SON OF A SERVANT

Shaw was correct to detect that only the sour and rarely sober Norwegian Henrik Ibsen came anywhere close to Strindberg for innovation and dramatic power. Strindberg, like most Stockholmers, missed his city when abroad. For Ibsen, a fellow writer under the Swedish-Norwegian union, escape to Italy had been a liberating experience. Ibsen was seldom happier than when sitting drunk in the Scandinavian Club in Rome. Michael Meyer reveals how different it was for Strindberg. No sooner had he arrived in Paris than he was already longing to return to the country he had so longed to leave. He missed Swedish food, asked friends in Stockholm to send him split peas and dill, and vowed he would never leave Sweden again once he had returned. He described France as a damnable land where the people were all rogues. He couldn't eat the local dog food (as he called it) without getting ill. Worse:

> A hundred francs only lasts 5 days so I will have to write hard. No aquavit, no beer. To piss costs 5 centimes, to shit a franc at least, and Paykull and Drawer [two friends] who were here a few days ago say you can't fuck for less than 10 francs. This last doesn't concern me, but I still think it's too dear.

Strindberg had twenty-four homes in Stockholm town flats. They were a refuge, not a Grand Duke's palace. In his last move he shifted from Karlavägen to a new home at 85 Drottninggatan. Although its major architectural features were its central heating, elevator and a green tower, Strindberg nicknamed it "the Blue Tower" after a famous prison in Copenhagen in which some celebrated Swedes had been bolted to the walls. Strindberg worked in his three-room apartment on the fourth floor, a few minutes walk from the Intimate Theatre.

Born in Stockholm in 1849, Strindberg grew up in what was one of Europe's seediest towns. He developed an Oedipus complex, as his autobiography shows. He glossed over his father's wealth and explained that mother worship was a substitute for a lost belief in God. Strindberg experienced this when his father married one of his family's servants after his mother's death. Oscar's marriage resulted in the young Strindberg going down a class in the game of life. He was shifted from the respectable Klara School for upper- and middle-class children and relocated to the Jacob Parish Apologist School, the parish school which housed Stockholm's answer to Squeers; it was a working-class school and full of ragamuffins. Strindberg's obsessive focus on his position in Stockholm society never wavered and he moved around the town to live at several of Stockholm's better addresses. Strikingly handsome, he was married and divorced three times, once to Siri von Essen, one of the most beautiful actresses in Europe. Siri and August lived in five different apartments in Stockholm, one for each year of their marriage.

Strindberg always felt messed up—and to a large extent he was. At the height of his fame, his drinking friend Edvard Munch painted a portrait of Strindberg, mis-spelling his name so it came out as "Stindberg" and decorating the frame of the painting with larger-than-life sketches of sperm circulating round it. Born in a period of European revolution, when kings and constitutions were being flung aside right and left by armed bandits and nationalist patriots, Strindberg died as Sweden limped towards social democracy after neutrality in the First World War. He described social changes and incorporated them in his plays, but never felt the triumph that a different political setting would have given him had Sweden taken a rougher road to social democracy or, like Russia, France, Germany and Italy, adopted fascist and communist alternatives. Sweden did not break out the revolutionary barricades during the 1848 revolutions, preferring to leave constitutional change to Louis de Geer, working quietly on a new constitution in the Zoological Gardens. Strindberg moped over what did not happen in Stockholm (revolution) as well as what did (his three divorces and his father's second marriage).

As a young man, like his despised Norwegian neighbour and competitor, Ibsen, Strindberg had experimented with historical subjects. They proved theatrical rat poison. His *Master Olof*, finished when he was 23, was rejected by the critics and resulted in years of brooding and critic phobia. Shit rebounded on Strindberg's head—to use a Swedish expression he was fond of. Not until he was middle-aged did he become internationally famous by writing *Miss Julie* (1888), a play so shocking that it might be taken as the dramatic expression of the iconoclastic spirit of Stockholm on the eve of the gay nineties.

MISS JULIE: SHOCKING STOCKHOLM

Miss Julie left no taboo untouched on its opening night. The play opened on Midsummer's Eve in the kitchen of a Swedish count. The count never appeared on stage but during moments of high emotional impact and turning points of the action, barked his orders down a speaking tube to his *dräng*, his menial, churlish and chauvinistic manservant, Jean. As the dust mites from the rising curtain fell on the floor boards, two representative personifications of high and low culture—the count's daughter Julie and the cook Kristin—discussed secret women's business of a particularly unpleasant nature. It was revealed in a rather stagey way that Miss Julie's bitch had been put in pup by the gamekeeper's dog. "On midsummer night anything could happen," thought the more perceptive audience members: "like mistress, like bitch". Tradition in Stockholm allowed a degree of familiarity between the classes on Midsummer Night, not permitted officially on any other night, and Miss Julie, who had just broken off her engagement, was ready to rebound into the arms of the improbably well-informed and sophisticated valet—or so the front stalls feared. The events of the next minutes unfolded before the audience in real time, as if they were happening in their own lives.

Strindberg's famous preface to *Miss Julie* spells out and highlights the power of ancient Greek Naturalism. I once had what Sir Kenneth Clark would call a "serious aesthetic experience" in seeing the play, performed at the Royal Dramatic Theatre and directed by Ingmar Bergman himself. It was faithful to Strindberg's visions in costume, set and intent and as fresh as if the ink had dried on the manuscript that very afternoon.

Jean entered the kitchen, asked what was cooking, and was told to buzz off. Undeterred he pressed his question and as the minutes passed the audience learned more than it probably wanted to about Miss Julie. She was having her menstrual period and was quite mad, raging with hormonal imbalance. Jean, the stage cad, was a familiarly simple character. He played Julie for a fool with a complex set of unlikely bounder ruses. Strindberg had Jean on the one hand feigning despair that Julie was so far above him on the social scale as to be almost unattainable, and on the other showing a class reversal of unlikely proportions, Jean preferring to drink Bordeaux from a stemmed wine glass while Julie guzzled beer from a beaker. The audience was left in no doubt that Jean and Julie exchanged not only class stereotypes but also bodily fluids while Kristin was off stage taking a nap after her hard day's work in the kitchen.

Even Stockholm was a little shocked by what they saw. Where was romance? Where were boots and uniforms? Worse was to come. There was no interval and no dramatic respite in ancient naturalistic Athens, and no quarter was given in nineteenth-century Stockholm either. Miss Julie explained, as any woman would, that Jean ought to have said he loved her. Jean thought this would be an admission too far but for a while they both desultorily discussed marriage. Jean was taken by the idea that they should flee Sweden for Switzerland to set up a hotel business to prey on honeymooners who would book for two weeks, quarrel and leave after one. Was this typical of the Swedish tourist? In Jean's system Julie would be the attractively baited female hook at the cash register while he would sit around drinking wine from stemmed glasses and, somewhat implausibly for a butler, studying *Cook's Railway Guide*. For a moment Jean considered buying a count's title from a Romanian vendor of honours he knew. At this point Julie woke from her dream of love. She was already a countess. What she did she did for love. Nevertheless, leaving Jean's deficiency in emotional development and incapacity for love aside, Julie was prepared to leave Sweden provided she could take her pet caged bird with her.

Bitch in pup, bird in cage—Strindberg's metaphors were basic. Jean and Julie were then attacked by second thoughts, and drink. Matters were made worse for the audience, squirming on their seats, when the cook returned to the kitchen and confronted Jean with what her eyes could hardly communicate to her brain: her fiancé, Jean, had mated with the mistress of the manor. For a castle cook, a working-class pillar of Stockholm social probity, this was too much. Kristin could not remain in the employ of such a debauched household, lacking appropriate class distance and reserve, and she left the stage to go to church to pray for divine intervention in much the same spirit that a train traveller would complain to management about the unreliability of trains on a particular route.

While Kristin was getting dressed appropriately for church, Jean and Julie sobered up. Jean, with post-drunken brutality, explained to Julie that he never even liked her. His sweet words of seduction were nothing more than cynical Machiavellian manipulation. At this Julie screamed at Jean to stand up when he spoke to her and Jean barked back that Miss Julie was not very particular about her personal habits. What was left of the first night audience then wondered if the trip to Switzerland was off.

Julie decided to give it one more shot. She reappeared on stage, kitted out to travel south, although a little grubby about the sleeves of her shirt, carrying her pet bird. Jean wearily agreed to go, but without the bird. Everyone in the audience knew that this trivia was the sort of thing unhappy couples bickered about. After some to-ing and fro-ing, Jean decided to cut the Gordian knot by decapitating the bird. (Remember that this is naturalistic drama.) The play opened with a real stove on stage, with real fire. No painted backdrops. Real people in real midsummer night clothes, ready for the annual orgy. The axe fell on the avian neck with a mighty crash. Julie's scream was so piecing it might have been she who felt the blow.

Strindberg struck a further blow for the Stockholm working class against aristocratic ineptitude and hypocrisy before the night was out. Jean mesmerized Julie into suicide. In a play with more blood than *Macbeth*, Julie cut her throat with Jean's razor and the curtain fell.

Strindberg died in 1912. The Blue Tower is now furnished and decorated as if the author had just been carried out to be buried. His spectacles were left on his study table, along with his camera, plate, guitar and some of his printing. His bedroom and dining room have not changed for a hundred years. Nothing gives any clue to his early terrors as a schoolboy. It is as if he lived a life that left no damaging physical memento. But Strindberg never forgot the cruelty he suffered at school. In *Gamla Stan*, he recalled:

> Every schoolboy at Jacob counted the day when he escaped beating as most unusual. After morning prayers came the moment of punishment for those whose beating had been postponed from the preceding day and then the lashes rained during every hour lesson.

Strindberg remembered more fondly how his chums had ulcerous noses, ugly facial features and stank. While the students at Jacob were notorious for their disorder, fighting long-running schoolyard battles among the carts, barrels and hawkers' goods that crossed their playground, the teachers were systematic in their cruelty. They kept a selection of carpet beaters in each classroom—long, medium and short. As Kenne Fant explains in his superb biography of Strindberg's classmate Alfred Nobel, "thrashing was considered an effective cure for intellectual shortcomings.

A student who had made six spelling mistakes could be called to the teacher's desk. 'Put your fingers on the edge!' Then the teacher raised the carpet beater and dealt six stinging lashes across the fingers." No wonder Strindberg and his schoolmates slipped out for an aquavit during their lunch break.

GRAHAM GREENE: SENTIMENTAL HUMILITY AND DEEP HIDDEN ARROGANCE

It was a chance professional writing interest in Ivar Kreuger that first drew Graham Greene to follow Shaw and travel to Stockholm. In March 1933 to make some money Greene sketched a biography of Kreuger for *The Spectator*. Ivar Kreuger was a household name in the 1930s, while Graham Greene was relatively poor and unknown. Kreuger was one of the thousands of Swedish engineers who changed the world through a combination of engineering know-how and business craftiness. He turned out to be a signal bad apple in the barrel, but in his twenties he worked well and professionally as a civil engineer in the United States and South Africa, returning to Sweden on the eve of the First World War.

In 1913 the Kreuger family owned two firms making safety matches. By 1918 Kreuger had taken over the entire Swedish match industry and consolidated it into a single firm, Svenka Tändsticks. He then used American capital to buy out match production and marketing rights in dozens of countries outside Sweden. On the eve of the Great Depression Kreuger controlled half the world's match production in an era when matches were one of life's necessities in rich and poor countries alike.

So far so good, but "the Match King" diversified his business empire by lending huge, unsecured loans to out-of-pocket sovereign states in return for match-making monopolies. Typical was a deal with Germany by which Kreuger obtained a match production monopoly agreement in return for an unsecured loan of $125 million. He even diddled the pope with a similar scam. His loan business expanded well beyond his resources and Kreuger took suicide to be the only way out of a life that had been built around almost unimaginatively huge corporate crimes, forgery and fraud. He shot himself in the head in Paris in 1932, bringing catastrophe to his immediate circle but having carved a niche for Swedish industry that continues to this day. Almost a century later, strike a match, look at the matchbox and it will probably say "Made in Sweden".

When Graham Greene first visited Stockholm he was well on the road to becoming a spy. (John Le Carré pointed out that the life of a writer and the life of a spy were perfectly compatible. Le Carré saw Greene as his mentor because Greene changed Le Carré's life by providing him with the phrase "the spy who came in from the cold".) Moving on from his article on Kreuger, Greene blended fantasy and reality in the Scandinavian anti-hero of his 1935 novel *England Made Me*. At first sight the title suggests a book that had nothing to do with Stockholm, and Greene could have described the two major characters, a brother and sister, as living anywhere in the world. A practised cadger like all authors and spies, Greene talked the Göta Canal Company into giving him a free ticket for part of the journey to Stockholm where he intended to gather material for his *England Made Me*. He travelled with his brother Hugh, leaving his wife, five months pregnant, in Oxford.

Greene's plan was to take the Göta Canal boat from Gothenburg to Stockholm in August, the height of the summer tourist season. He knew it would be as cold in Stockholm in mid-summer as it was in northern Scotland, the coldest spot he had experienced, and accordingly packed extra supplies of warm underpants. In later life he remembered walking alongside the boat on the towpath in the warm, soft summer brilliance of the Swedish midnight, among the silver birches. Greene was swept off his feet by the peculiar emotions stirred by being awake in a night when the sun hardly seemed to set. As all who first experience this as adults, he loved the magical atmosphere.

Down to earth, Greene worried and fretted. Could he establish himself as an author and novelist in Stockholm? Could he meet publishers and lawyers to handle any contractual matters if he were lucky enough to find a Swedish agent? As it turned out, *England Made Me* was less informative about Stockholm than the article Greene wrote when he returned home. Published in *The Spectator*, it described his distaste of Stockholm-style pacifism. Greene was sensitive to cant. He thought he saw Sweden edging towards fascism, masked by his Stockholm contact's insincere protestations of humility. Describing experiences in Stockholm, he sketched Swedish militarism through a picture of the moon glinting on the sentry's bayonet parading on the palace terrace and, at midday, a beating of drums, flashing of swords and prancing of chargers as the royal guard changed at the city's royal castle. When he met new friends Greene memorized this dialogue. "Our little country, our little country," the Swedish lawyer and the Swedish publisher kept repeating, said Greene "with sentimental humility and a deep hidden arrogance." In Oslo (he mocked) they said "our small country, our small country", meaning the latest census result, or the extent of herring fisheries.

Greene was not, like de Botton, an enthusiast of Swedish domestic interiors. For him a Stockholm home was a stage set. Greene described a formal house, where every piece of furniture was like a child in a charity school, well-scrubbed, in place and at attention. He noted that on home ground the Swedish pacifist supported war between races. He was furious to observe how the pacifist grew excited at the thought of Russia, spoke of the glory involved in implementing an extermination policy: "poison gas, germs, aerial bombardment, savouring the words; after the schnapps and the beer and the wine (*Skål*, with the glass held at the fourth button of the waistcoat, while the charity children stood stiffly around) and the glasses of punch and three whiskies and sodas, he became vehement about women, ears back, eyes popping: no woman has character... made to be the mates of men."

In a practical, non-social-democratic, Oxford sort of way, Greene took it upon himself not only to defend the rights of women and children, but to unmask the hypocrisy and insensitivity of Stockholm reactionaries. He wrote:

> The publisher with the military carriage and the bristling red moustache said, "If the socialists really came to power, I should be first to take up arms. I do not, of course, believe in God, but if our Church was threatened, I should be the first..." He said, "We haven't any need of Socialism here. I will show you how the workmen live. Poor, but so clean, so contented". He thrust his way into strangers' cottages, leant in at their windows, opened their doors...

By the time *England Made Me* was made into a film in 1973, a lot of water had sloshed past Slussen and lapped on the capstones of Stockholm harbour quays. Kreuger had been transformed by the British director Peter Duffell into the corrupt financier Krogh, played by the Australian Peter Finch. The following year Finch picked up another Scandinavian role as an unconvincing cardinal in *The Abdication*, also a British film directed by

Anthony Harvey. Liv Ullman was Finch's co-star, reinventing Greta Garbo's role as Queen Christina. Finch failed to provide a challenging test of the sincerity of Queen Christina's conversion and the film was described as plodding.

The filmmakers of *England Made Me* believed that a 1970s generation would not understand why Greene chose Stockholm as the background city to illustrate the moral collapse of capitalism. To magnify the point that Stockholm was decadent and rife with sexual unconventionality (however staid municipal politics might be) Greene added incest to lust. Michael York was convincing as Anthony Farrant and Peter Finch was a one hundred per cent success as Kreuger turned Krogh. Only the Berlin cabaret and the German Nazis instead of the Stockholm variety rang false. Greene might also have wanted to know why a story about Stockholm, hijacked to Berlin, was shot in Yugoslavia. Like the book, the film was, as the critics say, "unappreciated" in its initial release, but repaid second viewings for its absorbing, thoughtful fare.

As a young novelist, Greene did not look further than his old public school experiences and his life at Oxford for an odious stereotype to illustrate the corruption of western capitalism. In creating Minty Greene overbalanced the novel, Minty being a more convincing Stockholm resident than the suicidal Swedish capitalist Krogh. Stockholm, then as now, was full of Mintys, trading on the public school ethic, respecting the old school tie and organizing Harrovian dinners to raise funds for schools or their colleges.

Greene visited Sweden again during the Cold War. During the Second World War he had worked for M16 and controlled a non-Swedish master spy code named, rather unimaginatively, Garbo. Greene chose the Royal Dramatic Theatre for a swansong. This premiere of his play *The Living Room* looked out of place performed in the luxurious ambience of opulent marble staircases and halls, gilded stucco and impressively painted ceilings on the Nybroplan site. Greene started work on *The Living Room* in Vietnam in 1951 and finished it off in Kuala Lumpur, where he was much more at home. As an elderly gentleman he did not pack his extra warm underpants on this occasion even though the developing ex-colonies in the humid tropics suited his muse more than the chilly northern capital of a major world economic power.

In October 1952, when the play was staged, Greene had never been more famous or more depressed. It was an effort to travel to Stockholm for the first night. When he stepped onto the stage to receive applause, it was as one of the greatest novelists of the twentieth century. To members of the first night audience it seemed that the applause would never end. A friend of Greene's in the world of criticism recalled that the world premiere gave the impression of a gala with the whole of Stockholm crowded about the object of the gala—the author. But the predominant feeling among the audience at this most remarkable Dramatic Theatre first night was, one of them put it, of uneasiness, deep emotion and sometimes agony.

After the performance Greene left Stockholm for the last time. He was in the same bitter state of mind that struck him on his first visit, feeling that nothing had been resolved since the 1930s and that the Swedes remained cultural barbarians. Stockholm is not a city where hosts ignore being baited. Many believed, and used the verb, that Greene had deliberately "tortured" his Lutheran audience. Artur Lundkvist, then known as the grand old man of the Swedish Academy and Nobel Literature laureate king-maker, had the last word as far as the Stockholm view of world letters was concerned. Lundkvist boasted that he had stayed alive with the express purpose of stopping any chance Greene had of gaining the Nobel Prize for Literature. Lundkvist considered that Greene turned out "Catholic propaganda of the most vulgar type". In case his readers missed the point, Lundkvist added that Greene's degeneration had long been suspect, describing him as a morally dangerous writer in league with the darkest of present-day western reactionary powers. Lundkvist ended by saying that on any occasion when Greene's work was performed in Stockholm "the plague flag should be raised over the Dramatic Theatre."

BLACK HOLE

Despite repeated cultural misunderstanding, Stockholm remains still a black hole that sucks in creative writers. It is hard, even in the early twenty-first century, for any novelist, prize-winner or duffer, to avoid having one of their characters visit the place. Ian McEwan, author of many books including *The Comfort of Strangers*, *The Child in Time*, *Black Dogs*, *Enduring Love* and *Amsterdam*, the "best novelist in Britain" (*Financial Times*), referred to Stockholm in *Saturday* (2005). McEwan put the mother of the novel's hero as "swimming for Britain in the Stockholm Olympics of 1912—the first ever women's swimming event."

Translation traffic, apart from Henning Mankell and Stieg Larsson, is largely one-way. Stockholmers read many English authors in translation. *Ring for Jeeves* is very popular. Judging from the appearance and expression of many elderly professors in Stockholm I have met, P. G. Wodehouse is the only English-language author they have read. Anachronistic greetings and accents make you blink to confirm you have not actually met Bertie Wooster. While McEwan puffed Stockholm for its pioneering acceptance of female sporting equality, A. J. Cronin saw the city as it appeared to its detractors as the last place in the world one would like to work. It was a realm to send and forget failed professionals. In *The Spanish Gardener* (1950), Cronin created an English diplomat as stereotypically misguided, bloodless and infantile, a plum role for Michael Hordern when the book was filmed in 1956. Dirk Bogarde, convincing as the honest peasant, tried to liberate the diplomat from his heartless and careerist pursuit of rising status. The feeble and failing diplomat's last post before Sweden was Spain. In Spain he distinguished himself by wrongly accusing his gardener of stealing from his residence and made things even worse by insulting the Head of Mission, the British ambassador. To complete the picture of misery, his wife deserted him and went to live in Scotland, denying access to his child. In Cronin's day, the London Foreign Office had only one destination for such a failure: the British Embassy in Stockholm. The FO view was understandable. There seemed no point in wasting time building up relationships with a country whose people and government were determined and clever enough to remain neutral in major world conflicts. In Tokyo, however, Stockholm was seen as a plum appointment.

MOTOJIRO AKASHI: THE JAPANESE JAMES BOND

Colonel Motojiro Akashi is known to his fellow Japanese with an interest in espionage as their own James Bond. His appointment to the Japanese Embassy in Stockholm during the Russian-Japanese war was a sign of things to come as Stockholm became a central clearing house for spies and intelligence specialists for the next hundred years. When Japanese torpedo boats attacked Russian warships in Port Arthur in February 1904, Colonel Akashi moved his desk from St. Petersburg to Stockholm overnight. Michael Futrell, in *Northern Underground* (1963), described Stockholm's key strategic location and Akashi's role as an agent of influence. English sympathies were with the Japanese. Japan became an ally of England in

1902 and, notwithstanding Pearl Harbor, remains a friend of the UK and the US today. Colonel Akashi's mission was to organize gunrunning into Finland to divert Russian resources and to arm revolutionary Finns who wanted to cut their constitutional links and create a workers' state. Akashi purchased weapons in Switzerland, and stored them in a London bookshop until he found ships and crews to charter for the adventure. Only one vessel, the *John Grafton*, reached Finland where it ran aground in the Finnish archipelago and had to be scuttled. The gunrunners escaped through the connivance of the Finnish police, making it across the border to Stockholm and safety. Akashi's role became public and he was recalled to Japan. He continued to spy with distinction, dying in 1919 with the rank of general. By then he was famous for the string of brothels he organized on the route of the Trans-Siberian Railway to carry and hide his agents from Japan to Stockholm via Russia. As part of his role as brothel keeper as well as spy, he developed a reputation as a womanizer especially irresistible to western females.

The Russian revolutionaries never forgot Stockholm's role in their struggle against the Tsar, and Lenin made a celebrated trip to the city. The Bolsheviks and the Russian Red Cross both bought pharmaceutical drugs and medical supplies in Stockholm to get them through the war. Lenin's contact in Stockholm was Jacob Fürstenberg, who lived on a diet of pancakes and ice cream in a villa near Saltsjöbaden. After 1917 he left Stockholm for the Soviet Union where he had a successful career as a diplomat, which ended in his murder during a purge in either 1937 or 1939.

Lenin's simple instruction to Fürstenberg was: "don't spare money on connections between Petrograd and Stockholm." Lenin, accompanied by both his wife and his mistress, made a trip to Stockholm on 12 April 1917 and was photographed carrying an umbrella. He was entertained by Swedish socialists and left Stockholm by train in the evening for Haparanda, Finland and Russia, arriving in the Russian capital on 16 April. Lenin spent only nine hours in Stockholm where he found time to buy a suit and an overcoat at the PUB department store. Stockholmers thought that he looked like a workman on a Sunday excursion in unsettled weather. During this time he set up a Bolshevik centre to represent him abroad and appealed for money to meet his travel expenses. The Swedish foreign minister chipped in, saying he did so "gladly, as long as Lenin leaves today." Lenin left and Stockholm remained a strategically located centre for intrigue in the years that followed. A measure of the closeness between Bolshevik intellectuals and their Swedish friends was the marriage of Strindberg's daughter, Karin, to Vladimir Smirnov, who became Soviet consul general in Sweden after 1917.

MAROONED IN THE GRAND HOTEL

Justin Cartwright, listed for the Booker Prize and winner of the Whitbread, continues the tradition of piling Stockholm into a novel. In this case, the references are apposite. In a thinly disguised attack on Isaiah Berlin, Cartwright describes Stockholm through the eyes of Elizabeth Partridge as seen from a balcony of the Grand Hotel during the Second World War. The novel, *The Song Before It Is Sung* (2007), describes Elizabeth looking out across the famous harbour. Down below the ferries are setting out from the quays to the islands as if everything in the world was ordered, unruffled and calm. The madness and destruction of the war seem to her to belong to another world. Elizabeth Partridge finds wartime Stockholm quite literally unreal, "but of course it was real. All too real. I sat on the terrace of the hotel in the warm sunshine, my heart full of bit-

terness and shame. How had we allowed our world to be destroyed? Why had our wonderful, enchanted lives been ruined, our friends killed? Here in orderly, sensible, calm Sweden, the folly of war was so overwhelmingly obvious."

Stockholm was, in countless ways, modified by its contact with visitors and the Grand Hotel was often the scene where Swedes did things some found distasteful: entertain German officers during the Winter War and imprison British citizens for not paying their hotel bills during the Cold War. In London's world of the literary imagination, the British Ambassador in Stockholm was more an agent of the Howard League for Penal Reform than an intelligence-gather for M16. On arrival in Stockholm, British diplomats were popularly perceived stereotypes like Lord Tilmouth. In London, Gainsborough Films, at the opposite end of the cultural spectrum to Svensk Film Industri, in 1948 produced a stagy piece of theatre set in post-war Stockholm, *Traveller's Joy*, in which His Excellency Lord Tilmouth is a foil for the dramatic skills of Googie Withers and John McCallum. Lord Tilmouth, a chinless moustachioed aristocrat, has been transferred to Stockholm from Cairo, from one extreme of climate to another. In a farcical episode in his early life as a young diplomat he has shown Googie Withers around the pyramids and accidentally triggered her divorce from a spectacularly handsome, jealous husband. Years later Googie, her ex-husband and Lord Tilmouth meet again in Stockholm where Googie is selling Harris Tweed to the Swedes. Although Gainsborough's magic lantern never left London, the film shows three of Stockholm's most attractive water panoramas in evocative moving sequences: the view across to the Town Hall from Södermalm, traffic moving to Gamla Stan across the water and, most impressive of all, the Grand Hotel as seen from the Royal Palace.

The plot called for Googie Withers to be marooned in the Grand Hotel with her (male) secretary and her ex-husband. The trio have run out of money and cannot pay their hotel bill. The hotel manager explains that, while he is happy to let Americans run up bills because they can pay them, the British are required to put cash on the nail. Post-war exchange controls prevented the British taking anything except a small allowance for business travel purposes. In one scene two Swedish policemen, with sabres rather than baseball bats at their belts, arrest UK citizens in the Grand Hotel lobby and march them off to prison where they are to stay until their bills are paid. Not by the ambassador. The ambassador visits defaulters in prison in his time off from hosting crayfish and aquavit parties at which the British diplomats and their guests drink twenty shots of vodka during a meal and master *tack tack* (the all-purpose Swedish phrase) convincingly when speaking to the embassy servants.

At that period in history Stockholm was a place to leave, not to visit. Googie Withers herself was a thespian war heroine. She survived a direct hit by a V2 on an Antwerp theatre where she was performing when the German flying bomb killed over a thousand of her audience. Googie chose to live and work in Australia rather than post-war Europe. At one stage in her life her husband invented, for television, a marsupial equivalent of *Inspector Rex*, a kangaroo named Skippy. Kangaroos had limited skills as actors and 35 were required, with various attributes. One could get in and out of a car, for example. Skippy turned out to be a bestseller but not initially in Stockholm. Swedes declared that it was improper to mislead their children by telling them that kangaroos could do things that they could not, like operating police radios, which even the police had difficulty with.

Chapter Four

MONEY, MONEY, MONEY

INDUSTRIALISTS AND PHILANTHROPISTS

ALFRED NOBEL: GRUMBLING BEAR

Googie Withers' film *Traveller's Joy* described what it was like to be stranded in Stockholm without currency after a business trip. Everyone in Stockholm knows that it is complex to live in a rich man's world, especially around wartime. When Justin Cartwright's fictional character Elizabeth Partridge ordered lingonberry tart during the Second World War, Stockholm was "full of Nazis and agents from every power", trying to make money. The Swedish stock exchange, banks and the financial system, in peace and war, were first-class in generating wealth in a capitalist free for all.

Stockholm is unusual as the home of the world's only sensationalist business newspaper, *Dagens Industri*. This publication reads as if the pink pages of the *Financial Times* have been spiced with tabloid page-three girls. The executive off-bourse activities of daily industry in Stockholm have always been sexy. From Alfred Nobel through Ivar Kreuger and Axel Wenner-Gren to the Barons of Bofors, financial journalists have had rich pickings. Attached to the Swedish dictionary definition of *industri*, industry, alongside the respectable definitions of trade, manufacturer and employer of skilled labour, are the words *industri-riddare*, industry knight. So that English speakers can understand the colloquial impact, the extended meanings of swindler, adventurer and "swell-mobsman" are added.

Nobody personified the famous openness of Swedish financial opportunity better than Alfred Nobel, the most celebrated of the industrialists to illustrate the spirit of philanthropy that characterizes the Stockholm mindset. Among the knights of the adding machine and the calculator Alfred Nobel became a template for the Stockholm inventor. His apprenticeship in St. Petersburg made him appreciate that responsibility came with opportunity and that life among the champagne bottles was but a short mishap away from bankruptcy.

As a seventeen-year-old Alfred was apprenticed to John Ericsson, the most important inventive Swedish genius of the time who played as significant a part in American history as he did in telecommunications. Swedish know-how was on the winning side in a significant battle during the American Civil War when Ericsson's iron-plated Union warship *Monitor* defeated the Confederate *Merrimac*. Ericsson's celebrated warship design had been mocked as a cheese dish on a breadboard. Its deck was only two feet above water and in its crew of 57 were six Swedes. Ericsson built the *Monitor* in 118 days and it saw off the *Merrimac* only to sink in a storm shortly afterwards.

In Ericsson's day a lexicon of derogatory epithets reported that the word "Swede" was usually coupled with the word "dumb". Unintelligent persons were often derogatorily referred to as Swedes, while ethnic Swedes themselves were more specifically taunted as "dumb socks" or "herring-chokers". For a time Swedes were rated with the Irish as the United States' most stupid immigrants, a reputation Ericsson and Nobel dispelled.

Ericsson became rich after he turned to the defence industry in a career path that Nobel followed. Typically for a Stockholmer, Alfred said virtually nothing about his teenage contact with a role model to envy and emulate, but there is no doubt that both Ericsson and Nobel were at one in believing that although they were one hundred per cent Swedish they worked for mankind as a whole.

Although the Swedish Academy in Gamla Stan shares its address with the Nobel Museum—the most moving and impressive exhibition of power, good taste and philanthropy in the world—the house where Alfred Nobel was born on 31 October 1833 no longer exists. It was demolished a century later as part of the progress inevitable when obsolete property was requisitioned for inner-city development. Nobel was born on the second floor at the back of the three-storey apartment at 9 Norrlandsgatan. As a child he, like August Strindberg and Greta Garbo, lived among the urban poor. Nobel's first home was icy cold in winter, its rats were said to be fatter than humans, garbage was tossed into the backyard and lay around the outdoor lavatories, and epidemics of cholera, typhoid, diphtheria and whooping cough killed many of his friends.

When Alfred was four years old his father Immanuel went bankrupt and sailed east to Åbo, Finland, to avoid debtors' prison. The father (which sounds like a good title for a play) left his wife Andriette and her three children to support themselves until he got back on his feet and could return home, taking advantage of the fact that Finland was then no longer part of Sweden, but a Russian Grand Duchy. Alfred, as an eight-year-old, saw Immanuel make influential friends within the Russian defence ministry, and his pioneering development of land and sea mines had laid the foundation for the expansion of unimaginably large wealth. Towards the end of the nineteenth century, through the unanticipated global success of his company's weapons, explosives manufacture and by being pioneers in the oil industry, the Nobels had become the Swedish equivalent of the Rothschilds, Rockefellers and Morgans.

The young Alfred soon tasted the fruits of wealth in the family mansion in Russia and absorbed his father's stern Protestant work ethic. His father had been fortunate with the timing of his brave burst of entrepreneurial energy. The Russian acquisition of Finland from Sweden at the end of the Napoleonic era gave imaginative Swedish citizens the chance to make fortunes in a developing despotic region under centralized control where Swedish influence, wielded by Swedish-speaking Finns, was still important. The Crimean War allowed Immanuel the opportunity to demonstrate that his mines were superior to both the British and the Russian versions. Nobel-designed mines were laid along the Gulf of Finland from Kronstad to Sveaborg and Reval, and kept the British enemy away from St. Petersburg—although not from Bomarsund. Alfred's father went bankrupt a second time when the Crimean War ended. After Tsar Alexander II signed a peace treaty in Paris, the Russians, like bookmakers at a race meeting, defaulted on their debts to the Nobel family. The Nobels returned to Stockholm where they remained optimistic that better luck was just around the corner.

Corporate reconstruction of the most complex kind once again transformed the Nobel fortune. Alfred has taken the lion's share of historical attention away from the family through his legacy, the Nobel prizes, the courage of his enterprises and his amassing and retention of capital to an extent never to be seen again in Sweden. Not that everything was always rosy. Having just succeeded in detonating nitroglycerin, Alfred wrote a Freudian note to his father warning him not to claim credit for his son's ingenuity, ending by saying that he would not allow himself to be treated like a schoolboy.

Like the house where Alfred was born, the factory where he experimented with nitroglycerin production has vanished. The building on Långholm Bay was demolished quicker than the apartment in Norrlandsgatan. It disappeared in an instant in an eruption of yellow flame and broken glass panes on Kungsholm. Until then, the development of nitroglycerin had been seen as relatively harmless, but human error in storage of larger quantities of explosive, at that stage kept in open containers, dismembered Stockholm residents and Nobel's workers and management alike.

Having resolved his rivalry with his father, Alfred became the family's most daring and clever chemist. He received his first Swedish patent to manufacture nitroglycerin and for almost a year worked to build up a stock of about a quarter of a ton of highly explosive oil. He stored this in an old coach house within the grounds of his factory. Nobel's biographer, Kenne Fant, recalled how during the eleven months before the tragedy Alfred's neighbours felt, not without justification, that they were living on top of a volcano and they complained to the landlord. Both Alfred and Immanuel were unaware of the devastating power of nitroglycerin. They were concentrating on getting the explosive to detonate and assumed it to be relatively safe, an assumption based on wishful thinking. They did not want to believe that an accident could happen and assured everyone there was no reason to worry; their experiments, they believed, were completely harmless.

The yard outside the main building was deserted when catastrophe hit on 3 September 1864. The laboratory exploded with a thunderous roar. A Stockholm newspaper reported that the source of the blast was a building on the Heleneborg estate "where the engineer Nobel had constructed a nitroglycerin factory. In the capital people heard the violent sound of the explosion." The newspaper reported that a much more terrible sight awaited at the site of the accident. There was nothing left of the factory, a wooden building adjacent to the Heleneborg estate, except a few charred fragments thrown here and there. In the houses nearby, and even those on the other side of the bay, not only had the glass panes been smashed but also windowsills and moulding. The horrified readers then learned

> Most ghastly was the sight of the mutilated corpses strewn on the ground. Not only had the clothes been torn off but some had their heads missing and the flesh ripped off their bones. These formless masses of

flesh and bone bore little or no resemblance to human bodies. The effect of the explosion could be judged by the fact that in a nearby stone house, the walls facing the factory had split open and a woman who had been standing by her stove cooking had part of her head crushed, one arm torn off and one thigh terribly mauled. The unfortunate victim was still alive and was carried to the hospital on a litter, looking more like a bloody mass of meat than a human being. Mr. Nobel was not himself present, but one of his sons is said to be among the victims, and another son sustained major head injuries.

Alfred Nobel survived the blast, his face bloodied and damaged by flying wood and glass. For the next thirty years he stayed away from hands-on involvement in the explosives industry and lived mostly off-shore in Paris and San Remo, getting richer and gloomier by the minute. During the last three years of his life, as Kenne Fant points out, absence had made the heart grow fonder and Alfred grew closer to his birthplace, Sweden. In middle age he fell in love with Sophie Hess, whom he came to describe as "the Troll". Sophie was twenty-three years younger than Alfred when they first met at a Viennese spa, and his jealous thoughts about his young mistress turned him, by his own admission, into a grumbling bear. During their twenty-year relationship, Alfred never managed to control Sophie as he controlled ICI in Scotland and many other enterprises. Alfred dominated the oil industry in Russia for a time, still referred to as "the Nobelski era" in Baku, and broadened his mastery of dynamite to create gelignite and manufacture improved hand grenades. One of the richest bachelors in the world revealed in a typically private letter the extent of his personal confusion.

Stockholm, Hotel Rydberg
September 27, 1878

Dear child,
You complain that my letters are too brief and reticent, but you seem not to want to understand the reason why, although it is evident: everyone is an egoist, especially women who think only of themselves. Though I knew this at the beginning of our acquaintance, it is now even clearer to me that your view of life has been twisted. I am therefore forced to

remain aloof to prevent your affection from becoming too deeply rooted. You may believe yourself to be fond of me. But it is merely gratitude, perhaps respect, and such feelings are not enough to fill the need for love in your young soul.

The time will come—perhaps fairly soon—when your heart will be filled with love for another man. How you will blame me then for the way I tied you down with an ardent lover's inextricable bonds. I see this clearly and therefore rein in my feelings. Do not believe, however, that I really have a heart of stone, as you so often charge in your letters.

More than most, perhaps, I have lived with the pressure of desolate loneliness, and in the past have sought an intimate communion with someone. But this someone could hardly be a twenty-one-year-old with whose philosophy of life and spirituality I have little or nothing in common. Besides, your star is rising in the heaven of fate while mine is descending. Youth lends colours to your hope, while in me the bright colours are few and more reminiscent of those in a sunset. Two such essentially different people do not fit as lovers, but in spite of this can remain good friends.

Nobel was not drawn to Stockholm by the food. From the Hotel Rydberg he wrote to Sophie:

The food served here is very bad, and since I don't like to eat alone, I suffer stomach aches most of the time. Being careful doesn't seem to help. Though I neither smoke nor drink wine, my headaches are so terrible that life seems filled with bile. I hope you are feeling better; judging from your letters you seem to have forgotten all about me already. That is not nice of you, since you live always in my thoughts and in my heart.

For a long time Nobel survived love and food poisoning and desolate loneliness. He died of a stroke on 10 December 1896. He was not buried alive, as he had feared during countless bouts of insomniac nightmares at the Hotel Rydberg. He was definitely dead when his body was taken in its coffin from the ceremony at Villa Nobel to the San Remo railway station to be sent on to a Stockholm graveyard. Nobel made sure that this element of his burial was double-checked after life was pronounced extinct by a second medical opinion called for in his instructions.

Nobel's funeral procession took place in the Swedish capital on a wintry afternoon, with torch-carrying outriders and illuminated cabs. The church was decorated according to his older brother Emanuel's instructions. Kenne Fant described how the guests entered through the large portal, to be met by the sight of laurel trees. The centre aisle was transformed into an alley of palm trees with garlands joined by a canopy that was, in accordance with Italian custom, held up by a white dove. The coffin was made of olive wood and had silver handles. At the head of the coffin was a silver plaque inscribed with his birth and death dates. Although the funeral was one of the most extravagant ever held in Stockholm, no representative of the Swedish royal family was present; they continued to sulk over the controversial terms of Nobel's will.

The ceremony included a recital by the opera singer Carl August Söderman, who sang a selection from Verdi's *Requiem*. Around 4.30 p.m. the coffin was carried outside, where the crowd had assembled. The funeral procession included forty carriages, of which four were filled entirely with wreaths. Thousands of people lined the road to the crematorium at Norrtull, and more torch-bearers on horseback joined the procession. "The light from torches and cressets at the graveyard threw a magical glow over the white snow drifts," read an account in the *Dagens Nyheter* newspaper, which went on: "Outside the crematorium at the Northern funeral grounds, the lid was unscrewed and a white inner coffin was carried inside to be entrusted to the oven's fires. The clergyman said a few last words, an organ hummed, and the mechanism by which the coffin is loaded into the oven rattled while the torches outside blazed."

Ingvar Kamprad: What is IKEA?

While Nobel accepted British, American and European business models, a later generation was impressed by Adolf Hitler's systems. Stockholmers were Germanic after all, and during the First World War their neutrality masked community disagreement on whether a German or a British victory would be better for the town. In the 1930s enthusiasts for german industry and pubic policy were thick on the ground and among them was the young Ingvar Kamprad.

Ingvar Kamprad had personal wealth greater than almost every human on earth. In 2008, according to *Forbes* magazine, he was the richest European-born person alive, with a net fortune estimated at $31 billion.

Kamprad reasonably feared what the wealthy take to be the vampire-like fangs and vulture-like talons of the Swedish tax office. While the delicacies of the Swedish welfare state have to be paid for, no-one likes paying taxes, especially the mega-rich. Stockholm's most famous prime minister, children's author, tennis champion and film director all felt the tax office's sting. Olof Palme was in hot water with them for not declaring a small lecture fee; Astrid Lindgren was distraught and confused, and cried that they wanted to tax her 150 per cent of her earnings, and humiliate and discredit her; Wimbledon champion Björn Borg settled for a time in Monaco; and Ingmar Bergman left Stockholm claiming he had been roughed up by the tax department muscle men. Bergman, Borg and Lindgren all finally came to terms with the inevitability of death and taxes, and returned home.

Kamprad's emporia are sited at the opposite end of the furniture market to high-class Svensk Tenn. IKEA caters for "everyman". You can buy sofas in transactions sweetened with meatballs and lingonberry jam in IKEA stores from Dubai to Adelaide. Kamprad has had an impact on lifestyle in Stockholm and the world, turning consumers into do-it-yourself enthusiasts, scratching their head every week trying to put together the flat pack products shown in the IKEA catalogue. Kamprad's IKEA catalogue is read by more people than the Bible. Almost one million people enter an IKEA store somewhere in the world each day.

You have to look hard to find someone who has not recognized Kamprad's achievement. Journalist Lesley White found one of the few in 2006. Interviewing Antony Armstrong-Jones, the ex-husband of Princess Margaret, White became irritated by his continual use of his title "Lord Snowdon". Describing the "Lord of the Lens" as a mischievous toff, White illustrated the point by reporting Snowdon as so out of touch with the twenty-first century that he could ask, when the subject of interior decorating arose, "what exactly is IKEA, darling?"

Even among interior decorators Snowdon is in a minority. IKEA is an acronym of Ingvar Kamprad's name, and the names of the farm where he was raised and the closest town, hence I for Ingvar, K for Kamprad, E for Elmtaryd and A for Agunnaryd. Ingvar was written off by his father when he was four years old because he was too lazy to milk the cows on Elmtaryd, the family farm in the one-elk town of Agunnaryd situated south of Stockholm. Maybe Ingvar's father should have invested more energy in his son, who was once richer than the richest Saudi prince and has retained more money than Bill Gates.

It seems that entrepreneurial spirit is born in many, but for most it fades over time. It was not unusual for a five-year-old to sell matchboxes, cards and pens, or for an eleven-year-old to pick and sell berries. What was unusual was entrepreneurial star quality, a quality Kamprad always had. At around the same age that Ingrid Bergman was trying for drama school, Kamprad had sufficient confidence to found IKEA, opening his first store in Älmhult in 1958. The local competition was so small that Kamprad found himself with too many customers to service. He was selling hand over fist, so he invented the retail equivalent of user-friendly dynamite, a system whereby customers went to a warehouse and picked up their furniture at bargain prices, then carted it home to unpack and assemble themselves. His success irked his jealous rivals, who persuaded furniture makers to boycott Kamprad because he was undercutting them. In response, Kamprad created the IKEA in-house product built by his own workers and made do-it-yourself easier by inventing the successful marketing of the flat pack system of furniture packaging.

Even though Kamprad had the customary oversupply of the wealth enjoyed by all of Stockholm's major inventors and sports and movie stars, he tried to keep a level head, so much so that he developed a reputation for stinginess. Kamprad was genuinely uneasy about the expensive nature of his hobby vineyard in Provence. Many Stockholm tycoons had similar getaways in Umbria, Tuscany and even the Barossa Valley in Australia, yet few emulated Kamprad by driving eleven-year-old Volvos, travelling economy class, staying in down-market hotels and refusing to pay more than $15 for a haircut. "I'm a bit tight with money, but so what?" he said. "I look at the money I'm about to spend and ask myself if IKEA's customers can afford to spend it."

Kamprad dresses casually, insists that his staff "call me Ingvar," and buys fruit late in the afternoon (so it is said) when prices have dropped. There is a messianic edge to him, just as there was to Alfred Nobel. To Kamprad the IKEA catalogue is not like the Bible, "it is the Bible." Echoing Nobel's famous will, Kamprad has devised *The Furniture Dealer's Testament*, which contains the commandment: "IKEA people do not drive flash cars or stay at luxury hotels."

All of Kamprad's skeletons are out of the IKEA cupboard because,

after all, IKEA itself pays huge corporatation tax and Kamprad has the quality most Stockholmers prize above all else: honesty and ordinariness. Kamprad, as a young man, was briefly a supporter of Sweden's pro-Nazi movement. He bitterly regretted his totalitarian flirtation and told all his employees so in an IKEA-style brochure, *The Biggest Mistake in My Life*. Kamprad was not unique in sympathizing with the small organized fascist movement. Ingmar Bergman's circle of friends included a large number who wanted Germany to win its wars, and who saw the Nazis as idealistic, fun and appropriate to young people. Herman Lindqvist in *A History of Sweden* (2002) reproduced a colour photograph of Swedes sympathetic to Germany and Nazism. They are marching behind three flags, the first a blue ensign carried on a spear-tipped pole in the unmistakable colours of Sweden: a Swedish blue field with a swastika in Swedish yellow. They are all in step, all wearing blue shirts and yellow ties, and all are teenage girls.

The Gnomes of Gamla Stan

Nobel and Kamprad worked in an orderly financial climate where the rules of the game were clear: failure meant bankruptcy, jail or suicide, and success meant limitless wealth. Prudent banking policies were the rule. Stockholm was not Shanghai. Stockholmers were obsessed with the possibilities of association, incorporation and the power of patent law. The city's bankers led the way in creating a rich man's world. For a long time motor vehicles were the most obvious sign of Swedish economic strength. Cars and trucks were bigger than matchboxes or vacuum cleaners, more explicable than gas accumulators or roller bearings, even if they were not more profitable. Not much remains of the Swedish car industry, once the flag carrier of national identity. Having fallen victim first to globalization and then global economic crisis, no longer do Volvo and Saab proclaim the longevity and strength of Swedish steel, the predictability of Swedish reliability and the masterful nature of Swedish innovation. Although they still try to camouflage their Americanness, General Motors and Ford have controlled these former icons for decades even if they have been tempted to try to on-sell the trademark to other manufacturers. Saab began producing cars at Trollhattan in southern Sweden in 1949. After the firm was sold to General Motors in a corporate takeover, Saab owners claimed that GM has run the company down. By 2001 it was making a loss and in 2009, amidst recession and declining sales, GM tried to obtain aid from the Swedish government to rescue Saab before it went bankrupt. Nor should the expression "bloody Volvo driver" now be taken as anti-Swedish, as the doctors' favourite station wagon no longer originates exclusively in Sweden: ten thousand Chinese workers are now making them. At one stage the Volvo S80 had a V8 engine made by Yamaha, a division of Toyota. Even so, motoring writers have described the Volvo S80 as having styling "unerringly functional in an IKEA sort of way", but the Volvo is a luxury the US car industry cannot now afford.

Long ago Hallendorf' and Shuck's *History of Sweden* (1929) proudly described the extent of Swedish engineering and banking development just as the first Volvos were beginning to rust on the eve of the Great Depression. Nobel was the most important of the engineers, bankers and company directors who in their thousands are dead but not forgotten. The governors of the State Bank of Sweden, the National Debt Office and the rulers of the empire founded by A. O. Wallenberg, the Stockholms

Enskilda Bank, are all to be visited in Swedish cemeteries, most—but not all of them—in the capital.

The most famous family member of the Wallenberg dynasty disappeared helping save Jews from the Holocaust, most likely murdered by the Russians during the Cold War. The Nobel empire overshadowed in popular imagination, although not necessarily in economic importance, Swedish insurance companies, copper mines and electrochemical firms. The inventor J. Wenström patented inventions that made Allmänna Svenska Elektriska (ASEA) the world leader in transformers and electrical engineering. A forge established at Bofors in the seventeenth century grew into one of the world's most important arms manufacturers.

The Aga: Simple, Sweet Tempered and Smart

Stockholmers built not only refrigerators, vacuum cleaners, milk containers and telephones, but also produced the world's best lighthouses and stoves. Many Swedish companies were run by scholars who left the birch groves of academe and turned their intellectual curiosity to the benefit of their community. Gustav Dalén was one who was at home in learned professional societies and company boardrooms. It was hard to find a more gifted theoretical physicist turned practical man. He invented a system for dissolving acetylene, developed aeronautical beacons, traffic signals and locomotive lighting and, from his desk at AGA, AB Gasaccumulator, oversaw in 1922 the development and marketing of a cast iron stove which allegedly liberated women. The British have pushed back the invention of the Aga stove to the foundation of the English Coalbrookdale Company formed by the great iron master Abraham Darby in 1709. Under the slogan "cook better, eat better, taste better and live better" Rayburn advertised that most people associated the name Aga with a fine food and good living, "and, although it's often thought of as quintessentially British, the Aga actually began life in Sweden."

The Aga legend was that Dalén was appalled by the amount of time his wife (and their maid) spent tending their cooker so he set out to design a stove which by the year 2000 the BBC placed in the three top design icons of the twentieth century (alongside the Coca-Cola bottle and the Volkswagen Beetle). In a dubious public relations exercise not much different from Coca-Cola's spring-water spin, Aga's UK manufacturer traced the cooker in a direct and implausible line from iron wheels for railway engines, an iron bridge over the River Severn, Hyde Park's gates and iron garden furnishing.

Coalbrookdale was merged with a Swedish parent company in 1929 and manufactured Aga stoves for almost a century because it was the best available company skilled at handling scrap iron and pig iron molten metal, casting and blasting. Millions of households worldwide use the Aga cooker. In its time it has been used on the Persian state railways and trans-Atlantic luxury liners and was a feature of the homes of the middle classes. It was particularly popular in Britain during the 1930s.

The cookers had a vitreous enamel surface and in contrast to many marriages founded on an Aga purchase, they were long-lasting and scratch-resistant. Some Agas were colour-coded to illustrate the year of manufacture and have become collectors' items. The porcelain arm of the Rayburn conglomerate even manufactured teapots modelled on the Aga design, which are as gorgeous and functional as the original metal icon. The Aga stove could run on every sort of fuel, including wood, gas, electricity and oil. Best of all, perhaps, the Aga provided continuous hot water on tap for a cup of tea after love in the afternoon.

SHIPS AND MATCHES

Sweden's heavy defence industry was the backbone of the nation's economy. The country owned one of the world's biggest shipyards at Malmö, founded by F. H. Kockum in 1840, and many other yards built civil and military vessels. Some defence industries had long histories. Husqvarna Vapenfabriks manufactured small arms from 1689 onwards; three centuries later its diversified output included household hardware and world-beating chainsaws, motorcycles and sewing machines. By the 1920s directors K. F. Göransson, Axel Wästfelt and Björn Prytz were in charge of Sandvik, Separator and SKF, the latter established in 1907 to manufacture self-regulating ball bearings. The Separator Company capitalized on the invention of the milk-cream separator by Gustav de Laval, which, like the safety match, was a Swedish application of an invention so superior that it had no world peer and was exported everywhere as a consequence. Sandviken, the largest steel works in Sweden, began in 1862 and exported 75 per cent of its output in the 1920s, when its highest priority was to exert "the greatest care for the comfort and well being of its workmen". For different reasons, Svenska Tändsticks and

Telefonaktiebolaget L. M. Ericsson are still famous today.

Telefonaktiebolaget L. M. Ericsson, recalled Hallendorf and Shuck, was established in 1918 and originated in A. B. Ericsson & Co., founded in 1876, this latter concern having been at a later date combined with the Stockholm Telephone Co. and the Allmänna Industribolaget. L. M. Ericsson's telephone apparatus was known all over the world at the beginning of the twentieth century. The historians boasted that the company's production consisted of all kinds of telephone material, line material, electric cables and wires, telegraphic apparatus and electricity meters. The company had affiliated manufacturing and operating companies as well as agencies in all continents.

Hallendorf and Shuck then proudly described how Svenska Tändsticks A.B. (the Swedish Match Manufacturing Company) was established in 1917 and was formed by a fusion of Jönköpings and Vulcans. In a burst of immodest praise, which fate was shortly to destroy, the pair stressed that the firm

> was incomparably the largest enterprise of its kind in the world, and during the last few years the Company, partly with the help of foreign capital, has acquired a very extensive influence over the match industry in various countries so that, at the present time, more than one-third of the total match-production of the world is under Swedish direction. At its Swedish and foreign factories the company produces 10 million boxes of matches, which is at the rate of 30,000 matches per second. The skill with which this all-embracing, international business organisation has been built up by the world-renowned Swedish financier, Ivar Kreugar and his partners, has assured the Company lasting control over all its most important markets, thereby further contributing to the future success of the Swedish match-industry.

It is very easy for a historian to speak too soon, especially about an *industri-riddare*.

ETHICAL INVESTMENTS: AN ARM AND A LEG

The Swedes are well aware of—and very defensive about—ethical and moral problems that have always existed within their prosperous industrial world. In *The New Totalitarians* (1972) Roland Huntford described the root of their anxiety. Swedes have always provided war material for their combatant distant and near neighbours. The recent Swedish economic miracle was founded on a combination of defence industry expertise and a foreign policy of neutrality. In two world wars the Swedes have been non-belligerents. Their cousins in Finland, Norway and Denmark chose not to forgive them for this. They believe that Swedes profiteered from their neutrality, selling arms to both sides until the victor was in the home straight.

Nor has criticism of the Swedish armaments industry diminished. I leave the last word on what arms manufactured by Swedish firms are contributing to death and injury in the current bleak international landscape not to Lady Diana, the Princess of Wales, but to Henning Mankell. There is no escaping the damage to life and limb perpetuated by the inventors of improved weapons transported during the Gulf War by Scania trucks, although the Swedes are not responsible for this. Although Swedish foreign policy is overwhelmingly pacifist and anti-war, the intellectual property of Swedes is so superior to its competitors that it is the preferred weapon of choice when it can be obtained. After a nasty murder in which a victim in one of his novels is blown up by a land mine, Henning Mankell illustrates this in a dialogue between his anti-hero detective Kurt Wallander and a fictitious Swedish army officer:

> "What can you say about the mine?" [Wallander] asked them. "Size, explosive power? Can you guess where it might have been made? Anything at all could be of use to us."
>
> "LUNDQVIST, CAPTAIN", it said on the identity disc attached to the tunic of the older of the two soldiers. He was also the one who replied to Wallander's question.
>
> "Not a particularly powerful mine," he said. "A few hundred grams of explosive at most. Enough to kill a man, though. We usually call this kind of mine a 'Four'."
>
> "Meaning what?" Wallander asked.
>
> "Somebody treads on a mine," Captain Lundqvist said. "You need three men to carry him out of battle. Four people removed from active duty."
>
> "And the origin?"

"Mines aren't made the same way as other weapons," Lundqvist said. "Bofors makes them, as do all the other major arms manufacturers. But nearly every industrialised country has a factory making mines. Either they're manufactured openly under licence, or they're pirated. Terrorist groups have their own models. Before you can say anything about where the mine comes from, you have to have a fragment of the explosive and preferably also a bit of the material the casing was made from. It could be iron or plastic. Even wood."

"We'll see what we can find," Wallander said. "Then we'll get back to you."

"Not a nice weapon," Captain Lundqvist said. "They say it's the world's cheapest and most reliable soldier. You put him somewhere and he never moves from the spot, not for a hundred years if that's how you want it. He doesn't require food or drink or wages. He just exists, and waits—until somebody comes and treads on him. Then he strikes."

"How long can a mine remain active?" Wallander asked.

"Nobody knows. Landmines that were laid in the First World War are still going off now and then."

AXEL WENNER-GREN: SWELL OR SWINDLER?

In the Swedish case it is often hard to judge whether a captain of industry is a benevolent pillar of society or a corporate crook. Axel Winner-Gren, who was to Electrolux what Dalén was to Aga, looked every inch the businessman. His silver hair and suave appearance made him easily mistaken for a man who sold vacuum cleaners, not invented them, and his life was ruined when the American and British governments decided that he was not a harmless swell but a spy and a swindler. Unlike Nobel, Wenner-Gren is all but forgotten, reduced to a couple of paragraphs and an inaccurate index reference in William Boyd's 2002 novel *Any Human Heart*. His legacy is a 24-floor eyesore skyscraper that disrupts the stunted but homely silhouette of the Stockholm night sky, the Wenner-Gren Centre. Opened in 1962, it has 155 apartments housing foreign scientists undertaking long-term research in Sweden. At subsidized rents, they use their scientific skills, if Wenner-Gren's wishes are being observed, "to solve mankind's problems."

In 1940 he was one of the richest men in the world, the epitome of the rich, cosmopolitan peripatetic Swedish magnate. His yacht was not named the *Southern Cross* for nothing. Wenner-Gren sailed it from hemisphere to hemisphere as a relief from the cares of business administration and as a break from his hobby of property development. He had extended his business interests far from refrigerators and vacuum cleaners to a crayfish cannery in the Bahamas. He lamented that he was "so international a figure as to be considered a spy in any country."

Axel Wenner-Gren was born in 1881. Like many of his countrymen he was a brilliant engineer and inventor, using inventions made elsewhere, especially in the United States, for his models. Seeing the potential of an industrial empire based in Sweden manufacturing and exporting vacuum cleaners and refrigerators, Wenner-Gren founded Electrolux in 1919 and within ten years derived a large, relatively untaxed income that he spent on travel, philanthropy and property development.

In passing he picked up some of Ivar Kreuger's assets in the fire sale that followed Kreuger's suicide and, among other achievements constructed Disneyland's monorail and was among the first to market embryo computers. As was common with Swedish tycoons he was resident abroad most of his life. He married an American and took a fancy to Delaware but became disturbed and preoccupied by the probability of a European war in the 1930s, fearing it would wipe out his investments and ruin the world. He had the self-confidence of Nobel or Kreuger added to the determination to play a major part in global politics during his lifetime.

Wenner-Gren thought he could change the direction of history and lobbied King Gustav V, President Roosevelt and Neville Chamberlain with suggestions on potential mollifying international alliances that might defuse the explosive situation that had developed following Hitler's aggressive foreign policy. He saved his most implausible advice for the Germans. Trading on his Swedishness—and the Swedishness of Hermann Goering's wife—Wenner-Gren had two meetings with Hitler's closest advisor. The meetings were at Karinhall, which the uxorious Goering named after his spouse in much the same implausible spirit that Sibelius called his house in Finland Ainola. (Karin was important to the ideologists devising racial Nazi theory who argued that the Valkyrie spirit was Nordic as well as German and thus deserved a much wider credibility and following. Valkyries did not just reside in Berlin, the arguments ran, and Karin, before her early death, was idolized as a Scandinavian role model and personification of pure Aryan Nazi identity.)

Knowing all this, Wenner-Gren reported the agenda of his meetings with Goering to Swedish Prime Minister Albin Hansson. Goering was derisive, explaining that the very suggestion that Hitler should back down on issues like the Jewish question would only enrage the *Führer*. Wenner-Gren ignored Goering's pessimism, pressed on and published his views, trying to distribute them to the most influential contacts he could envisage. Having failed to influence the Swedish king, the American president, the British prime minister or Hitler, Wenner-Gren then tried his luck with the Duke of Windsor. As the Duke of Windsor also had an American wife, Wenner-Gren was generous enough to offer the duke use of one of his houses in the Bahamas, Shangri-La. Wenner-Gren's yacht was often moored in the Bahamas where he had decided to sporadically settle in tax exile from Stockholm. The malevolence of the British royal family by chance later turned Wenner-Gren and the Duke of Windsor into neighbours. The post-abdication duke only accepted "with profound gloom and despondency" his colonial posting as Governor of the Bahamas. Wenner-Gren asked himself "how can they deport such a fine man to so uncivilised a place, where one needs a hide of steel to survive? How can they expect him to survive?"

The relationship ended when the Japanese entered the war. Wenner-Gren was at sea in his yacht bound for Nassau when he heard of the attack on Pearl Harbor. Within weeks the president added Wenner-Gren to the State Department's blacklist and he was turned into an outcast. The US assets of Electrolux were sequestered for the duration of the war and he was banned from visiting the US or doing business with Americans. The UK also prohibited him from sailing there. The Duke of Windsor's pressure on the Foreign Office to convince M16 that Wenner-Gren was not a spy failed to help. Wenner-Gren ended his career all but forgotten and only remembered when considered as a criminal and compared with Lord Lucan. The US in a public relations campaign successfully branded him as a spy for Germany and he was smeared as a murderer in cahoots with the Duke of Windsor when Sir Harry Oakes was killed. Wenner-Gren's yacht was said by witnesses to be nearby when Sir Harry, the most important man in the Bahamas (besides the Duke of Windsor) and the richest baronet in the Empire was found burnt and battered to death in his Nassau bed. This crime was unsolved.

Like much else to do with Wenner-Gren, improbability and uncertainty were left in the air. He probably did not guide U-boats to their targets during the Second World War but was rescued from mortal danger during an impromptu tiger hunt, saved by Paul Fejos, a Spanish cinematographer working for Swedish Film in Southeast Asia. In an extraordinary sequence of events Wenner-Gren then became Father Christmas to anthropologists until the 1970s, transforming the discipline through his benevolence. He set up the Viking Fund as a charitable trust under Delaware state laws and appointed Paul Fejos as research director. The Royal Anthropological Institute from Queen Anne Street, London, was among the most important of all those who thanked Wenner-Gren for all the financial jam their benefactor spread, knowing nothing about anthropology. In 1981 the RAI news summed it up like this: "Once upon a time (ie 1938) there was an internationally celebrated Hungarian/American film director (Paul Fejos) who had abandoned Hollywood to operate freelance in a more professional style. He was currently making ethnographically based films in South East Asia on behalf of the Swedish film industry." Enter multi-millionaire Swedish-American financier Axel Wenner-Gren, touring the world in his luxury yacht. Fejos and Wenner-Gren became acquainted and Fejos was persuaded to organize a tiger hunt in the course of which he saved Wenner-Gren's life. "This puts Wenner-Gren in Fejo's debt and he becomes his patron and financial backer... he seems to have imagined that when the war was over he would be able to get the money back again." He was not.

FAMILY BUSINESS

Imagination and good fortune were not confined to the nineteenth century and Nobel's generation, although inherited wealth provided the usual springboard to financial consideration and increased power. Among the world's top twenty billionaires are three Swedes whose various paths to fortune have endowed Sweden and Stockholm with an indecent share of global wealth. Living in Stockholm, content to pay local taxes, enjoying common hobbies and pursuits with his fellows is Stefan Persson. In 2007 *Forbes* calculated that Persson was worth $18.4 billion, pipping fellow Swede Birgit Rausing at $11 billion and behind Ingvar Kamprad, who from time to time nudged Bill Gates for pole position as richest person in the world.

Stefan Persson is the chairman of Hennes & Mauritz, a public company that produces and sells clothing and cosmetics. Like IKEA, H & M has (as

it coyly explains) a price point in the discount fashion market but also markets its brand to high end customers. Stockholm is full of high end consumers who want to be ordinary and so H & M combines plebeian and exclusive alternatives. Stefan inherited the business from his father, Erling. Erling began by selling women's clothing in Västeras. He called his shop Hennes, "hers" in Swedish. In 1968 Erling bought a hunting and fishing store in Stockholm from a man whose Christian name was Mauritz. Mauritz sold men's clothes as well as shotguns and fishing rods to hunters like Axel Wenner-Gren who emerged from the shop clad like Rambo. Erling renamed the store Hennes & Mauritz, which did not make a lot of sense, even in Swedish, so the name was abbreviated to H & M.

Although H & M grows stronger by the minute in a geometric progression of imaginative expansion and brand incorporation—Karl Lagerfeld, Gap, Madonna, Stella McCartney—it is a robustly ethical business. Not only is the Church of Sweden a major shareholder, but Swedish Christian ethics inform company policy. To complete the image, Stefan Persson has homely hobbies with which his customers from Stockholm to

San Francisco and Dubai can identify. H & M is also tough on drugs. In September 2005 Kate Moss was dropped from an advertising campaign for autumn clothes. The company explained that Kate Moss's image had become inconsistent with H & M's clear disassociation with narcotics.

The Tetra Pak was perfected in 1951. It began as packaging for storing milk. Erik Wallenberg, Harry Järand and Erik Torudd designed a long cylinder lined with plastic, twisted one way at one end, another way at the other, forming a pyramid. A prototype was ready by 1944, driven onwards by Ruben Rausing, dead set on being the first to produce a paper milk packet. Rausing's wife Elisabeth solved the problem of filling the tetras based on a method she used to stuff sausages. Milk was filled from the top and each tetra was snipped off a little below the liquid level. No air entered and the milk remained bacteria free. The TetraBrik was added to the range in 1969. Birgit Rausing, the latest family member to inherit the fortune derived from the invention by Tetrapak, has not followed Stefan Persson's example; she lives in Switzerland.

Birgit inherited $11 billion and Swiss banks proudly advertise that the Rausing roost in Montreux is an example of how friendly Swiss banks are to the very rich who wish to live tax free in a secure, non-murky environment. Yet Rausing and Persson are tycoon pygmies compared with Ingvar Kamprad, who could give every person alive in China ten krona and still have enough left for some discount shopping.

Chapter Five
STARS AND SLY BITCHES
STOCKHOLM AND CINEMA

SCREEN GODDESSES

There were no swells or mobsters in the Swedish film industry, which has always been a serious business conducted by the ethically committed. From its beginning entertainment came second to moral education in the messianic minds of filmmakers. Swedish cinema was always economically successful enough to be able to afford to produce thoughtful films that disturbed the audience. *Pengar är inte allt*, money isn't everything, is a common phrase in Stockholm, and it certainly applies to movie box office receipts. Movie-going was an egalitarian communal pleasure that could be shared on the long dark winter nights. It was not just coincidence that Prime Minister Palme was assassinated after leaving not parliament but the cinema.

Swedish cinema is a marriage of industry and art, although sometimes the directors prefer to call it science and art. More often than not it has been possible to make money and present an improving tale: Greta Garbo's first talking film was based on a Eugene O'Neill play with an uplifting story. In 1930 Garbo was cast as Anna Christie, acting her role as a stereotypical young woman "with a shady past" whose experience proved it was better not to drink too much, and best to avoid sailors.

The Swedish film industry survived the cultural imperialism of Hollywood in the 1930s and 1940s, and the welfare state set up Svensk Film Industri along the lines of many similar institutions designed for the public good. Funded by the taxpayer, it had a very large budget and complete freedom to produce what it liked. In 1971 the Swedish film industry put most of its activities under one roof at Filmhuset, film house, near Karlaplan. Its brief is to produce quality films and guard the country's cinema heritage, contained in an archive of 18,000 films.

From the outset Svensk Film Industri often went into co-productions with other countries. Two extremes illustrate the width of its horizon. The

The young Ingrid Bergman

first concerns the Stockholm love affair with Italy. When it joined the European Union, Sweden was able to capitalize on the stereotypical reciprocal interest Italian men had in Stockholm women. An obvious opening was taken by Svensk Film Industri when it collaborated in *carabinieri* versus mafia tele-movies based on Sicily's answer to Kurt Wallender, Inspector Montalbano. In one episode the Italian detective is called upon to massage the ankles of Ingrid Sjöstrom, a Swedish actress wearing little more than knickers. At five feet eleven inches Ingrid towered over Montalbano, and the bald and swarthy *commisario*'s indifference towards Sjöstrom's attempt to seduce him was less convincing than other scenes in the film. In one of these a giggling Sjöstrom drove backwards at very high speeds, illustrating the perception of the otherwise patronizing Italian men that Swedish women are natural rally drivers. The plot also required that the Swedish woman have an affair with her father-in-law, be set up as a killer, and be found not guilty of murder, but convicted for "licentious behaviour", as the Italian audience would have expected.

While Inspector Montalbano massages Ingrid Sjöstrom's ankles round the clock on world television, some serious co-productions are seldom aired. Svenski Film Industri and an Australian company made an ironical and moralistic movie with a distasteful racist theme. *The Stuart Case* was about the trial of Rupert Max Stuart for the rape and murder of a young girl in on a beach in Ceduna, a remote outback town. The television Sicilian policeman, Montalbano, was fiction; Stuart was real. Stuart was also an Aboriginal who got frontier justice. He was found guilty of murder, sentenced to death, reprieved after a long campaign against capital punishment and spent decades in prison. On his release he was elected a tribal elder and was given an audience with his queen, Elizabeth II and her consort, the Duke of Edinburgh, on one of the many British royal visits to their Australian subjects. Robert Carlisle played the lawyer who saved Stuart from the gallows, but this film, like many other uplifting Svenski Film Industri ventures, was born to blush unseen. Not so the performances of Greta Garbo, Ingrid Bergman and Anita Ekberg.

The West could not get enough of films starring Garbo, Bergman and Ekberg. They were more than movie stars. What happened in their personal lives not only resonated in Gamla Stan but created the popular view in the English-speaking world of Stockholm, Sweden and Swedes. The three women were poles apart in their careers. Ingrid Bergman refused to conform to un-Swedish expectations and continued to work all the days of her life, avoiding the company of celebrities and the famous whenever possible. Greta Garbo made a brilliant but difficult transition from silent movies to the talkies. She was always the product of a myopic Hollywood, which cast her in unsuitable roles, trading on her exotic private life in the absence of good scripts and creative insight about her real identity. As time went by, Garbo became afraid of Ingrid Bergman and went to great lengths to avoid her. Anita Ekberg's career was intertwined with the perennial dream of Swedes, which is to lead a sweet life in a sunny climate. All had in common a Queen Christina-Pippi Longstocking view of the integrity of their persona and despite their numerous ups and downs they resisted attempts to sway them from a Swedish determination to remain as simple and normal as possible, even if they had all turned out to be both rich and famous.

GRETA GARBO: I WANT TO BE LEFT ALO NE

Some significant sites must remain in the imagination. The exact place where Greta Garbo first excited her captive audience has, like much of Stockholm, been knocked down by developers. It was a barber shop that gave Greta her first pay. Her parents, Karl Gustafsson and Anna Karlsson, were drawn to Stockholm by the hope of work and housing just as poor peasants in Ireland were drawn to Dublin at the end of the nineteenth century. Karl and Anna met in 1896, the middle of the gay nineties, the decade when Bram Stoker's *Dracula* had as much resonance in Södermalm as Southwark. The working class believed they were having their blood sucked dry by the middle class who exploited the desperate need for work. Alcoholism was a common response to the unresolved class war and Karl, like many Scandinavians, was drunk more often than not.

Greta was born on 18 September 1905 in a part of town that is not now as it was then. She had a Stockholm working-class slum upbringing in a street whose name meant wan, pale and bleached. Her family lived in a rented one-room apartment on the fourth floor of a two-storey tenement off Götgatan, the street which marks Södermalm's main axis. In those days the rays of the sun always seemed dim. Her earliest memories were of her mother beating her father. Working-class poverty was worse in Oslo, but before social democracy transformed Stockholm's medical system travellers compared these two northern Scandinavian capitals with Calcutta, such was the death rate from tuberculosis and cholera. Greta's sister Alva had tuberculosis and Greta herself suffered a bout of the potentially fatal disease as a child. By the time she was fifteen, Greta had experienced so much trauma in her life that playing Anna Karenina was an exercise in empathy.

Greta was the family breadwinner in the era before social security payments. She spent summer mornings sitting on the roof of the family's outside lavatory and dreaming of what life would be like in a warm climate. Her first job was to lather the piggy bristles of a shaving brush with soap, then slop it on the whiskered faces of the beery customers sitting in the chair of her local barber shop. As Greta soaped a man's chin it was a Lolita-like experience, with a touch of *Miss Julie*, when the cut throat razor appeared.

God took a hand. In a nasty childhood moment, Greta's monstrous mother denounced her as a masturbator and suggested a dose of church attendance as an antidote to self-abuse. Greta's mother at the time was in love with the Södermalm pastor. In Stockholm deals are done in church, not on the golf course. Another parishioner, Paul Bergström, was roped in to give Greta a better job than that in the barber shop in his prestigious but unfortunately named department store, PUB, an acronym for Paul U. Bergström. Pastor Ahlfeldt's motive was to be repaid in bed by Greta's mother who became his mistress-housekeeper. Greta's unauthorized biography noted that this was an agreeable prospect for Anna, as her husband Karl's brewer's droop had made him somewhat unresponsive to his wife's affectionate advances, which often ended with him being belted over the head with a chair.

Thanks to Pastor Ahlfeldt's intervention, Greta left hairdressing and began a short sales career at PUB in July 1920. Good fortune followed as another of Ahlfeldt's contacts, Lars Ring, left the Swedish army to seek his fortune in the new field of filmmaking and made a bee-line for Greta to star in a small PUB product promotion, the 1920s equivalent of *What Not to Wear*, called *How Not to Dress*. As Ring had predicted, Greta looked special. Starry eyed and with asymmetrical beauty, she was encouraged by the reception to her advertising film to hone her acting techniques and enrolled accordingly as a student at the Royal Dramatic Theatre.

After she graduated from Dramaten Greta's life was changed by the director Mauritz Stiller, who persuaded her to try her luck as a film actress in America. Greta caught the train from Stockholm to Gothenburg on 27 June 1925, leaving Södermalm behind and sailing away on the Swedish steamship appropriately and evocatively called the *Drottningholm*, or Queen Harbour. Her first feature film, *Gösta Berlings Saga*, was made under her birth name, Gustafsson. She signed on with Goldwyn and Mayer, and changed her name to Garbo at the MGM studio's insistence (much to the amusement of her Australian audience, as "garbo" is the word used as a job description for Greta's father, from whom she inherited a very large frame appropriate to a life of carrying garbage bins in the world of city rubbish removal).

Before she retired at the unbelievably early age of thirty-six Garbo was discovered many times: tradition has it by the cabin steward on her ship to America and certainly by John Gilbert, who broke her heart. For her near half century of reclusive retirement in New York Greta perfected a personal version of Swedish armed neutrality. Her variously quoted motto was said to be "I want to be left alone." Although childless, Garbo's films *Queen Christina* and *Anna Karenina* were her best performances, informed as they were with poignant personal knowledge of what she had lost by moving from Stockholm and what sorrow felt like.

Photographs of Greta at her seventieth birthday in 1975 with her friend Countess Kerstin Bernadotte show a strong, determined Stockholmer with big feet and a deliberate tread, stuffing food into her mouth. By then her stage name had become totemic and was used to encourage a variety of causes, ironic and appropriate, trivial and momentous. In public Garbo wanted to be alone; in private she preferred the company of members of the Swedish royal family, or the insincere misogynist Somerset Maugham. Garbo was at home in the garden of Villa Mauresque at St.-Jean-Cap Ferrat, and it was perhaps with this in mind that one of the three divisions in "Operation Dragon" was codenamed Garbo Force by the Allies, the United States and the United Kingdom during the Second World War. As part of the assault on German-held Fortress Europe the recapture of Provence was as important to General Dwight Eisenhower as any other military objective. While Garbo Force was named thus to raise the spirits of American GI moviegoers, and indeed took St. Tropez, one day after H-hour on D Day, it is doubtful if the so-called *Goums*, the hundred thousand Muslim Algerians, Moroccans and Tunisians, disguised in British issue helmets and carrying American MI carbines, could have known they were fighting in the name of a Swedish screen goddess.

INGRID BERGMAN: THE PALMOLIVE GARBO

Ingrid Bergman knew she walked in Garbo's footsteps even if the *Goums* did not. Bergman found "nothing very exciting" about Dramaten, which was after all just a couple of large rooms on the upper floors, but she was impressed to stumble on a "big desk where everyone carved their names: a lot of famous names then and afterwards. Greta Garbo, Mai Zetterling… I felt I belonged to something at last."

Ingrid Bergman never forgot her experience as a young woman, walking along the bright, open quayside of Strandvägen on the way to take her audition and, perhaps, to begin a new life. Miss Bergman was number sixteen on Dramaten's list and waited in a small park across the road from Lake Mälaren spending tense minutes looking at the bearded bronze head of John Ericsson, who she recalled was the Swedish engineer who invented the first armoured battleships and played such a crucial part in the American Civil War.

As an old woman who had survived cancer and Hollywood, Ingrid Bergman explained her feelings when she arrived to take up the audition. The theatre had a massive, pale grey façade. Beyond it stretched the waterfront, backed by the symmetrical curve of seven-storey apartment buildings, shops and offices, surrounded by domes of copper cupolas, tarnished to a pale sea-green by the salty winds blown in from the northern seas. Bergman, like Garbo, knew that she belonged to a particular city of lakes and ferry boats and glittering water. She had been born no more than a hundred yards from the theatre in an apartment above her father's photographic shop, on Strandvägen itself.

She made a fool of herself in the audition and wandered back to a little kiosk where the ferry tickets to Djurgården and Skansen were sold. There was no-one around. A few seagulls screamed in the distance, two or three floating on the surface. Across the water she could see the graceful golden tower of the Nordiska Museet. She thought life wasn't worth living and struck a theatrical pose: "there's only one thing to do. Throw myself into the water and commit suicide." Her memory was as follows: the water looked dark and shining. She took a step closer and peered into it. It was indeed dark and shining and dirty. She worried that she would be covered in dirt when they pulled her out. She'd have to swallow that stuff. Ugh! That was no good. Temporarily suicide was set aside. Ingrid was accepted for the course and, like Garbo, was head-hunted by filmmakers. By the time she was twenty she had appeared in the first three of her fifty films. The critics had only one word for her first performance—"hefty", referring to her weight, not her talent.

Although her supporters assured her she had star quality, Ingrid did not believe them and threw herself into married life with Petter Lindström, a little older than her and a sophisticated, successful dentist. Lindström was not a Stockholmer. Petter and Ingrid lived in the centre of Stockholm in a smart little modern apartment with a red awning and a black cat. And when Ingrid's "star quality" resulted in earning lots of money, they moved to a yellow cottage in Djurgården, where Ingrid was no good at cooking, yet boasted:

> but housework I was very good at. The scrubbing and cleaning of house or apartment from top to bottom has always satisfied my Scandinavian soul. One of my friends always says "how you have wasted all these years being an actress when you could have been the best char woman in the business?"

Ingrid's mother was German and naturally Ingrid's second language was German. While vacuuming she decided there was no way she was going to remain in Sweden as Swedish pictures were not the beginning and end of acting. Although she knew that France had marvellous movies and wonderful actors and Hollywood had talented directors with big budgets, she set her sights on Germany as a stepping stone while she worked on her French and English language skills. It did not take long for her to get into trouble in Germany by acting the Swedish neutral and declining to raise her arms in a Nazi salute and shout "Sieg heil" during a rally at a stadium in Berlin. She not only amazed her terrified companions by her non-conformity, but made things worse by emphasizing it and retorting, "Why should I? You're all doing it so well without me." Although one of her celebrated countrywomen was married to a major Nazi figure and Swedes were welcome in Berlin, Bergman guessed that since Goering's most famous boast was that "when I hear the word culture I reach for my revolver" there was not much chance of independent, creative filmmaking in Germany after 1939.

Bergman duly moved to Hollywood. She wanted to act, not just to sign contracts as many of her contemporaries had done. The English-language remake of her Swedish movie *Intermezzo* was such a success that it was reviewed by Graham Greene for *The Spectator* in January 1940. He could not resist saying: "This film is most worth seeing for the new star Miss Ingrid Bergman who is as natural as her name. What star before has made her entrance with a highlight gleaming on her nose tip?" Stockholmers were—and are—great consumers of chocolate and ice-cream and the star of *Intermezzo* tucked into confectionery and became even heftier. She made things difficult by refusing to change her name from Bergman. She knew there was an enormous gap between the cultural values of her new Californian friends in Benedict Canyon and the comparatively suburban priorities of Stockholm's Strandvägen.

Although *Casablanca* was the highlight of a career with countless memorable roles, Ingrid's love affair with the United States was always difficult. She could not understand the need for stars to have status symbols: "Why do I have to have a mink coat"? she asked. Nor could she understand how Americans felt about Christmas and New Year. Ironically for a Stockholmer, she criticized their heavy drinking:

> I couldn't believe my first New Year in America because in Sweden it was such an important day. A family day. You waited for midnight; you talked about the past and what the future might bring; and then of course you made various resolutions like, "I'll stop smoking," things like that. Then, at the stroke of midnight, all the church bells broke out all over the country, and on the radio one very famous actor… would read Tennyson's "Ring out wild bells". It was broadcast all over Stockholm from loudspeakers. You could hear it in every street in the city—you didn't even have to listen to the radio. Quite different from America… by that time half the party had passed out.

The United States discovered who Ingrid Bergman really was after her sensational elopement with the famous Italian film director, Roberto Rossellini. A representative statesman and popularly elected politician Edwin C. Johnson spoke for middle America when he said: "Even in this modern era of surprise it is upsetting to have our most popular but pregnant Hollywood movie queen, her condition the result of an illicit affair, play the part of a cheap chiselling female to add spice to a silly story which lacks appeal on its own." He concluded by calling for actresses, producers and films to be licensed by the Department of Commerce, and described Ingrid Bergman as "one of the most powerful women on earth today—I regret to say, a powerful influence for evil... When Rossellini the love pirate returned to Rome, smirking over his conquest, it was not Mrs Lindström's scalp which hung from the conquering hero's belt; it was her very soul."

Nor was Rossellini popular in Stockholm, where he arrived with two cars—a Ferrari and a Rolls Royce—but no evening dress. Rossellini did not understand that Stockholm was not the city in which to flaunt wealth. But it was vitally important, if one was likely to be presented to the sovereign or to move comfortably in society, to have a white tie and tails hanging in the wardrobe. This understandable comprehension gap between Rome and Stockholm continued and grew greater during Ingrid Bergman's married life with Rossellini. While Rossellini could share Ingrid's bed he could never share her mind. After Ingrid fell out of love the divorced couple raised their children in between bitter court battles for custody and charges of stealing the children from one another.

Ingrid wanted her European children to know the life of Stockholmers and took them to the island summer house of her new partner Lars Schmidt. Ingrid recalled that Rossellini had protested. She recalled: "If Roberto had his way he wouldn't allow it. Sleep in a wooden house? Far too dangerous! Wooden houses burn down. Someone told him that Swedes lived in wooden houses... In Italy, if it rains you stay indoors, but Swedes can't do that because then you might be indoors all year round. So we bought the children rubber hats and trousers and they never had so much fun."

Ingrid's Italian nanny, Elena, who was Rossellini's spy, grew bad tempered because her idea of summer was not that of a chilly Stockholm in July, but of long hot days lying in a deck chair on a crowded beach. Then there was the sauna. In Sweden there is no association between sex and sauna. Children may be born there but they are not conceived there. Ingrid introduced her children to the sauna on one of the thousands of typical islands around Stockholm. The children were taught to spend a short time in the dry heat, and then splash in the cold water. They screamed with delight. Elena thought it was absolutely diabolical. She thought the children were risking their lives in such water. Bergman recalled:

> Of course we always swam without bathing suits; there wasn't a soul within miles. That horrified Elena. She screamed, "Wait until Mr Rossellini will hear that Mr Schmidt is naked when he swims"… gambolling about naked in the cold Swedish sea just went against her nature. She didn't realize that all Sweden bathes naked. All she knew was that in Italy even a year old baby is put into a bathing costume.
>
> The difficulties with the children got worse and worse. When they came to us from Italy they were filled with the idea that we were Protestants and they were Catholics. They had been told it was a deadly sin for them to pray with their Protestant mother. I used to say a little Swedish prayer, and one day they refused to say the prayer with me. I asked, "Why don't you pray with me?" They said, "Father says you're a heathen."

It was not just Rossellini who gave Ingrid a hard time. While Rossellini had managed to charm the King of Sweden by chatting about their mutual interest in Ferraris, the Swedish press gave Ingrid the worst reception she had endured anywhere in the world. Eventually the crying actress left Stockholm, driven out, she said, by "the rotten press atmosphere", adding "probably I will never come back again." She gave up on Stockholm completely after the Swedes complained that she had disgraced their national flag. Before leaving she paused to buy furniture at Svensk Tenn, "the most beautiful shop in the world", because although she was loathed she was loaded, and carefully scripted a hectoring speech to be broadcast on Swedish radio. She concluded with glee: "I won't come back". After this, in echoes of the cancelled suicide, she added a postscript before saying goodbye to Stockholm for the last time and farewell to everyone from her life in Sweden with the words: "Maybe. The children loved the snow after they got used to it. It is so beautiful, lots and lots of snow."

ANITA EKBERG: *LA DOLCE VITA*

Wrongly famous for her body not her brain and staying power, Kerstin Anita Marianne Ekberg was born in Malmö in 1931, and was celebrated for the size of her breasts rather than her movie star quality. Her disdain for women's liberation as it was applied in Sweden made her a natural citizen of Italy, where she spent most of her life. She made a transition smoothly from Sweden to Hollywood to Rome.

Stockholmers would never rate as important the "vital" statistics of bust, waist and hip measurements. Yet initially it was not possible to write in the English language about Ekberg without describing her body in inches, 40-22-36. Although ignored in Stockholm, Ekberg was always popular in Hollywood and Rome. Among her coterie were Tyrone Power, Errol Flynn, Yul Brynner, Frank Sinatra and Gary Cooper. She was married to the British actor Anthony Steel for three years. If ever there was a stereotype of the dumb Swedish blonde, Anita Ekberg milked and promoted it, Bob Hope quipping that "her parents received the Nobel Prize for Architecture."

Anita Ekberg was as sensible and intelligent as her two older role models. Like Ingrid Bergman, Italy changed her life. Ekberg cheerfully admitted that she stalked and manipulated Federico Fellini, overwhelming him with her charms, which she advertised by driving in ostentatious circles around his film studio. Eventually Fellini spotted her and, familiar with the history of Swedish acting talent, gave her a starring role as Sylvia in *La Dolce Vita*. In Anita's view, however:

> It was me who made Fellini famous, not the other way round. When the film was presented in New York, the distributor reproduced the fountain scene on a hoarding as high as a skyscraper. My name was in the middle in huge letters, Fellini's was at the bottom, very tiny. Everyone said I didn't have any talent, only long blonde hair and a marvellous bust, but *La Dolce Vita* was a piece of cake for me; I could have done it blindfolded. They're always showing that scene again on the television. The commentators never say "Fellini's *Dolce Vita* with Anita Ekberg", but "Anita Ekberg's *Dolce Vita* with Fellini", or simply "*La Dolce Vita* with Anita Ekberg."

When the author Constanzo Constantini, interviewing the director in *Fellini on Fellini*, asked him what he remembered about *La Dolce Vita*, Fellini recalled that for him the film was largely about Anita Ekberg. Asked what was she like and what initial impression she made on him, Fellini replied:

Anita Ekberg in the Trevi Fountain

She possessed incredible beauty. I met her towards the end of 1959 in the Hotel de la Ville, the hotel in the centre of Rome where she was staying. I had never seen anyone like her; she made a great impression on me. Later that day I met Marcello Mastroianni, who later told me that Ekberg reminded him of a stormtrooper in the "Wehrmacht", but really he didn't want to admit that even he had never before seen such marvellous and unbelievable beauty.

Ekberg was no German stormtrooper, but rather more Swedish stainless steel. Before taking the role in *La Dolce Vita* she wanted to know who the other actresses were and what her character was like. Ekberg asked Fellini, "Where is the script?" and when told there wasn't one exploded: "I told you this was a joke. This man isn't a director, he's a madman. How can you make a film without a script?"

Ekberg complained to her agent that Fellini's offer to her to write her own script was unacceptable. "I've never written anything, except for letters to my mother in Sweden. He doesn't want me to have a part in his film, but maybe he's after something else from me." Fellini admitted that he asked her if she liked the rest of the cast and promised, "If not we'll change them."

Constantini:	Ekberg immersed herself in the Trevi Fountain without difficulty?
Fellini:	Ekberg came from the North, she was young and as proud of her good health as a lioness. She was no trouble at all. She remained immersed in the basin for ages, motionless, impassive, as if the water didn't cover her nor the cold affect her, even though it was March and the nights made one shiver. For Mastroianni it was a rather different story. He had to get undressed, put on a frogman's suit and get dressed again. To combat the cold he polished off a bottle of vodka and when we shot the scene he was completely pissed.
Constantini:	How long did you take to shoot that scene?
Fellini:	It took eight or nine nights. Some of the owners of the surrounding houses would rent out their balconies and windows to the curious. At the end of each take the

crowd would cheer. A show within a show. Every time I
look at the picture of Ekberg in the Trevi Fountain, I
have the sensation of reliving those magic moments,
those sleepless nights, surrounded by the miaowing of
cats and the crowd that gathered from every corner of
the city.

Anita Ekberg and Federico Fellini were a partnership that showed how
positive the Swedish-Italian, Rome-Stockholm axis could be in engineering changes in artistic public opinion and moving social progress forward.
But the stress was too great for the honeymoon to last and it turned malevolent in the end. Ekberg and Roman Catholic conservative Italians never
saw precisely eye to eye. Constantini asked:

Fellini: Is it true that when the film was screened for a gala
evening at the Capitol in Milan on 5 February 1960, an
infuriated member of the audience spat in your face?
Marcello and I only just saved ourselves from a lynching.
I was spat at in the face and he received insults like
"layabout", "scoundrel", "debauchee", "communist".
The *Osservatore Romano* retitled the film *The Disgusting
Life*. Some went so far as to demand that it be burnt and
I be deprived of my passport. In truth, Italian critics
were very favourable, but it was abroad that it enjoyed
widespread and immediate approval. The evening of its
official screening at Cannes was memorable. Anita,
Marcello and I along with the rest of the cast walked
back to the hotel, flanked by a delirious crowd. Georges
Simenon and Henry Miller, president and member of
the International Jury respectively, had fought for the
film to be awarded the Palme d'Or.

In 1988 Fellini wrote the screenplay for *Intervista*, a film about his
own relationship with Cinecittà, the Mussolini-inspired film studios near
Rome. *Intervista* is the story of shooting a non-existent film. Its theme is
that the only reality is creative imagination, as everything is an illusion
created by the writer of the screenplay. But Ekberg's life was no illusion.

For three years she was in love with Fiat Chairman Gianni Agnelli. The life she built in Castelli Romani exemplified the attainment of a perennial Swedish ambition: to live in a warm climate, surrounded by olives, vines and chestnuts in the rich volcanic soil of Monte Porzio Catone, with holidaying popes as neighbours.

BO WIDERBERG: MASSACRE AND WHITEWASH

The home-grown Swedish film industry has more often reflected gritty social realism than life in the Trevi Fountain. Screen directors show that Swedes in Stockholm, unlike the nationals of other European capitals, have always been interested and engaged in how the lives of country Swedes affect the metropolis. Whatever dismissive thoughts the rural cousins have about their capital, the truth is that a massacre in far off Ådalen hurts the shoppers in Östermalm, the workers in the Ericsson telephone factories and the Pripps beer brewers.

At noon on 31 May 1931 all work stopped in Stockholm and every human activity was halted in the capital while ten dead Swedes were buried in Norrland. The citizens of Stockholm did not have to be told for whom the bell tolled. It tolled for them. The coffins contained the corpses of Swedish workers who were shot and killed by Swedish soldiers while marching under the red flag and singing the *Internationale* during a peaceful demonstration that turned to tragedy.

Bo Widerberg's 1969 film, *Ådalen 31*, describes the events and background more eloquently than words. During the hiatus between the First and Second World Wars, fights between capital and labour in Sweden were grim and brutal. At Fränö, on 14 May 1931, a rally of striking Swedish paper workers' unions, sawmill unions and communists affiliated with the Russian workers confronted strike breakers brought in to get the timber works rolling during what was termed "industrial volatility". The Great Depression had reduced the demand for Swedish paper and the workers had gone out on strike in response to management decisions to shorten working hours and reduce wages.

During spring the weather in Fränö was beautiful. Rocks had been thrown at strike breakers and workers earlier on 13 May, but the picnic atmosphere of the demonstration was unmistakable except, unfortunately, to two army officers and the local sheriff. The workers decided to march to Lunde, where they were blocked by Swedish cavalry troops and were asked to disperse three times. The happy but emotional crowd of about 5,000 did not move. They were then fired on. Swedish troops had never before fired live ammunition at Swedish workers and their families and the central government in Stockholm quickly decided that they never would again. In the Swedish way, an inconclusive inquiry was held which found that no-one was responsible.

The inquiry into Ådalen 31 may have found no scapegoats but, as the Irish might say, at least they did not find them quickly. The report ticking off those responsible for the order to fire, followed by token minimal punishments and a general amnesty for all involved, was sorted out in a couple of months. It took five years, however, before the Swedish Confederation of Trade Unions started to make serious headway in their efforts to regulate the labour market and it was not until December 1938 that representatives of capital and labour made short trips from Stockholm to the beach suburb of Saltsjöbaden to conclude the basic agreement between workers and bosses that was destined to serve Sweden—so it seemed— forever; certainly for half a century. *Ådalen 31* was not Bo Widerberg's only film but it was his best.

INGMAR BERGMAN: THE DEVIL'S EYE

Widerberg has always been overshadowed by Ingmar Bergman, who died in 2007. Leonard Maltin's indispensable *Movie Guide* dismisses *Elvira Madigan* as a true story filmed like a shampoo commercial, and brushes off *Ådalen 31* as an appealing mix of romance and history, concluding cattily that no-one would ever mistake Widerberg for a filmmaker of gritty realism. Gritty realism was for Ingmar Bergman.

Ingmar Bergman personified the Swedish film director and was responsible for creating the image of Sweden where Satan ruled. Swedes did not thank him for his popular celebration of the darker elements of their culture. Like Strindberg, Bergman's output was Herculean. It was largely an introspective look at the darker preoccupations of the director himself. Over thirty films found appreciative moviegoers in New York and Paris, but not in Stockholm. His themes were too unpleasant and confronted the Gamla Stan audience with a self-portrait they flinched away from. In *The New Totalitarians* Roland Huntford rightly singled out Bergman as the best exponent of "the blighted Swedish soul", the unwanted ideologue who described a society untouched by the gentle wand of humanism.

The Seventh Seal

Smiles of a Summer Night, Summer with Monica, Sawdust and Tinsel and *A Lesson in Love* Stockholmers could sit through. *Wild Strawberries* had its moments, unless one was an elderly professor with a premonition of imminent death. But what was meant by *The Seventh Seal*? On the one hand, it might have been one of the greatest films of all time, up there with *Casablanca*. Critics agreed that it was a one of a kind masterpiece which made Ingmar Bergman famous. Max von Sydow was cast as a knight heading home to Sweden after a crusade and for 96 minutes he played chess with Death, who had given him a short reprieve. Von Sydow did not come up with the meaning of life, but he did launch his own brilliant career. For most, however, 96 minutes was too long. *The Devil's Eye* was meant to be funny. The plot began with the devil having a sty in his eye, caused by the virginity of a beautiful woman. Bibi Andersson was cast in this role and Don Juan was called up from hell to seduce Bibi Andersson and, by magic, restore the devil to full vision.

My favourite Bergman film is *Winter Light*, which critics have described as a difficult film for non-Bergman buffs. There were few of these in Stockholm by 1963, when the film was released. It covered elements of Swedish behaviour that mystify outsiders. A simple plot dealt with God, suicide, guilt and anxiety. The small cast comprised a priest who did not believe in God, the only female member of his congregation, who was the priest's mistress, and the single male member of the congregation who in a powerful end killed himself by jumping into a winter river when he could not get pastoral advice to dispel his irrational anxiety about Red China and the effect Chinese foreign policy might have on Sweden. It is, naturally, filmed in black and white.

The Silence, Persona, Hour of the Wolf, Shame and *Cries and Whispers* provided more grist to the mill for those who believed Swedes were neurotic, suicidal, fascist cowards cringing away from their imminent death at the end of a holocaust which would leave Stockholmers the only survivors of a global nuclear war. While *The Magic Flute* and *Fanny and Alexander* provide some relief from Bergman's pessimism, there is a scene in *Cries and Whispers* where a wife performs genital self-mutilation with a broken wine glass to prevent her horrid husband obtaining his unmerited conjugal rights. This was usually enough for most cinema-goers to turn to Truffaut or Renoir for their new wave experiences. Bergman may not have a magic lantern but he does possess the devil's eye.

Ingmar Bergman was a magnet drawing interested foreigners to his studio. An artist in a different medium, the painter Lucien Freud, followed George Bernard Shaw and Graham Greene to Stockholm to make some money out of a famous Swede. The chances of Freud succeeding where Shaw and Greene failed were slim. Freud had nothing in common with Bergman. Freud was a painter who moved in celebrity circles. He counted among his friends Francis Bacon, Picasso and a couple of gangsters called the Kray twins. He confessed that he liked very grand parties with newspaper proprietors and whoever was the prime minister. He had found Queen Elizabeth very open-minded and had always admired her. With the exception of the Kray twins none of these characters was likely to be cast by Bergman. Freud complained that Bergman was rude, forbade him to smoke and refused to work on Saturdays because he spent the weekend mornings in bed with his wife. Bergman was such an uncooperative model that Freud left Stockholm, grizzling that "while he was working, he kept going off to have Bibi Andersson, or one of the other actresses."

Bergman was not the self-centred Swede Freud described. On the contrary he, like Strindberg, was awake to foreign talent and made a pilgrimage to Cinecittà to talk with Italian directors. The Italians, like the English, found conversation difficult with Swedes. Fellini was particularly distressed when Bergman, in an echo of Strindberg and his vomit cue, announced he wanted to have a pee. Fellini's concern was that, coming from a country famous for excellent household appliances, Bergman would be shocked by what he saw in the Cinecittà staff toilets. He was.

While Bergman was embarrassing to most Stockholmers, his work changed western values and ideas when his light first flickered in world cinemas. Sages as wise as the 12th Earl of Drogheda, writing in the *Cambridge Alumni Magazine* in 2007 of "my time in Cambridge", was thrilled at what he found, especially at the Arts Cinema where he remembered, in particular, Ingmar Bergman's *The Seventh Seal*. Also reminiscing in the same volume of *CAM* was a "legendary rock photographer who shot the seventies", who lacking writing skills began to think in terms of movies. "In Cambridge you could see a fantastic mix at the Arts Cinema, off the marketplace. I liked Bergman (especially *Persona*), which is full of extreme facial close-ups".

The age of greatness for Swedish film is now past, sunk by global pressures. But high and low culture are still informed in Stockholm by entertainment and education combined in appealing mixes, which show how imagination benefits, and is rewarded by, cultural diversity. As in *My Life as a Dog* (1985), which opened eyes to the canine downside of the Russian space programme, *Jalla! Jalla!* describes through comedy how seemingly irreconcilable differences between Lebanese and Swedish mindsets can be washed away, both the two male heroes of the film being coincidentally "garbos", one a Lebanese immigrant, the other local native-born Swedish. Swedish films, made by directors without an obvious sense of humour, will never make *Bend it Like Beckham*, *Stolen Kisses*, *Muriel's Wedding* or *The Castle*, but in Stockholm, when "the end" comes up before the credits, nobody in the audience has any illusions. The directors, cameramen and stars are not only expected to excite the audience's imagination, they are expected to devise a spooky, transforming effect and to make the film buffs better citizens when they file out toward the *tunnelbana* and home in the suburbs.

Chapter Six
A Man after Midnight
Sex, Gender and Equality

ABBA: The Game is on Again

When they sang "Gimme gimme gimme a man after midnight," ABBA were influential in perpetuating the image of Sweden as a country where women were predatory, self-indulgent and overwhelmingly sexy. The title and first line of their hit "A Man after Midnight" promoted the view of Stockholm as a place where females prowled the streets like tigresses—a vision reinforced by the costumes of the two women group members who often dressed like big cats.

The song's title was misleading. What the lyrics said, quite literally, was that without a man in their lives to hear their prayers, and help them through the darkness to the break of day, the women felt helpless in trying to chase away the shadows of the night. These words could have been written by a bishop of the Church of Sweden. The song is also about summer light and winter darkness. Sweden's normal weather patterns move from extreme cold to tepid warmth. The weather changes are an element in daily life that produces overwhelming patterns of thought difficult for outsiders to understand. One of ABBA's members, Anni-Frid Lyngstad, originated from a region of Norway where polar ice and the midnight sun were as common as continuous summer light. The others were from a country where population density is so low that long-distance travellers see few other humans on a trip to Stockholm, the magnet that attracts about twenty per cent of the country's people. In this sense, ABBA were no different from other Scandinavians. An empty landscape represents purity, innocence, divinity, the absence of human sins and pollution. The Stockholm apartments they lived in were extensions of the landscape, and as the seasons changed, winter darkness, the freezing cold, the snow blizzards and the thawing ice on the city streets represented danger, anxiety, and death.

Anni-Frid (Frida) Lyngstad and Agnetha Fältskog were in fact ordinary housewives moving from their daytime personae to night-time careers dressing up and singing songs and living with men who were typically un-remarkable and as such very Swedish. The change came when the group came together and decided to promote themselves with one of many Swedish acronyms. With their relatively simple language, somewhat basic Germanic grammar and penchant for one-syllable vocabulary, Swedes like to use the initial letters of a series of nouns to facilitate quick and clear communication: examples include IKEA, SKF, SAAB and hundreds of other companies. Acronyms are easy to understand and remember, even if initially it might have been possible to confuse ABBA with ABB, Asea

Brown Boveri, a Swedish-Swiss multinational working and dominating the world of heavy engineering. Perhaps to make sure the first B was later reversed and became part of the band's trademark.

The two A letters stood for Anni-Frid Lyngstad and Agnetha Fältskog, the Bs for Benny Andersson and Björn Ulvaeus. When they left Stockholm and first performed internationally, ABBA were as unknown as the first Volvo to roll out of its Gothenburg workshop. Yet the members of ABBA sacrificed their individual identities to create a memorable trademark. In the beginning they were feted by a small local market only, but this changed when they were chosen by Sweden to be the country's flag carrier in the Eurovision Song Contest in 1974. Opportunity knocked softly. Little was known about ABBA. Their work, although striking, was derivative and without the future uniquely abbaesque identity. Certainly Agnetha had her own successful band and was making money from albums. Björn Ulvaeus sang and played the guitar for the Hootenanny Singers (so you can imagine where his musical values came from). Benny Andersson modelled himself on a Beatle and played keyboards. Agnetha Fältskog was dismissed as "a beautiful blonde in her early twenties and Benny's girlfriend." They had a manager, Stig Anderson. Half the population of Stockholm is called Anderson spelt in various ways, but before long he was to become the most identifiable Anderson in the land. In a touch of Cinderella, ABBA nearly missed their ball. Their trial piece for the competition, "Ring Ring", its English lyrics partially written by Neil Sedaka and Phil Cody, was given third prize by the Stockholm judges, but Stig had no trouble mobilizing public opinion and after an efficient campaign ABBA was on the plane to the United Kingdom.

The competition that year was held in Brighton, and the song they performed, "Waterloo", had triumphant nationalist military associations in Britain. To underline this message the conductor wore a totemic Napoleonic hat. A close look at the lyrics suggests that the anxious artists were expressing not the aftermath of loss after a feat of arms, but how to cope with a broken relationship. In the latter case they had plenty of practice.

Musicologists have spent years trying to work out how ABBA did it and have failed to produce a convincing explanation for the group's phenomenal popularity. Dozens of tunes have provided the material for countless karaoke sessions and the hugely successful musical and film *Mamma Mia!*: "Knowing Me, Knowing You"; "Take a Chance on Me"; "S.O.S."; "Chiquita"; "Fernando"; "Voulez-Vous"; "The Name of the Game" and so on. They came up with the idea of a wall of sound, and over-dubbed the voices of Agnetha and Anni-Frid with multiple harmonies. The complex music and simple lyrics created by Andersson and Ulvaeus have defied dissection. My view is that they were successful because when they were not recording they were continually flying around the world on promotional campaigns, following Volvo's lead in not neglecting previously untapped markets. The hit albums remain crisp distillations of exactly what the listening and watching public wanted at the time, and if the extraordinary revival of *Mamma Mia* is to be counted, well into the future. Benny and Björn and their female partners were agents for musical change and have been almost impossible to copy, plagiarize or improve upon. For a short time the group was composed of two married couples, but as their agents put it "relationships between the couples inevitable strained" and they all went their separate ways and the story of ABBA as a performing group was over, leaving in their music "a magnificent reminder of an era when four young artists from Scandinavia were the biggest group in the world."

"Waterloo" won the 1974 Eurovision competition, but the ABBA image took skill and energy to promote and fine tune into the dominant brand name in their field. It took years of hard work, as it took masses of Swedish steel combined with exemplary labour relations in the factories to turn Jakob into Volvo, and make the car's name into a household word across the world. There was a short period when only Volvo earned more foreign exchange than ABBA for Sweden. Benny and Björn worked as if on the car assembly line, six hours a day, mechanically turning out their creations and inventions for ten years. One did bodies, one did engines; Benny the music, Björn the lyrics. Their later hit "Money Money Money" did not really represent their lifestyle. Like everyone else in Sweden, they had to work all day to pay the bills they had to pay. But ABBA never dreamed about the time coming when they would be able to being able to fool around and have a ball, wouldn't have to work at all. They knew that they lived in a society where seventy per cent of all people between 16 and 64 were gainfully employed. The welfare state saw to it. They were conformists and were conditioned to like working; off stage they dressed and looked like assembly workers and spoke in the metaphors of finding the right vehicle. Unless one likes hillbillies one would not have looked twice at the men. Their wives provided glamour.

During the Eurovision contest the BBC even thought that Ulvaeus would turn off the audience and the viewers would switch off their sets, so they blanked his image, leaving just his sound. Ulvaeus laughed about it, admitting that in a black jacket with pearls and satin trousers tucked into silver boots, he "looked like a fat Christmas tree." But the banging rhythm of the repetitious jingle was more successful than the revolutionary French army in capturing hearts and minds. The expression "to meet your Waterloo" had been first popularized in Stockholm by Karl Gerhard in a revue during 1923. In the 1970s the arcane reference to Napoleon's fate in 1815 was overwhelmed by references to the role of fate and destiny in destroying love. Around the world hundreds of thousands of teenage girls who did not understand the emotional context loved the tune and sang and danced to it, swept up at a deeper level by the hidden complexity woven into the song by the talented and imaginative song writers. Benny and Björn composed the classic song "The Winner Takes it All" for the album *Super Trouper* in 1980 when ABBA was nearing the end of its run as an ensemble.

> The winner takes it all
> The loser has to fall...
>
> The game is on again
> A lover or a friend.

Agnetha Fältskog later commented that this was the group's favourite song. All members of ABBA lived lives that conformed to the spirit of mantras embracing winning, losing and playing games with friends and lovers.

Public opinion looked for exceptions to the rule, and often described Anni-Frid Lyngstad as not being Swedish. I suppose you could say that she did not look Swedish if you believe in national stereotypes. Her marketing image was headed "dark haired siren". She came from frontier Norway on the desolate north-east coast, the scene of strategically vital battles during the Second World War. She was a war baby, born near Narvik on 25 November 1945. By then the war was over, but not for her. Her mother Sinni had married a German sergeant during the occupation and experienced most likely the scene of German victory as Norway's gold reserves, its foreign minister and its king sailed away leaving British, French and Polish forces defeated. At the time of Anni-Frid's birth it was normal to hate Germans. Collaborators were driven out of Norway, and Anni-Frid, her mother and grandmother all fled to safety in liberal Sweden, which welcomed refugees from all war zones where they could. Anni-Frid grew up in and took her cultural values from Sweden. She also lived ABBA sound tracks. Her third marriage in 1992 was to Prince Heinrich Ruzzo Reuss von Plauen, and, as with much of her life, the wedding had sad consequences as the prince died prematurely in 1999. In a never ending series of personal setbacks, Anni-Frid's father turned out not have drowned conveniently during the Second World War, (as she had been told as a child) and in a serial progression of Waterloos she always seemed to lose the closest and dearest members of her family at the time of her greatest adult happiness.

JUST A HOUSEWIFE

Anni-Frid did not spend her waking hours trying to lure men onto rocks, nor was she was "just a housewife", a common Swedish expression at one time. By the end of ABBA's youthful years this tag was an anachronism. ABBA spoke for a generation of young women. Paradoxically, while proving the limitless possibilities that women could have in their lives, ABBA contributed to the widespread misunderstanding that characterized Stockholm as the capital of a land where love was free. During the 1960s Colin Simpson's view was typical of outsiders. In his book *The Viking Circle* (1966) he spent over ten pages on Swedish sin and sex during a perceptive comparative analysis of the Nordic nations. At the end of his research he ruled that it was wrong to use Sweden and sex as synonyms. Conscious of worldwide preconception about promiscuousness and free love, Simpson reported that "Stockholm has struck me as being a more inhibited, less exotic city than Tokyo, Paris, Vienna or Copenhagen." As a good journalist, he asked representative local female informants for their views. Did all Swedish girls subscribe to the mantra "Take a chance on me"? Were they sexually "free" in every sense of the word? Simpson's representative source, Gunilla, suggested that the idea that Swedish girls were promiscuous devotees of scandalous behaviour was "formed by people who had never been to Sweden."

In 1968 Paul Britten Austin linked the bemused and prurient world press reaction to Swedish sexual behaviour to the very large role women have always played in that country. He described how the Swedish woman, feared by Strindberg in the nineteenth century, realized herself completely in the twentieth, standing on her own two feet and distributing her favours where and how she wished, making no bones about her right, whether married or not, to take a holiday in Italy and there to find a lover who, though he might not be sincere, was at least polite.

At some length Austin explained how Swedish woman managed to survive, and thrive. Brought up in the old Swedish style, she had seen father and mother favour her brothers, and well understood the domesticity which men required of her: the cakes that had to be baked at Christmas and the proper cleanliness of a Swedish kitchen floor. On reaching adolescence, Austin said, she became aware that just to be a female, however beautiful, a mere housewife, *bara en hemmafru*, simply would not do. Two not easily reconciled roles were required of her. More often than not she rose to the challenge.

Austin's *On Being Swedish* praised this representative Swedish woman as speaking four languages fluently, driving the family Saab or a Volvo in motor rallies, an excellent cook, perhaps trained as a conference or air hostess; she was the apotheosis of beautiful and capable womanhood, well adapted to the rigours of modern living. Austin described this female type as more than able to hold her own against all comers and as being the despair of the Frenchman. "His holiday in Sweden, land of free love, is apt to turn out not at all as he hoped! Instead of a melting silly female creature, he finds a very clear-headed, poised sort of girl, who knows very well what she wants and doesn't want, who isn't going to submit to cavalier blandishments aimed at undermining her autonomy and on whom, therefore, his seductive techniques, fruit of a thousand years of French culture, are simply wasted."

ANTONIO'S TEMPTATION

The Italians of the 1960s were no wiser and fared no better than the French. Gigolos and Romeos were unable to grasp the Nordic indifference to nudity. The sexual cultural conflict was most obvious, comical and touching in the French and Italian new wave film industry, where the Latin approach to Anita Ekberg set the benchmark for mutual incomprehensibility. Fellini's exploitation of the young Ekberg has a lot to answer for, as *La Dolce Vita* imprinted an incorrect view of Swedish women. Ekberg's role required her first appearance to be at Campino Airport. She was cast as Sylvia, a Swedish-American actress who was chased from the airport by Signor Paparazzo, a photojournalist. (Paparazzo was soon to baptize a whole occupation with his name.)

When Ekberg reached her Roman hotel she was asked a series of stupid questions that revealed more about Italian preoccupations than Swedish reality. Sylvia was asked: "Is it true that you take a naked bath in the snow?" Sylvia replied: "Oh yes, every day." A second journalist asked:

"Madam, which is the thing you like most in life?" To which Sylvia replied: "There are a lot of things that I like, but particularly three: love, love and love." Undeterred, the Italian interpreter asked: "One last question, madam. What do you think of Italian men?" Sylvia: "Italiano? Oh…" (she looked across at Marcello Mastrioanni) "give me a couple of days to answer."

Anita Ekberg was a brilliant actress but the way she was promoted did nothing to help the status of Stockholm's women abroad. She was cast as hedonistic and a fool for not knowing whether Giotto's most famous bell-tower was in Florence or in Rome. But by the end of her cinema career her place in Italian society was respected and valued, and Italian banks and land agents were thrilled to have her as one of their wealthy clients.

Fellini followed up *La Dolce Vita* with the collaborative *Boccacio '70*, of which his episode was entitled *Le Tentazioni del Dottor Antonio*. This cinematic exercise again showed the huge gap between the Swedish and Italian minds. Fellini's description of a particular way of behaving was incomprehensible in Stockholm. In the opening scene Dr. Antonio finds that in front of his house in a large uncultivated field a group of workmen are putting up an enormous hoarding. It carries the portrait of Anita Ekberg stretched out in a provocative manner with a glass of milk in her hand. Commissioned by a dairy co-operative, it bears the advertising slogan "Drink More Milk". Dr. Antonio is shocked by the actress' "rather pronounced bosom" and, after linking it to the slogan, he goes mad and dreams he has killed the actress. For the film Fellini constructed a forty-foot statue of Ekberg so the deranged doctor could imagine he was sitting on her breast. In the surreal scene Dr. Antonio destroys the temptations posed in the poster by shooting ink pellets at the hoarding in the name of morality. The authorities respond by ordering that the poster be covered provisionally by small pieces of white paper.

The critic agreed that Fellini's move from *La Dolce Vita* to *Le Tentazioni del Dottor Antonio* did not come off. It certainly did not come off in Stockholm, where pictures of a beautiful, naked, pregnant woman were placed by the thousands at underground stations to illustrate the positive and healthy consequences of male-female equality in carrying out parental roles in rearing children. The posters, placed within arms reach of passengers moving on the *tunnelbana* escalators, were left untouched by graffiti sprayers and not even glanced at by the majority of commuters.

A SOLITARY BEACON: STOCKHOLM AND PROSTITUTION

In *La Dolce Vita* Fellini cast, as well as four photo-journalists, four prostitutes. Prostitutes, like paparazzi, were part of Roman life, then fashionable celebrities. Stockholm's citizens, on the other hand, were determined
to stamp prostitution out, and there was no place for sex workers in
Swedish popular culture. It takes a village to make a prostitute, and
Stockholm was a village, in this sense at least, and no exception to the rule.
But with their instinct for devising systems, Stockholmers have managed
to build the foundations of an effective wall between sex and commerce.

At the end of the twentieth century Stockholm attracted planeloads
of Japanese businessmen, twenty years ahead in the field of information
technology but twenty years behind in their lubricious research on Swedish
free love and Nordic permissiveness. Reforms by Swedish social democrats
had by then all but put a stop to paid-for love. Even so, human nature
meant that it took more than prostitution law reform to stop call girls
sneaking in from other parts of Europe to earn a few euros. The collapse
of the Soviet Union made the achievement of routine acceptance of gender
equality more difficult, as thousands of women from the Baltic and Eastern
Europe streamed into Stockholm to become the backbone of "apartment
prostitution".

In a clandestine world of non-conformity the exact number of sex
workers arriving on the Finnish or Estonian ferries was hard to estimate,
but at an individual level the costs were well illustrated by the 2002 film
Lilja-4-ever. This was a movie about the life of Dangoule Rasalaite, a
sixteen-year-old Lithuanian girl who jumped out of a Stockholm window
in June 2000 after being smuggled into the country a year earlier to work
as a sex slave. Almost a decade later, episodes of the Danish television cult
crime series *The Eagle* are often shot in modern Stockholm, which is
shown as a city where child prostitution is confronted and extinguished.

The system devised to interdict the purchase of sexual services was as
simple and ingenious as the ideas behind the alcohol-controlling *systembolaget* (of which more later). The government considered it was not reasonable to prosecute the person giving the service and changed the law
accordingly. Stockholm's lawmakers were also realistic enough to see that
client criminalization is never more than supplementary in stopping prostitution. Knowing that immigrant women were not as easy to convince as
those whose grandmothers and grandfathers had been taught to use

gender-neutral language, and who had gender-neutral values in their schools, the National Police Board set up an anti-trafficking reporting system. The Immigration Board also did what it could to conform to values that were established by the European Union to end trafficking across member states' borders.

Four years into the social experiment, Karin Grundberg reported results to Agence France Presse, whose journalists were naturally intrigued by the law reform, seeing implications for their readers well beyond Montmartre. After the law changed and it became illegal to purchase sexual services, Sweden's techno-savvy prostitutes quickly decided to use the internet to attract clients. In Stockholm free websites with unrestricted access advertised young women seeking generous men for pleasant encounters at home or in a hotel. Some claimed that more often than not women offering their services on the internet suffered violence and other forms of abuse. Stig Larsson, Professor of Social Medicine at Lund, disagreed, commenting that historically street prostitution provided the worst conditions. He cited madams and drugs as determining factors in abuse and he claimed that in reality, in spite of the reforms, neither had disappeared from the streets of Gamla Stan.

Only foreigners, mostly Finns, Germans and Japanese salary-men, slipped furtively into the grimy seats of the empty blue-movie theatres that were systematically firebombed by Stockholm's more militant feminists. As potential Japanese sex tourists crossed flight-paths with the more educated and savvy Swedes heading to Southeast Asia for what was not locally available, the censorious captains of SAS knew that their cargo of middle-aged Swedish men would return home to plan yet another politically incorrect visit the following year, while the white-gloved Japanese pilots, who had done their own research, for their part knew that there would be very few Japanese men heading north for sex more than once.

An ominous trend was detected in the last decade of the twentieth century, when public violence against women increased and it was not uncommon to see a man hit a woman on the tunnelbana or for their shouting match to be broken up by irate spectators. The practice of onlookers was to hector the male assailant, protecting the woman and, in such a well-ordered social democratic community, advising the man to seek professional help for his aggression. Such active intervention in domestic disputes was rarely seen in other capitals around the world, and the Swedish par-

Gender equality in action: the Riksdag

liament added a raft of ways to protect "a woman's integrity". The definition of rape was widened and it was made an offence to neglect to report
sexual crimes.

In Stockholm prostitution is thought of as violence against women.
The absence of patriarchal dominance in the Riksdag (over 45 per cent of
members were women following the 2002 elections) made passage of the
necessary law reform smooth. The high degree of gender equality in all
areas of Swedish government, the low unemployment rate of Swedish
women and the ease with which women could find well-paid legitimate
ways of supporting themselves made it easy to persuade public opinion. In
Stockholm society men and women usually work as a team, from the
home, combining parental and breadwinning responsibility.

In the third millennium Sweden has been hailed around the world as
having found a solution to prostitution, and Stockholm indeed seems the
world capital most successful in tackling it. A Californian women's justice
centre in Santa Rosa queried in Spanish "why hasn't anyone tried this
before?" A mainly Hispanic audience, who knew all about the problem,
were told that one country's success stood out as a solitary beacon light-

ing the way. In just five years Sweden had dramatically reduced the number of women in prostitution. In Stockholm, street prostitution was reduced by two-thirds, and the number of clients by eighty per cent. There were other major Swedish cities where street prostitution had all but disappeared. Gone too, for the most part, were the renowned Swedish brothels and massage parlours that had proliferated during the last three decades of the twentieth century when prostitution in Sweden was legal. In addition, so Californians were told, the number of foreign women being trafficked into Sweden for sex was relatively small. "The Swedish government estimates that in the last few years only 200 to 400 women and girls have been annually sex trafficked into Sweden, a figure that's negligible compared with the 15,000 to 17,000 females yearly sex trafficked into neighboring Finland. No other country, nor any other social experiment, has come anywhere near Sweden's promising results."

Sex tourism is clandestine and hits at the central values of social democracy. It is difficult and unpleasant to investigate and to describe, but Henning Mankell does it well. Mankell is well placed to understand his fellow countrymen. When he is not writing—he has dominated the world's bestseller lists with detective novels such as *Faceless Killers*, *The Dogs of Riga*, and *Firewall*—or travelling, he spends his time helping African charities working with HIV/AIDS patients. Mankell tackles serious issues and accordingly has his hero, Inspector Kurt Wallander, Sweden's answer to Inspector Morse, go through the morale-sapping self-loathing common in many middle-aged Swedish men. In Mankell's *The Man Who Smiled* (2005) Inspector Wallander personified Stockholmers as world leaders in not only inventing such life-changing products as the Aga stove, the robot vacuum cleaner and the roller ball bearing, but also in devising efficient methods to enjoy and promote sex tourism abroad. Mankell describes how his hero Wallander staves off drinking himself to death with an annual package holiday to Thailand. When he returns from vacation, like many thousands of Swedish men, he spends the following winter back home fearing he has contracted HIV. Mankell writes:

> For more than a year Kurt Wallander, a detective chief inspector with the Ystad police, had been on sick leave, unable to carry out his duties. During that time a sense of powerlessness had come to dominate his life and affected his actions. Time and time again, when he could not bear

to stay in Ystad and had some money to spare, he had gone off on point-
less journeys in the vain hope of feeling better, perhaps even of recover-
ing his zest for life, if only he were somewhere other than Skåne. He
had taken a package holiday to the Caribbean but had drunk himself
silly on the outward flight and had not been entirely sober for any of the
fortnight he spent in Barbados. His general state of mind was one of in-
creasing panic, a sense of being totally alienated. He had skulked in the
shade of palm trees, and some days had not even set foot outside his
hotel room, unable to overcome a primitive need to avoid the company
of others. He had bathed just once, and then only when he'd stumbled
on a jetty and fallen into the sea.

Late one evening when he had forced himself to go out and mix with
other people, but also in order to replenish his stock of alcohol, he had
been solicited by a prostitute. He wanted to wave her away and yet
somehow encouraged her at the same time, and was only later overwhelmed by misery and self-disgust. For three days, of which he afterwards had no clear memory, he spent all his time with the girl in a shack
stinking of vitriol, in a bed with sheets smelling of mould and cock-
roaches crawling over his sweaty face. He could not even remember the
girl's name or if he had ever discovered what it was. He had taken her
in what could only have been a fit of unbridled lust. When she had ex-
tracted the last of his money, two burly brothers appeared and threw
him out. He went back to the hotel and survived by forcing down as
much as he could of the breakfast included in the price, eventually arriving back at Sturup airport in a worse state than when he had left.

His doctor, who gave him regular check-ups, forbade him any more
such trips as there was a real danger that Wallander would drink himself
to death. But two months later, at the beginning of December, he was
off again, having borrowed money from his father on the pretext of
buying some new furniture in order to raise his spirits. Ever since his
troubles started he had avoided his father, who had just married a
woman 30 years his junior who used to be his home help. The moment
he had the money in his hand, he made a beeline for the Ystad Travel
Agency and bought a three-week package holiday in Thailand. The
pattern of the Caribbean repeated itself, the difference being that catastrophe was narrowly averted because a retired pharmacist who had sat
next to him on the flight and who happened to be at the same hotel

took pity on him and stepped in when Wallander began drinking at breakfast and generally acting strangely. The pharmacist's intervention resulted in Wallander being sent home a week earlier than planned. On this holiday, too, he had surrendered to his self-disgust and thrown himself into the arms of prostitutes, each one younger than the last. There followed a nightmarish winter when he was in constant dread of having contracted the fatal disease. By the end of April, when he had been off work for ten months, it was confirmed that he was not in fact infected; but he seemed not to react to the good news. It was about that time his doctor began to wonder if Wallander's days as a police officer were over, whether indeed he would ever be fit to work again, or was ready for immediate early retirement on the grounds of ill health.

THE SINGHA TSUNAMI

Even Mankell, with his ingeniously unpleasant fictional content, could not have imagined the tragic end of so many Swedish tourists. On 26 December 2004, 543 Swedish holidaymakers in Thailand were killed by a tsunami caused by an undersea earthquake that devastated coastal areas of Southeast Asia. Waves thirty feet high hit tourist resorts, villages and fishing grounds as bodies and debris swirled around in unimaginable devastation. Thailand was a favourite holiday destination for the zero-eighters, many of whom were among the 20,000 Swedes taking in the sun and having a Singha beer when a white wall of raging water appeared to come from nowhere and killed or injured about ten per cent of them.

Stockholm mourned its dead for twelve months. A year after the event the injured and shocked remained traumatized by the Asian tsunami, which cost Sweden more lives than any other western nation. Stockholm staged a tsunami exhibition featuring reports from Asian and Swedish children, which aimed to help those who lost loved ones or survived the waves. This was a typical response from victims: "In a way, I am feeling worse (than right after the tsunami) because in the beginning I was in a state of shock. But now I have realized that I will feel like this for the rest of my life."

More Swedes died in the tsunami than when the *Vasa* went down (see p.163). King Carl XVI Gustav emerged from the tragedy with his reputation enhanced. He told survivors and relatives of those killed that he wished he could put everything right again, like a fairytale king. "We are all just humans without clear answers," said the king, "what can I say that could be more helpful? It feels as though there are no more words or that they have never existed." Leading a national ceremony in Stockholm on 10 January 2006 in which he shared the nation's grief, he recalled the touching story of his father dying in a plane crash when he was a very young prince. From Sweden's old colony, the *Helsingin Sanomat* commented with approval that Carl XVI Gustav had appeared as a father figure to his people.

Although figures are, for obvious reasons, unavailable, one can assume that the majority of Swedes who travelled from Sturup or Stockholm were heading for Thailand to see the elephants, swim and drink beer. But sufficient Kurt Wallander clones fasten their seat belts for Sweden's premier glossy travel magazine to publish in each issue a full-page warning under the rubric "Eclipse of the Sun". The grim reaper message is combined with a black and white moral lesson: "Do not spoil a holiday and lazy days in a tropical pool by buying child prostitutes." A full page advertisement in black and white informs its hedonistic and wealthy readers: "There is something which darkens the sun for many tourist trips". In smaller print a helpful website is advertised and in five bleak paragraphs the curious are told that Sweden has already moved to stop the trafficking of prostitutes at home. Now the day has come to use the power of Swedish public opinion to end child sex tourism. Stockholmers, it is explained, are like other men. They can, and do, buy boys and girls in Third World countries on the internet. There are Swedish men and Swedish women who plan their holidays around child sex tourism. Child sex tourism exists because of the co-operation of taxi drivers, hotel porters, bartenders and crooked policemen. The "Swedes against child sex tourism" lobbyists argue that paying children for sex is not the way to raise the living standards of underdeveloped countries and that the morals of Stockholm should apply equally in Bangkok.

Foreigners should not be blamed for being confused. Stockholmers and Swedes in general can transmit very mixed messages. On 7 July 2004, the day *Expressen* devoted the whole of page 12 to a lampoon of the prime minister and his ginger cat, page 11 was centred on a similarly large photograph of a Swedish girl, Leona Johansson, described, in case the readers could not work it out, as having sex on stage with her Norwegian friend in front of 4,000 rock fans, followers of the Norwegian band, the

Cumshots. While the prime minister patting his cat was ridiculed, Leona Johansson was applauded for her project "Fuck for Forest" (*sic*). The public and the police had been warned, but for good form they took photographic evidence, sold it to the press and said they were shocked. But ultimately, as Tomas Kvarnkullen wrote in *Expressen*, pornography had been used for a good cause, protecting the environment and saving the tropical rainforest. With the slogan "we did it for the environment", the Cumshots concert raised money for a region in the world which Swedes were worried about and often visited on their annual vacations. The Cumshots, whose parents no doubt conceal their empty alcohol bottles when putting out their rubbish, had no inhibitions about combining nudity and sex to promote politically correct causes.

TATTOOS AND TAKEOVERS

Not everyone agrees with the consensus that public opinion and government policy have combined to eradicate conflict between men and women—so far as human nature makes it possible. Stieg Larsson is the most prominent dissident. After a career as a crusading liberal journalist, Larsson delivered three novels to his Swedish publisher Norstedts and died suddenly shortly afterwards, only to become a bestselling author. Larsson's *Män som hatar kvinnor* (men who hate women) was on sale in Stockholm in 2005 as the first volume of a series which Larsson called the "millennium trilogy". The millennium referred to was a fictional magazine named *Millennium*, which crusaded against Sweden's financial mafia. The villains in the novel had names reminiscent of but not quite the same as Sweden's most famous and successful entrepreneurial leaders of the past. Larsson's choice of the fictional name of one of the novel's basest characters could not have failed to raise eyebrows among the residents of the Wenner-Gren Centre.

Larsson has drawn a long bow by constructing a provocative link between capitalism, fascism and the abuse of women. The first volume runs to 533 pages, stuffed full of issues not much discussed by Stockholmers, who have nevertheless rushed to buy the book. Badged as crime and detective fiction and called in English in a misleading and sensational title, *The Girl with the Dragon Tattoo*, it is a novel about feminists, anti-racists and environmental activists who are all in the gun sights of conservative forces. Larsson describes anti-Semitism in the 1920s. A typical character is shown as representative of those who joined the first Nazi groups. A member of the Swedish national fascist organization, he fought in the Winter War (by then a captain in the Swedish army) as a volunteer. He was killed in February 1940, and, in the words of the text, "thereby became a martyr in the Nazi movement and had a battle group named after him. Even now a handful of idiots gather at a cemetery in Stockholm on the anniversary of his death to honour him." Larsson talks through other characters of "bursting the biggest bubble in the financial world since the Kreuger crash of 1932."

In what might be taken as lies, damned lies or statistics Larsson injects disturbing polemical wake-up calls and sets out to prove that there is a correlation between corporate crime and offences against women. His technique is striking and melodramatic, using almost full blank pages with capital letters in different sizes spelling out his concerns. Underneath IN-CENTIVE on the otherwise blank page in capital letters we are told: 18% OF THE WOMEN IN SWEDEN HAVE AT ONE TIME BEEN THREATENED BY A MAN. Another almost blank page called CON-SEQUENCE ANALYSES claims: 46% OF THE WOMEN IN SWEDEN HAVE BEEN SUBJECTED TO VIOLENCE BY A MAN. MERGERS, informs readers that 13% OF THE WOMEN IN SWEDEN HAVE BEEN SUBJECTED TO AGGRAVATED SEXUAL ASSAULT OUTSIDE OF A SEXUAL RELATIONSHIP. HOSTILE TAKEOVER reports that 92% OF WOMEN IN SWEDEN WHO HAVE BEEN SUBJECTED TO SEXUAL ASSAULT HAVE NOT REPORTED THE MOST RECENT VIOLENT INCIDENT TO THE POLICE. Whatever the truth of his statistics and the accuracy of his perspective, his message, now posthumous, has got across. His work has sold millions of copies, and is most popular in Denmark, where it is second only in sales to the Bible.

Stockholm snowstorm

Chapter Seven

THE SYSTEM

CONFORMITY, CONTROL AND THE DEMON DRINK

HELAN GÅR: THE FULL DRAM GOES

It is by being systematic that the Swedes hope to abolish evils like prostitution from Stockholm. *System* has only a short entry in the Swedish-English dictionary, but master the importance of systematic philosophies to Stockholmers and their way of life is easier to follow. Swedes love to plan. Systems are revered. When they fly out from Arlanda airport they prefer to use Scandinavian Airlines System. It is the system in the SAS logo that reassures them. They are not primarily interested in new aircraft. When Swedish passengers fasten their seatbelts and hear the ominous litany of safety warnings and commands they think that their system will save them. They do not care about seat pitch, video games, in-flight telephones and certainly not about the stewardesses. They accept being bumped when the system requires it.

The creation of SAS was a good idea but insignificant compared with the attempt to invent a system to stop heavy drinking. Alcoholism has been the curse of Sweden since Viking times. In an effort to stop it, Swedes set up the *systembolaget*, the state alcohol monopoly, by far Stockholm's most effective combination of company and system. Ever more surprising, Stockholm accepted the marriage between the head of the parliamentary system and the dominatrix of the state alcohol distribution network, thus merging Sweden's two premier institutions

Göran Persson may not have known the name of his cat, but he did know how to get a drink after hours in Stockholm. In the third millennium Prime Minister Persson wed "the spirit mogul", VD (managing director) Anitra Steen, head of the systembolaget. At the time of his nuptials Persson, who first became prime minister in 1996, was charged with running one of the richest countries in the world. By then Sweden had nine million citizens with an average household income of $51,000 and a

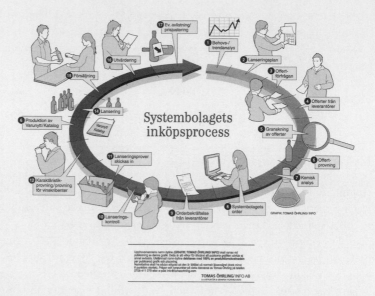

gross national product of $258,319 million. Almost a million citizens lived in Stockholm and the prime minister lived in a capital city famous for inebriation where premature death from alcohol abuse had been a fact of life for a thousand years.

Anitra Steen controlled 420 stores, most of them in Stockholm, and about 590 local agencies. However, at the time of her marriage to the prime minister, she had problems in her shopping trolley, as eighty of her store managers were defending charges of accepting bribes from alcohol suppliers (a situation that did not go unquestioned outside Sweden). "How can ministers supervise the State business which their boss's lover is running?" asked Katherine Butler in London's *Independent*. The issue raised eyebrows as far away as Singapore. According to *The Straits Times*, the prime minister, who had been married twice before, had pestered his girlfriend for years until she finally said yes. In the Swedish language, Anitra was described as Persson's *sambo*—a word with offensive connotations in the United States, but simply meaning "same residence".

The wedding closed the gap between political power and drink. Free alcohol was served when the scowling bridal couple officially stopped living in sin. Not that such a concept was widely held in Stockholm, although guilt was another matter. Their union made Göran and Anitra for a time the most important couple in the nation and the symbolism of their match was immense.

DRUNK AS A SWEDE

So how did Stockholm's alcohol problem begin? History blames it on too much salt in the diet and unsafe drinking water. Swedish food in the Middle Ages and during the Vasa period was salted to preserve it, and everybody drank lots of beer, which was said to be safer than water, to slake their thirst. Beer was supplemented by home distilleries. Stockholm quickly developed London-style gin-shops, frequented by drunks and prostitutes, often both at once.

Hallendorff's *History of Sweden* (1929) freely admitted that "intemperate habits had long been common among the Swedish people." Like many others, they gave the credit for devising the systembolaget to Dr. Ivan Bratt. Indeed, in its early years it was alternately known as either the Stockholm System or the Bratt System. Bratt became interested in temperance watching the Stockholm wharf labourers drinking heavily during working hours. He rarely saw a sober wharfie and there were huge numbers of industrial accidents. Wages usually balanced the dockworkers' booze bill and often the breadwinners returned home to their wives with nothing but a sore head.

The worldwide temperance movement, which campaigned fiercely during the First World War, was very successful in Stockholm. T. K. Derry's *History of Scandinavia* (1979) explains how the puritan element in the Lutheran Church made prohibition a major social issue. By 1917 the alcohol restriction system had been extended to the whole country and a state-controlled systembolaget took over the nationwide monopoly of the sale of alcohol. A national referendum rejected total prohibition by a small margin but the community, being naturally compliant, accepted rationing. Under the new rules income earners over twenty-five were eligible for a *motbok*, a ration book. Married women were disqualified, as were old age pensioners, sitting it out and waiting to die in their otherwise excellent retirement homes. The motbok could be withdrawn if the holder was charged with drunkenness, had defrauded the taxation department or was receiving national assistance. The systembolaget, as described by Irene

Scobbie's 1977 book *Sweden*, changed in 1955 when it was decided to abolish the motbok. Scobbie explained that one of the systembolaget's chief objects was to discourage customers, and she assumed that it selected its unsmiling personnel accordingly. Scobbie reported how a curiously oppressive mood descended on customers as they entered the shop, cheerful comments were assiduously avoided and, if a red light went on by the side of the cash-register, the customer was required to show identification. A blacklist signal included a register of alcoholics who were refused any kind of alcohol. Purchases were placed into anonymous bags, presumably to avoid encouraging people met subsequently outside to follow suit and buy more alcohol, but actually there were few things more recognizable than the anonymous bags and most customers could be seen shamefacedly plunging them out of sight into their briefcases.

Scobbie noticed that the sight of a drunk on the street, not uncommon in certain parts of most Swedish towns, caused an almost neurotic reaction from those around, some muttering in annoyance that it ought not to be allowed and others looking acutely embarrassed. There were few English-type pubs or relaxing cafés in the French style, so it was difficult to see where those addicted to alcohol could go unless they could afford expensive licensed restaurants. Certainly no criminal was as quickly bundled out of sight by the police as a drunk. Scobbie found it strange that a nation so aware of the rights of minority groups and the problems of many emotionally deprived people felt so little sympathy for the drunkard. As she explained, Stockholm's drunken drivers were the recipients of Swedish commonsense. A very small amount of alcohol in the bloodstream (less than half the permitted maximum in the United Kingdom) led to a stiff prison sentence, and police roadblocks were set up quite frequently in the evenings to make random checks, although the kindly welfare state allowed a convicted driver "to arrange to serve his sentence at a convenient time, often opting to spend his summer vacation paying off his debt to society."

While the idea of creating a state alcohol monopoly is over a century old, the concept remained modern in Steen's view. The systembolaget's official history ran that copper mines in Falun reduced industrial accidents by rationing alcohol and building a wall between alcohol sales and private profit. Some Swedish ideas have changed the world, but not the systembolaget, even though it sells alcohol to about a quarter of the population of Sweden every week. Outside Sweden the systembolaget cheerfully pushed its 80° vodka to cinema audiences and others with seductive advertisements that were banned in Stockholm, before making a fortune from selling the Absolut brand name to Pernod Ricard in 2008. Millions of Swedish systembolaget customers share their experiences of state-controlled alcohol purchase with a bibulous select minority: Finns, Norwegians, Icelanders and some puritan pockets of imitators surviving in Canada and the United States.

On paper, the systembolaget, once it was dreamed up, should have solved everything as SAS efficiently organized Nordic world air travel. Inebriates should have disappeared from the streets, beaten wives should have vanished from casualty and drunken stabbings, robberies and brawls should have been non-existent. No individuals should have grown fat at the expense of the misery of others. The folly of prohibition should have been avoided, bootlegging and smuggling should have ceased. Crooked doctors should never have had to prescribe brandy for medicinal purposes, and the interior of every home in Stockholm should have looked as if Carl Larsson painted it on one of his most optimistic days.

The theory has always been that without any private profit motive, there is no reason to try to persuade customers to buy as much drink as possible. In practice, supply reduction through limited trading hours and the previous completely monopolistic rationing system have had the opposite effect. Maybe traffic through the turnstiles would be reduced if the French, Italian, Japanese or Australian customs of free and easy access to alcohol were permitted. Its defenders claim things could be far worse: the systembolaget boasts that while in 1800 Sweden had around the highest consumption of alcohol in Europe and the country's national hero, Carl Michael Bellman, was celebrated as an alcoholic who had made a career as a drunken poet, by 2000 alcohol consumption was nearly the lowest.

The Stockholm social engineers who were once so proud of the invention of a perfect alcohol monopoly worthy of Plato are now in a state of anxiety, fearing that it is in its dying days. Since Sweden joined the European Union, rival officials and functionaries in Brussels with different ideologies have challenged the Swedish government's systembolaget and the British have mocked it. Under the heading "Hagar the Hangover", Stephen Brown described Sweden as a Nordic Nanny State. He described the sight of Swedes singing the drinking song "Helan går", which he trans-

Shopping at the systembolaget

lated as "Down in One", as akin to other nationalities belting out their national anthem. The systembolaget directors have counter-attacked by trying desperately to convince the Swedish population to support the near-state monopoly in the face of EU integration pressures and nibbling by capitalist restaurateurs and small shopkeepers. At the moment the Danish saying "drunk as a Swede" is still literal rather than defamatory. One does not have to live in Vasastan to benefit from the all-embracing power of the systembolaget. If a customer resides outside Stockholm on Gotland or north of Sundsvall, for example, anything not in stock locally will be trucked to the thirsty Swede the next day.

Despite the introduction of self-service to Stockholm's systembolaget in 1991 and the subsequent dilution of the monopoly, visiting its premises is not, as claimed by the VD, a pleasant experience. Restricted opening hours under which alcohol sales were turned off on Friday and recommenced on Monday morning, even in the glossy systembolaget near Östermalm, led to panic buying and last-minute scenes of despair as a weekend of binge drinking was cut short by the closing doors (a limited Saturday opening was introduced in 2000). Moreover, the strategic plan to create a "healthy drinking culture" has done just the opposite, driving thousands of Stockholmers to the overnight ferry services between Sweden, Finland, Denmark and the Baltic States in a futile attempt to escape high liquor taxes. Even when not strictly necessary, pensioners, school mistresses—almost every group in society—take a ferry and come back with arms full of spirits, quite usually the worse for wear, occasionally suffering concussion as bottles drop on their heads when overloaded roof storage bins collapse.

The systembolaget gives no excuses for heavy drinking. It provides frequent health warnings and gives its customers a newspaper called simply *Bolaget*. Sure, there are other inventions, other companies—thousands of other companies—many of them household names throughout the world, but for Stockholmers there is only one newspaper from The Company. Typically, it is possible to find hidden in its journal an article or editorial praising alcohol-free drinks, and warning of the links between alcohol and diabetes. The health education message is concealed in a glossy format that not only gives information about Grenache from the Costa del Sol, why rosé is summer's best wine and what hours the boutique is open, but also has crafty illustrations of what happens if you drink too much. Alcohol-free products are not rushing off the shelves, as the concept of alcohol-free festivities is rather hard to swallow despite the gloomy illustrations of "before" and "after" women. "After", drab and downcast in brown and black, moodily contemplates her glass of spirits, while her four glamorous sisters on the opposite page display the charms of their sex and smile knowingly across their orange juice. Alcohol-free red, white and sparkling wine, alcohol-free beer, cider and San Pellegrino mineral water from Italy take up only a tiny part of the sales catalogue. The various available brands of Scotch whisky alone are larger than the entire range of beverages in the alcohol-free section.

One now famous name, Edradour, is missing among the systembolaget pantheon of scotches. This brand so took the fancy of two innovative Swedes that they tried to name their daughter after it. The Swedish tax office, which registers the names of newborns, was affronted and refused the choice, saying it was linked too closely to an alcoholic drink. Magnus and Maria Eklöf fought a desperate legal battle with the tax office to gain permission to break with tradition and move outside the approved list of Christian names to call their daughter after a dangerous substance. In the end the Eklöfs won. Magnus did not gloat at his unexpected victory, and pleaded that not only the whisky but also the village of Edradour itself had tickled his fancy as well as his palate. When Edradour Eklöf receives her first of many communications from the tax authorities (who will keep in close touch with her until they sign off on her death), her neighbours might have joined the trend, forcing the mailman to deliver tax forms and information to Laphroaig Lundberg and Glenlivet Gyllenborg.

While Edradour Eklöf's father drinks imported whisky, Swedish beer and vodka are high in the country's export earners. In Nuku'alofa the King of Tonga, a tribal ruler with similarities to a medieval Swedish absolute monarch, presides over an undemocratic political system and, his critics complain, controls a royal near monopoly in beer brewing. Many of his subject Tongans drink Royal beer brewed under licence by Pripps in Stockholm—Sweden's contribution to development and progress in the Pacific.

Carl Linnaeus: Gross Prurience

Carl Linnaeus was born in Uppsala in 1707. Three centuries after his birth his praises are sung for inventing the best and longest-lasting system for classifying plants. In 2007 Linnaeus was hailed as a hero of the gardening world by *Country Life* when the Royal Agricultural Society's flagship Chelsea Flower Show celebrated his 300th birthday. Linnaeus invented the system by which science continues to name living organisms. In 1739 he founded the Natural History Museum, which he linked to the Academy of the Sciences. Exhibits in the museum have grown to seventeen million over the centuries. To me the most interesting is the *Vega* monument, commemorating the name of Nils Adolf Erik Nordenskjöld's ship in which he was the first to sail through the North-East Passage.

By 1759 Linnaeus lived, lectured and stored his collections in a small manor house at Hammarby, sitting at a lectern he called the workhorse, trying to turn into a hermit, feeling tired and old rather than excited. The landscape architect, Ulf Nordfjell, designed the illustrative Linnaeus exhibit for the Chelsea Flower Show. *Country Life* cleverly described Nordfjell as avoiding the temptation to create "a sort of Stratford-Upon-Moominland". Instead, he conveyed a landscape that showed the intense excitement Linnaeus found in both wild and cultivated spaces, a sense of enlightenment inquiry and order being projected onto what was once more or less a wilderness.

The *Independent* magazine was more investigative than *Country Life*, as visitors to the Chelsea Flower Show might expect. Anna Pavord's look at Linnaeus' life, under the heading "A Class of his Own... the Swedish Genius of Botany", explained that Linnaeus was famous because he gave the world the system for naming plants. Linnaeus' great contribution was to use Latin as a universal language to designate—but not describe—plants. As Pavord put it, Linnaeus cut through the garbage that had accumulated through the centuries in naming plants and devised a two module name tag system. He saw himself as a celebrity, quipping "God created. Linnaeus set in order."

Before he became withdrawn and depressed he described one of his textbooks as the greatest achievement in the realms of science. Perhaps it was. The use of Latin did not hide the essence of Linnaeus' interest—he called his invention *Systeme Sexuale*. Linnaeus was as interested in goldfish and orang-utangs as marigolds and was undisturbed when a fellow botanist in St. Petersburg said that his nomenclature was "loathsome harlotry". Johann Siegesbeck posed the rhetorical question: "who would have thought that bluebells, lilies and onions could be up to such immorality?" Linnaeus also ignored the Bishop of Carlisle after the cleric remarked: "to tell that nothing could equal the gross prurience of Linnaeus' mind was perfectly needless". Thundering on the Scottish borders that Linnaeus' system was "enough to shock female modesty" was water off a duck's back.

Uppsala had Linnaeus on its books, if not as resident, then as a professor in the medical faculty, and was also home to Anders Celsius, born in 1701. Celsius was the professor of astronomy at Uppsala University (by whose standards of learning Stockholm had yet to reach red brick stage) between 1730 and 1744. Celsius also worked in Paris and Nuremberg, was a famous expert on the Aurora Borealis and is an everyday name now as the centigrade thermometer is called after him in a tribute to his scientific systematic description of an instrument which, whatever its various uses, never raises pulpit ire. Uppsala, as a former capital of Sweden, can be credited with impressing the need for systematic organization in Sweden; its most famous son invented a whole branch of science based on what he originally called "systematics".

Stockholm, the modern capital, should be acknowledged for developing the eighteenth-century rationalization personified by Linnaeus to its ultimate expression and confirming the spirit of Nordic enlightenment in the twenty-first century. It has always been mind after matter, not mind over matter in Stockholm. Swedes have given proper priority to staving off hunger, cold and death, as far as possible and for as long as possible. In Stockholm, to evade the system, to behave without a system, to pretend the system does not exist, to wander about and conduct life unsystematically is to ask for trouble. Conformity is often not a choice, but part of a failsafe built-in way of life. Whenever human nature or mechanical and electrical engineers can devise bullet-proof systems, self-harm and injury to others are prevented. Living with the system in winter is crucial to survival. To ignore traffic lights or warnings of countless kinds, walk in the wrong place, defy bylaws, show flippant disregard for custom and habit, to do what is not expected can leave you dead in a very hygienic hospital or locked up in a relatively pleasant prison. Designers compel obedience where obedience can be compelled, and as a result pedestrians do obey traffic signals and most vehicles halt at pedestrian crossings to allow people on foot to pass.

Some systems are so necessary and important that they are seen by the state as a matter of life and death. Volvo and Saab drivers have no choice about switching on their headlights when conditions are dark; nor do the drivers of non-Swedish manufactured vehicles moving about Stockholm. By law, engineers ensure that headlights are switched on every time a driver turns on the ignition switch. With so many obtrusive systems, Stockholmers have always been well aware that a danger existed in continually improving existing systems, whether on earth, in the mind or in heaven. New methods are not always the best methods. There is even a word for the zealot system creator—*system-makare*, system-monger.

In the first edition of Wenström and Harlock's dictionary *bolag*, "company", had roughly the same size entry as *system*. In later editions bolag is less defined, but the activities of Swedish companies have grown in inverse proportion to the interest of lexicographers. Stockholmers are inventive. They love to associate in partnerships. They like to go shares with each other in joint business, and *bolagaffärs*, business affairs, are what put Sweden near the top of the world in per capita income and standard of living. As James Proctor and Neil Roland observe in *The Rough Guide to Sweden*, it is hard to find truly disgusting service in Sweden and, for those used to British Rail and its privatized successors, Swedish railways are a revelation.

Swedes were initially cautious about embracing trains and abandoning horse-drawn transport. A German doctor convinced many of them that looking out of train windows at the proposed high speed of travel would cause them brain damage. This prediction proved incorrect. Proctor and Roland are right to claim that the public transport system in Sweden is Europe's most efficient, and train travel is a quick, easy and relatively inexpensive way of covering the country's vast expanses. While the pride and joy of Sweden is its high speed trains, the quickest and most useful form of transport for city dwellers is the *tunnelbana*, Stockholm's metro system.

TROLLS IN THE *TUNNELBANA*

There are many beer drinkers in the Swedish underground but no actual trolls, although one Swedish zoologist got so carried away with the urge to systematize and classify that he declared that trolls existed. It became official in Stockholm in 1911. The existence of God was hard to prove but a Swedish scientist was the first in Europe confident enough to declare the reality of subterranean creatures. The population of Stockholm obediently followed in the footsteps of the trolls on the city's underground railway system. On many platforms you feel as if you are in the halls of the mountain king.

As Stockholm is so far north, built on a series of islands and its terrain crisscrossing water channels, devising efficient wheels of commerce to move people and money around the city has always been difficult. Following the example of contemporary and comparable European capitals, Swedish engineers soon built a fine system of tram tracks. Many Stockholmers, ruled since the beginning of the nineteenth century by the Bernadotte dynasty, had a natural affection for France and opted for the Parisian metro as the model way to organize traffic. In Stockholm it was sensible to shift the tram system underground as lakes and granite outcrops, let alone the winter weather, disrupted the natural flow. Something about a system of tracks in a network of tunnels chimed in with a developing Freudian spirit in Stockholm, a recognition of the importance of the concealed unconscious. The railroad tunnel construction era took off in Europe and coincided with the beginning of psychoanalysis, which at that time was as attractive to Swedes as to Austrians.

Moving about like trolls beneath the islands and lakes suited the Stockholm psyche. The troll clones, heading down the escalators at the

Consstructing the *tunnelbana*

beginning of a trip and up to the natural light at the end, felt a coherent part of a necessarily underground community bent on efficient movement from place to place. Stockholmers were always thoroughly proud of being part of something larger than the individual and tunnel track traffic lifted their spirits rather than depressed them as they massed to use it. Swedes took to the tunnelbana as they initially took to the systembolaget; it was better than what preceded it. The quiet cleanliness and good order of the Swedish underground system was reassuring. It was not unlike an underwater birthing experience, emerging from the biologically warm, air-conditioned womb to the comforting smell of *korv* cooking at the hot dog stand in the fresh air. The emotional needs of Stockholm's Persephones were met when the pale city dwellers sprang out into the sunshine and had the chance to get a hasty warm snack, with or without mustard.

Many things are hasty in Stockholm, from *hastigt frukost* (hasty breakfast) to *hastigt samtal* (hasty meeting) and *hastigt samlag* (hasty sex). Swedes are far from prudes and would never cover their piano legs but, in a town where engineering and functionalism are prized, the tunnelbana sat well with civic duty inclination and everything was hidden that could be hidden. Beneath the rocky ground and water channels hundreds of miles of underground railway tunnels soon linked the humans, if not the trolls, to the downtown city.

With characteristic meticulousness, engineers and town planners took their time and mulled over dozens of ways to solve the engineering problems of moving the Stockholm populations around town by the tunnelbana. It took decades to start the blasting and earthmoving. Around sixty different underground schemes were discussed by the Stockholm City Council before the decision to dig was taken. The system began with a line from Hässelby in the west and ran through the centre of the city to Hagsätra, Farsta and Bagarmossen. Another ran from Ropsten in the east under the main waterway to the south-west, with two branches to Varberg and Fruängen. By the 1960s—late for undergrounds in French and English terms—the tunnelbana had reached Östermalmstorg, Sätra and Fasta-Strand.

Swedish trains, like Swiss ones, run on time. In the middle of winter a potential passenger has to know that when the train is due to arrive, it will arrive. It is not possible to stand around in sub-zero temperatures at underground entrances in February any more than it is possible to jump up and down on the spot to ward off hypothermia in a bus shelter while waiting for an overdue bus. At peak times trains run at two-minute intervals. When the work and school rush are over the intervals are between three and six minutes. Passengers have thirty seconds to get on and off. The trains run smoothly and quietly at around twenty miles per hour. The passengers are equally silent. I have only once seen a demonstration of emotion on the underground, when a Polish-born asylum seeker read aloud, with happy tearful hysterics, a letter telling her that her application for Swedish citizenship had been accepted.

Not knowing that after the post-war immigration boom Stockholm train drivers were almost all recent immigrants to the city, for a time I practised my Swedish pronunciation by imitating the driver chanting the litany of station stops—Vällingby, St. Eriksplan, Odenplan, Hötorget, T-Centralen, Slussen—and injecting into my social life what I took to be convincing conversations about life in the suburbs: "Have you been to Midsommar Kransen lately?" I gave that up when one of my friends asked, "How have you managed to speak Swedish with a Turkish accent?"

The Stockholm underground project was carried out with the same enthusiasm as Mussolini's *autostrada* and Hitler's *Autobahn*, which were being set in concrete at about at the same time. There were plenty of supporters of fascist-style public works in the planning departments of the transport ministry, as indeed there were supporters of fascist-style political institutions. By and large the technicians who worked on the Stockholm underground had the Germanic thoroughness of their cousins in Berlin and Rome but thankfully only a minority, who did not exercise political power, shared the racial views of the German Nazis and Italian fascists. The achievements of German and Italian road building engineers were awesome but the Stockholmers who mined their way through miles of bedrock granite have provided something to see.

Not having to plan their railway system with a passenger clientele of an anti-social or crypto-Bolshevik working class, the Stockholm underground managers worked out a simple system which, in Europe, would only work in Sweden, for Stockholmers are like the Japanese, overwhelmingly honest. From the beginnings of public transport they could be relied upon to place their correct fare in the box. It was just like going to church. The honesty box in the earliest tram was treated with the reverence of the collection plate in church: it was a secular manifestation of spiritual consciousness and a shared sense of responsibility. The Swedes did not need to devise mechanical people swatters like the Parisians, whose underground travellers have, when possible, reverted to revolutionary behaviour and slipped through without paying. Physical restraints that are now common were invented to prevent egress and ingress into a quarantined transport system. This is not so necessary on the Swedish underground, although heavy fines are levied if passengers are caught travelling without their ticket, or more commonly now without their monthly pass. The Swedish defaulter deterrent is based on a random selection of underground stations where all passengers being carried on a particular service are checked out by a platoon of inspectors sent there for the job on that day.

Stockholm, more than most European cities, has a large collection of former refugees and asylum seekers among its population, and many of these have not quite grasped the concept of the one-size-fits-all and the need to sacrifice the individual to the group. Although the recent new citizens carry Swedish passports, they have not had the benefit of the brainwashing of kindergarten, early and middle school education. Consequently they are a little behind the majority in shouldering their burden of fares, fees and taxes. Nevertheless, the non-native-born on the whole feel as at home on Stockholm's public transport in the severe, challenging climate of the north, for when they buy a ticket, show their pass and glance at the driver's cabin or listen to the station announcements, they are more likely than not to see a fellow immigrant.

Never missing an opportunity to inform, educate and improve the town's citizens, many underground stops are beautifully decorated with appropriate graffiti-proof popular art. Kungsträdgården Station, the king's vegetable garden, has fountains, statues and state-of-the-art decorative lighting effects; to travel by underground is to visit an art gallery more than fifty miles long.

Storm clouds the Drottningholm Palace

Chapter Eight

FAIRYTALE KINGS AND DANCING QUEENS
THE MONARCHY

The entrepreneur-artist combination of Stig Anderson, Björn Ulvaeus and Benny Andersson combined to provide the music and lyrics for ABBA's greatest single hit, "Dancing Queen". During the summer in 1976, and at receptions forever after, the King and Queen of Sweden could never escape hearing the verses, performed with varying degrees of skill, pomp and ceremony, which were played at their wedding reception on 18 June:

> You are the dancing Queen,
> young and sweet, only seventeen.

The total enthusiasm for the song identified with the royal family and celebrating the king's marriage in egalitarian Stockholm is a good humoured reflection of the even handedness of social democracy. Sweden is famously race, class and gender blind in regard to all its citizens, and no one sees any reason for the rich to feel their interests are neglected. Public opinion in Stockholm is as concerned about the welfare of its princesses as it is about the life choices of the town prostitutes or the problems immigrants have settling in. About five per cent of the population do not have Swedish passports and many live in an unsettling limbo and this applies equally to the diminishing pool of potential royal spouses. Unusually for Europe, the modern princesses have been protected from a potentially intrusive press by a society that respects the privacy of all its members.

All round the world, princesses are news. Dancing Queens were once dancing princesses, and the two Swedish princesses have been given opportunities that their cousins in France, Norway, Denmark and Britain must envy. Crown Princess Victoria was two years old when Sweden

Gustav Vasa

changed its constitution to allow her to inherit the throne; twenty-eight years later, like all young women in her city, she has made up her own mind on who her friends should be. And like many young women, her father disapproved of his daughter's choice and has kept her special friend, gym owner Daniel Westling, at arm's length and away from strictly noble occasions. She bears this with good nature. Yale University has schooled her in politics as well as international relations. Like her father she has done a stint in the Swedish armed forces and knows the importance of national security, to which she can herself contribute by smiling for the photographers. Looking every inch a younger version of her mother, she poses patriotically in a midsummer crown of flowers with the Swedish flag nestling in the crook of her arm. It is no wonder she is a happy Swedish princesses, for Swedish princesses can have their cake and eat it. One of IKEA's specialities in its fast food department is *princess tårta*, princess cake, and IKEA was not being ironical when it branded this delicacy "baked with love".

Born to Fight

Most of the first fifty kings of Sweden died violently, the majority at war. Leaders in battle, leaders in political affairs, they were always open to popular scrutiny of their intimate behaviour to an unusual degree. All Stockholm knew that on 12 February 1771 Adolf Frederick (Gustav III's father) died comforted not by religion but by eating his last cream bun, washed down with champagne. The current Swedish dynasty is the longest-lasting of all the Napoleonic creations, and functions better than most royal families in a world super-critical of kings and queens, jealous and resentful of their privileges and celebrity status. Not so in Stockholm. In modern Stockholm the sovereign is centre stage, especially on occasions when the eyes of the world are on Sweden. The crown plays a crucial part in the annual ritual when each winter is brightened up by the anniversary of Nobel's death. Today's laureates are duchessed by all Stockholmers from the king down. Hundreds dress formally for the occasion, a paradox in such a democratic and egalitarian country, and the king is at the apex of the social pyramid. Nobel Prize winners are put up at the Grand Hotel, Swedish television broadcasts the ceremony live, newspaper are full of details about the scientific celebrities. Each laureate is driven around in a limousine, is taught how to say *Skål* and drink *systembolaget* wine from

Orrefors glasses. The king and queen host dinners, formal and informal, at Drottningholm Court Theatre, where the waiters in wigs and gaiters look like they have stepped from the eighteenth century. Curious incongruities still abound. The footman standing behind the queen wears a large feather in his headdress so that the king, should he need to find her, can locate his wife in the socialite scrum. The laureates leave Sweden with their leather bound certificate and their medal puzzling over where to bank their new currency and what exactly was St. Lucia's Day all about? Why were girls processing with candles in their hair singing carols in the Stockholm darkness? The more scientific visitors know why the actual wax candles have been discontinued: too many singed girls ended up in the Karolinska Hospital casualty every December, but all laureates think they know the king as a person.

King Carl XVI Gustaf was crowned in 1973. The Swedish Institute recognizes that up to the end of the twelfth century dates are unsure and approximate. However, you would not be far out to identify Carl XVI Gustaf as the sixty-fifth Swedish sovereign. As a crown prince, Carl XVI Gustaf had more privacy than other modern European royal celebrities. Protected by the sentimental and romantic Finns in the outer islands of the skerries, he was able to conduct a normal love affair with his wife to be, unrecorded, unphotographed and undisturbed. As a young king, he was often seen about town, even once found rescuing an Asian tourist lost in the snow in the suburbs near his home. (Not that there is anything suburban about the Swedish monarchy. While the king is out and about, court bureaucrats enforce excessively efficient protocol, stiff formality and autocratic noble behaviour.)

Modern Stockholm evolved during the Bernadotte dynasty, although the actions of Carl XVI Gustaf's ancestors did not always create a stable relationship between the crown, parliament and the people. Karl XIV Johan was the first Bernadotte king. He abandoned France and championed Swedish interests from the moment he laid down his marshal's baton. Oscar II, his son, had the complex task of dissolving the Swedish-Norwegian Union without bloodshed. Karl XIV never spoke Swedish and governed his country in the French language. All government documents had to be translated into French before he could approve them. He was known for what he was not. He did not hunt or play cards, and hated the countryside and royal buildings in Sweden, except the small palace with echoes of Versailles he built himself at Rosendal on Djurgården island. He rarely left it. The only time he was glimpsed in the streets of Stockholm was during major fires, tradition requiring the king to personally lead the fire brigade. He spent most of life in bed as it was the warmest place in his palace. He did not smoke, drank a regular glass of red wine and sprayed visitors who stank of aquavit with eau de cologne. He began his working day at 10.30 with *café au lait*, at 12.30 his hairdresser appeared and curled his hair. Herman Lindqvist records in *A History of Sweden* that "the more refined men of court would be curly à la bernadotte." Towards the end of his reign he thought of himself as "a signature machine", calculating that he signed his name 13,000 times a year. He went to bed at midnight, eau de cologne by his side, a huge safe at the bed head full of bolt money. He was ready to flee, remembering Gustav III's murder, the coup d'état which put him on the throne and the recent killing of the speaker of the House of Nobility who had been trampled to death at Riddarholm.

Many of the early kings had comical descriptive appellations to distinguish them from commoners with similar names: Edmund the Old, Inge the Elder, Inge the Younger, Sverker the Younger Karlsson, Knut Holmgersson the Tall, Erik Eriksson the Lisping and the Lame. By the time Birger Jarl founded the Folkunga dynasty and was Romulus and Remus to Stockholm, names of the kings and the regents were no longer laughing matters but questions of life and death. Such was the merciless power open to the crown. The most important monarch ever was Gustav Vasa; the most interesting Christina.

THE VASA DYNASTY

The Vasa family took their name from the word "vase", an emblem they chose to illustrate their nobility and which they displayed on their coat of arms. It was not long before the Lion of the North was symbolized far and wide by a lion's head rather than a vase. Gustav started life as an aristocratic outlaw, fighting against the Danish King Christian II. Christian II laid claim to Stockholm and everywhere else for hundreds of miles. Swedes see Gustav Vasa as a combination of the Count of Monte Cristo, Bonnie Prince Charlie and Robin Hood. Certainly fortune favoured his star in 1518. As a 21-year-old, Gustav was imprisoned and held hostage by Christian II in Denmark. Twelve months into his captivity Vasa escaped to Hanseatic Lübeck where the powerful German League refused to hand him back to Denmark. An edge was put on his ambition in 1520 when his estates were confiscated by Christian. His father, brother-in-law and many other relatives were killed in what would now be defined as war crimes. Legend and reality are hard to distinguish, but Vasa certainly made Dalarna his Sherwood Forest. From there he launched a successful national revolution and re-took Stockholm. At Ornäs in Dalarna the farm still stands where Vasa hid in 1520. In January 1521 his hands-on help with harvesting and the authenticity of his peasant disguise encouraged the peasants of Dalarna to join his national resistance movement. The local miners, the labour aristocracy, also attached themselves to the rebellion, and one by one the doubtful members of what remained of the Swedish nobility after the war with Denmark inched into his network. When the Hanseatic League in Lübeck stumped up the money to bankroll a naval contingent, Christian II's viceroy, Archbishop Trolle gave up the struggle to administer an unwelcome regime. In the Swedish democratic tradition, an Assembly of the Realm was selected which, in June 1523, unanimously elected Gustav Vasa King of Sweden.

T. K. Derry, in *A History of Scandinavia*, got it right when he compared Gustav Vasa with Henry VIII, who broke the bonds of Rome and set up a Lutheran kingdom. Derry wrote that "Like our own Henry VIII, he was fortunate in his length of days—no later Swedish king before the twentieth century matches his reign of thirty-seven years—and in leaving three children who in various degrees carried on their father's work." He was a man of imposing presence; ruthless when crossed, charming when pleased; and a demagogic orator, who knew how to play upon the feelings of his subjects. Above all, Gustav was a tremendous worker, who watched over every aspect of his country's affairs as if it had been a private estate. The end-product of his energy was achieved by mid-century—a strong ruler reigned over a prosperous community.

Vasa's position was initially very weak. In 1524 the sequel to his capture of Stockholm was that his powerful allies in Lübeck negotiated his recognition as King of Sweden by the Danes. However, he had to give up the Norwegian border district and territory which he had occupied as far as Oslo. A year later the peasants and miners of Dalarna rose against the master they had so recently brought to power. No sooner were they put down than they rebelled again, this time in support of a noble pretender. To avoid relying upon feudal levies the king had to hire German mercenaries to defeat them. In 1527 the victorious Vasa addressed a Riksdag at Västerås. After he made loud threats of abdication, the parliament agreed that he might take possession of the wealth of the Church, the nobles being conciliated by fiefs of monastic lands and the right to reclaim recent involuntary gifts. At that point royal authority began to grow. In 1533, when the Dalecarlians had refused to surrender their church bells for melting down, they were crushed by executions and the confiscation of mining property. As Derry concluded the saga: "the poor southern province of Småland rose in 1542 under a peasant leader in a kind of Pilgrimage of Grace, with which the king found it necessary to temporize for a whole winter before making an end of resistance by a two-pronged advance across the province, followed by further executions, heavy fines, and deportations to Finland. The king was now indeed master of his realm."

Gustav Vasa ruled as a national hero. He drove the Danes out of Stockholm, ended the Kalmar Union and turned Sweden, for a time, into the major European world power. Vasa genes were for years the biological foundation of the Swedish state. Indeed, it was under Vasa that the concept of a Swedish state had meaning for the first time. There had been magistrates, rulers and regents since the Viking era, but the first real King of Sweden as an embryo modern European nation was Gustav Vasa. When Vasa was elected he was put in power to rule a country that had experienced 130 years of foreign occupation determined to never live under a foreign flag again.

Under Gustav Vasa Stockholm accepted and adopted Germanic ideas quickly, prepared by the long residence of German Hanseatic merchants and their families in the city. Lutheran heresy had riddled the Swedish Catholic Church before parliament ratified Lutheranism as the state Church and confiscated Roman Catholic property. The Swedish congregations saw their ministers change from priests to pastors overnight, and overall the citizens of Stockholm took it in their stride in as much the same nonchalant way as most reacted later when Volvo and Saab fell into foreign ownership. The more things changed, they more the stayed the same— except that the Lutheran pastors could enjoy the simple beauty of the puritan interiors of the thousands of Swedish churches (none of which were demolished, as happened elsewhere in the iconoclastic destruction widespread in post-reformation Europe) in the arms of their newly sanctioned wives.

Gustav Vasa's immediate successor, Erik XIV, was an aggressive regional warlord, but did understand the dynamics of European foreign policy. His wars with Denmark, his expansionary plans to take Estonia and "Finlandize" it, as well as occupying the strategic port of Narva could have turned Stockholm into a major business capital, but in the short term they did not work.

Erik XIV began with the bold and far-sighted vision to monopolize western trade with Russia. If Stockholm had become the clearing house for import and export business with the region's major locomotive of history, who could dream what wealth might flow into the treasury in Stockholm? In trying to make his ideas work Erik XIV overextended Swedish resources and was deposed rather than executed, an example of the Swedish middle way, a humane and sensible compromise not unusually followed by other Europeans.

Gustav Vasa's third son Charles IX had to wait for years while John III, his older brother, ruled. John III was King of Sweden until 1599, when he was deposed, making way for Charles IX to become Regent of Sweden. In a matter of a few years Charles IX proved himself so capable as to be offered the crown. However, he made a serious miscalculation in marrying Catherine, the daughter of the King of Poland. This marriage increased Sweden's influence in the north. Catherine was a Catholic, and Stockholm and its citizens had quickly adapted to the modified form of Protestant Christianity.

QUEEN CHRISTINA: HAIRY-LEGGED HUNCHBACK

While Gustav Vasa takes the credit for founding Sweden's most important dynasty, Queen Christina must take the blame for fatally damaging it. For a time Christina was the most imposing woman in Europe. She was born into a Stockholm described evocatively by Veronica Buckley in *Christina Queen of Sweden* as:

> ...a cold world, the worst time Europe had known for thousands of years, the "Little Ice Age" which balked the harvests and froze the seas. Fires blazed on ice-thickened rivers, and birds were seen to drop from the skies in mid flight... Court politics was a whirlpool... Christina's world was a world at war, the great thirty year war which raged across Europe

from 1618 to 1648, claiming countless lives, including that of her own great father.

At the time of Christina's birth, Gustav II Adolf and her mother Maria Eleonora had been married six years. They lost a stillborn son after a sailing accident off Skeppsholmen, when the royal couple, with Eleonora pregnant, had been caught in a squall inspecting Sweden's very large naval fleet in a very small yacht. At Christina's birth, whether through medical incompetence, wishful thinking or because Queen Christina had an enlarged clitoris and partially fused labia, the birth of a son was announced to the king near midnight. Although the gender was changed to a daughter in the morning, it caused Gustav II Adolf neither surprise nor disappointment. Princess Christina had an unambiguous antipathy to frilly femininity. In her own words:

> As a young girl I had an overwhelming aversion to everything that women do and say. I couldn't bear their tight-fitting, fussy clothes. I took no care of my complexion or my figure or the rest of my appearance; I never wore a hat or a mask, and scarcely ever wore gloves. I despised everything belonging to my sex, hardly excluding modesty and propriety. I couldn't stand long dresses and I only wanted to wear short skirts. What's more, I was so hopeless at all the womanly crafts that no one could ever teach me anything about them.

Queen Christina contained in her DNA the genetic codes of a family tree whose branches held about a dozen European monarchs: Gustav Vasa, King of Sweden; Johan III, King of Sweden; Karl IX, King of Sweden; Sigismund III, King of Sweden and Poland; Wladislaw IV, King of Poland; Jan II, King of Poland; Gustav II Adolf, King of Sweden; Karl X Gustav, King of Sweden; Karl XI, King of Sweden; and Karl XII King of Sweden.

In her father's absence Christina had her education as a Machiavellian prince at the hands of four regents under the control of Chancellor Count Axel Gustavsson Oxenstierna, Chancellor of Sweden for forty-two years. Not for Christina the park aunties and the sandpit. She was familiar with the thought processes of monarchs. Oxenstierna personified the sense of duty that gave Sweden a long line of impressive but understated tough negotiators, so useful in a changing twenty-first century world and later reincarnated in such diplomats as Raoul Wallenberg, Dag Hammarsköld and Hans Blix. In Stockholm it was more than acceptable to have a lust for public service and ethical administration. Oxenstierna took his calling as divine and held close to his heart the responsibility of being guru to the sovereign-in-waiting. Christina attended the meetings between sovereign and nobility when she turned fourteen, puberty and intense political education going hand in hand. All Stockholm acknowledged that Christina was a prodigy, but she knew how lucky she was to have Oxenstierna as her guide. He had all the qualities of charm, humour and human rapport to be found in Stockholm's higher echelons of governing bureaucrats. Oxenstierna proved his loyalty to Swedish social stability when, as the major public servant to King Gustav II Adolf, he finessed away a growing rift between the crown and the nobility, the sort of dispute which in other European countries had resulted in civil war, regicide and social revolution.

Whereas the title "public servant" is a term of insult in many cultures (curiously mispronounced but nevertheless illustrating the point by a Japanese scholar who proudly boasted that he himself had spent time as a "public serpent"), in Stockholm there was, and still is, no higher calling. Ending the battle for power between the knights and their sovereign, Oxenstierna did what Stockholmers do best: he invented a system. Oxenstierna loved systems. Before Christina's birth, Oxenstierna fixed up the constitution. In 1623 he straightened out local government practices so nobles, the crown and the bourgeoisie alike could co-operate with the workings of the Stockholm city fathers. Oxenstierna's most important systematic reform was to divide the nobility into classes with defined memberships and to provide them with a House of Lords.

Greta Garbo has provided the twentieth century with its totemic image of Queen Christina. Garbo's gloomy stare in the publicity release for the 1933 English-language *Queen Christina* showed a beautiful, serene woman. In real life, however, Christina was not a symmetrical beauty like Garbo, but a hawk-nosed hunchback who had been deformed shortly after birth, most likely by an attempt to murder her as a baby by flinging her onto the flag stones of her mother's castle.

How well-known Garbo's love affair with a Flemish beauty, the Flanders *femme fatale*, Maria Nys, was it is hard to say. But Hollywood directors exploited Garbo's ambiguous sexual preferences and in their characteristic casting inspiration turned *Queen Christina* into Garbo's best film.

As Leonard Maltin's *Movie Guide* put it: "...a haunting performance by the radiant star as 17th-century Swedish queen who relinquishes her throne for her lover, Gilbert. Garbo and Gilbert's love scenes together are truly memorable, as is the famous final shot."

When Garbo agreed to play the part, she rejected Lawrence Olivier as a proposed co-star in favour of John Gilbert, her current male lover. Director Rouben Mamoulian would have been closer in appearance to the mark if he had insisted Olivier play the part of the queen. He could have kept the costume and used it in 1955 for Richard III, as the real Christina was closer to Olivier's Richard III than to Garbo's creation. Almost everything in the Greta Garbo film was fiction but nonetheless riveting.

Outside Sweden Christina not only looked increasingly like Lawrence Olivier's Richard III, but she began to behave like him. Having decided to abdicate and turn Catholic, Christina summoned the senators to Uppsala to negotiate a comfortable royal pension. The Riksdag stamped her resignation at Uppsala Castle in 1654. Christina's ten-year rule was over. The same morning as Christina's abdication, Karl X Gustav was crowned King of Sweden, although hitherto his highest ambition had been to marry Christina. Christina's autobiographical notes are unreliable but Buckley summed up the real situation accurately: "After her abdication, Christina forsook the lovely island of Stockholm for the lovely hills of Rome. It was a bloody trip."

The Lutheran Riksdag reneged on its financial commitments to Christina. The ex-queen, at twenty-seven, discovered nothing more for the rest of her life than the joys of travelling the world in trousers. After she crossed the Rubicon, she was summed up by Buckley as reluctant to wear women's clothes or a woman's hairstyle. She appeared in public wearing men's flat shoes, often boots, and frequently a sword. Princes and popes would greet her with her legs showing and her feathered hat in her hand. Her speech grew coarse and her habits rough; even her voice deepened.

Christina was cruel, bitter and miserable for the rest of her life, but at least she was warm. Her memory of her German mother hardened into hatred. Her affection for Cardinal Decio Azzolino went nowhere. Even her funeral at Rome's most celebrated convent, magnificent though it was, saw her shunted off to the Basilica's crypt to be buried like a pet cat. Queen Christina did not lead the life she should have led. The only thing she learned from experience after abdication was that there was hardly "any difference between wild beasts and Germans". Christina had assured her friend Azzolino that of all the animals in the world, there was none less like a man than a German. German Jesuits were old, lazy and as cold as the climate. German surgeons were more dangerous than swords. In Christina's summary, it was better to be a heretic than a German animal. A heretic could at least become a Catholic, but a beast could never become a reasonable creature. "Curse the place," she concluded, "and the stupid brutes it produces."

Life among the Lilacs: Neutrality and Asylum

Christina's spells on the Germans had no impact on centuries of expansionary German foreign policy pressure and its growing effect on Stockholm. In the short sun-filled summer the almost continual daylight and relative heat after the wet winters make grass grow like tropical bamboos and the scent of summer flowers in the air drugs the bees and the somnolent citizens. When the city grew larger, life under the fairytale kings and dancing queens was better in their capital during the twentieth century than almost anywhere on earth. Happiness was the result of not only the standard of living, but also the warmth of communal inclusiveness that Stockholm displayed and which was extended to waves of asylum-seekers. During two twentieth-century world wars that Anglo-Saxons believed were started by Germans, Swedish neutrality offered the chance for escapees to start a new life safe from death and imprisonment.

Some refugees stayed in the city, others merely transited. All fugitives noted that the elective nature of the Swedish monarchy was a sign that anything was possible in Stockholm. Irène Nemirovsky personified the large group who passed through Stockholm to escape the chaos of the Bolshevik revolution and First World War. She had the misfortune to be born in 1903 in an area of Kiev called Yiddishland, where Russian Jews were cooped. Her father Leon was familiar with the term Yid from his youth, being caught up in pogroms from the 1880s. By 1917 Leon was one of the richest bankers in Russia. He lived in a St. Petersburg mansion where glamorous white and gold reception rooms housed a dysfunctional family. Irène's mother never showed the least sign of maternal love and hunted younger men for affairs, while Leon gambled at casinos from the Crimea to the French Riviera.

When the Russian October Revolution began to destroy the family's hedonistic way of life, Leon thought it wise to move to Moscow. He rented an apartment from an officer of the Tsar's guard who was on duty at the Russian Embassy in London. But the fighting in Moscow turned out to be fiercer than in St. Petersburg and Irène was trapped in the apartment with her mother, a bag of potatoes, some chocolate and a few sardines. The Bolsheviks put a price on Leon's head and, taking advantage of the fact that the borders had not been closed, Leon and his family fled to Finland, unconvincingly disguised as peasants. The family spent 1918 in Finland, where Irène learned Finnish and was as happy as she ever was.

When the First World War was over the Nemirovsky looked for and found greater security in Stockholm. Irène preferred Stockholm to St. Petersburg, which she described as "a collection of snow covered streets, swept by icy winds swirling over the disgusting, polluted canals of the Neva." By contrast, she saw Stockholm as an almost mythical, peaceful city, remembering most clearly the gardens and the sight and smell of the mauve lilacs growing in many of the home courtyards.

Leon made a long-term bad decision when the family left the safety of Stockholm after only three months. They settled in Paris where Irène's mother renewed her love affairs while her daughter nursed her hatred for her mama and the Russians. By the roaring twenties, the Nemirovsky family had re-established its St. Petersburg lifestyle in France. Leon had settled in and Irène led the life of a flapper celebrity, cashing in on the sensational overnight success of her first novel, *David Golder*. She dashed between parties, was assimilated into the top ranks of French society and spent her life in a whirl of champagne, casinos and luxurious holidays. She confessed in 1924:

> I have the wildest week; one ball after another, and I'm still a bit heady and finding it difficult to get back into the routine of work. I'm behaving like a mad women, it's shameful. I dance all night long. Every even there are very chic entertainments in different hotels, and as my very lucky star has blessed me with a few handsome young men, I'm enjoying myself very much indeed.

Stockholm gave Irène the chance of a new life. She was not the only beneficiary of Swedish neutrality. If Nemirovsky personified sanctuary seekers during the First World War, the Von Trapp family stands for the hundreds of thousands who were welcomed to Stockholm after 1939 when it was a staging point on an escape route to the United States. The 1965 film about the flight of the family from Nazi Austria famously focused on its title, *The Sound of Music.* When Georg Von Trapp, with the implausible occupation of commander in the Austrian navy, appointed Maria to tutor one of his children, he set in train an unlikely sequence of events, including an invitation (declined) to sing at Hitler's birthday party. Georg Von Trapp was called up to join the German forces, refused and fled to Sweden via Italy. The Von Trapps did not stay long in Stockholm, quickly moving to Vermont, where they served Austrian apple strudel, not Swedish meatballs, to the thousands of visitors who toured their music museum. They were untouched intellectually or emotionally by the nation which saved their bacon.

Nemirovsky was not so lucky. Irène married one of her young men, Michael Epstein, who had a degree in physics and engineering from St. Petersburg, but in France worked as a banker in the Banque Pays du Nord. Epstein's father had been president of the Union of Russian banks. In spite of her celebrity status—*David Golder* was filmed—Irène did not take up French citizenship and when the Germans occupied France in 1940 she knew she faced doom. She fled Paris with her husband to a small village in German-occupied France and began writing *Suite Française.* Racial laws passed in October 1940 declared her Jewish, and she and her husband lost the right to work and were forced to wear the Star of David. After the Germans invaded Russia, she was arrested, interned and exterminated. For Irène, the process took from 13 July to 17 August 1942. Moved from Auschwitz to Birkenau, she was gassed as the first of two million German soldiers were entering Stockholm to travel in uniform to occupied Norway under the supervision of Swedish soldiers who watched on without emotion. The Engelbrecht division entrained within a sniff of the lilacs that haunted Irène Nemirovsky.

Désirée and Cuckoo Kings

During the Second World War, when Sweden was again neutral, Annemarie Selinko was one of hundreds of Viennese Jews who fled from German-occupied Denmark. Spirited away through the mist in a little fishing boat, she crossed the sea to the safety of Sweden in the autumn of

1943. Selinko comforted herself by thinking about another émigrée in another war, Désirée Clary. Selinko recalled that while standing in front of the Royal Palace in Stockholm on a grey winter's day she fell to thinking that somewhere she had heard that a forerunner of the present Swedish Royal House had been the daughter of a simple silk merchant in Marseille. To ease the pain of her own unwanted, incongruous exile Selinko decided to write a book about Désirée. This curious bestseller was written as if by Désirée, looking back on her life from the time she was crowned Queen of Sweden. It is a sweet book, full of imagined dialogue between Désirée and the great figures of the Napoleonic era, one of which, her husband Jean-Baptiste Bernadotte, was a marshal of France.

The Emperor Bonaparte fell in love with Désirée when she was shy, sixteen, lisping and unable to spell. Napoleon wrote an improbable book, *Clisson et Eugénie*, describing his deep feelings at the time. As Nancy Mitford concluded, Désirée was born under a curious star. She nearly married Napoleon and she died Queen of Sweden. The Clarys were a family of prosperous silk merchants, and the penniless, ambitious Bonaparte brothers, Joseph and Napoleon, who were living in Marseille in 1794, had an eye on the dowries of Julie and Désirée. Joseph married Julie but Désirée was only engaged to Napoleon when he went to fish the troubled waters of the French Revolution. He never returned to her. He was caught up in the world of fashion and was soon bewitched by Josephine de Beauharnais. All the same, he kept a soft corner in his heart for Désirée. In 1823 Désirée went to Sweden for good and was crowned queen, though always keeping in the background of public life. She died in 1860, having outlived both her husband and her son. As an incorrigible Corsican romantic, Napoleon, as he was about to leave France forever and die in exile, reserved his last thoughts for Désirée, not Josephine, musing that he had had Ms. Clary's maidenhead.

The complex foreign policy negotiations that turned Bernadotte into a French traitor, a Swedish hero and a Norwegian war criminal are not easy to summarize. Bernadotte was adopted by the King of Sweden in 1810. Before he could accept the Swedish offer to become the next king he had to ask for Napoleon's permission to renounce French citizenship. Selinko reconstructed the dialogue when Bernadotte asked Napoleon for permission to leave the French army. After staring "viciously" at Bernadotte, Napoleon screamed like a madman: "How dare you appear here in Swedish uniform? You, a marshal of France?" Turning to Désirée, Napoleon addressed her as "Princess", saying:

> "I believe you do not know that the Swedish royal family is insane. The present king is incapable of enunciating clearly a single sentence, and his nephew had to be deposed because he is a lunatic. Because he is really— cuckoo!" He tapped his forehead. "Princess, tell me, is your husband crazy too? I mean is he so crazy that he wants to stop being a Frenchman for the sake of the Swedish succession?"

Bernadotte was far from crazy. Although it was taken for granted that a Napoleonic marshal would gravitate to French interests in foreign policy, as the pre-elected King of Sweden he negotiated with Russia and Britain. After Napoleon invaded Russia in 1812, Crown Prince Karl Johan and Tsar Alexander met in Åbo and signed a treaty. Napoleon's Grand Army perished in the retreat from Moscow. My clansman from the Outer Hebrides, Marshal MacDonald, by then famous for leading a French army over the Splugen Pass in winter, survived to limp back to Paris and turn Napoleon over to the British. In 1814, with Napoleon defeated at the Battle of Leipzig, the Treaty of Kiel was signed between Sweden and Denmark, under which Denmark ceded Norway to Sweden. Karl Johan had already agreed with Tsar Alexander that Finland would be lost to Sweden and that Sweden would never try to re-conquer it. The Norwegians rejected the Treaty of Kiel, met at Eidsvoll to adopt a constitution of their own, elected the Danish prince Christian Frederik as king, and rejected the Union with Sweden.

Selinko's dialogue may be imaginary but the sentiments are recorded accurately. "Papa said these Norwegians were marvellous. They had an army only half the size of ours and had hardly any ammunition at all, and yet they risked war. He was very touched and said he would give them the most liberal constitution in Europe." Selinko continued:

> But these marvellous Norwegians insisted on their independence, so Papa and his general staff went off to the campaign and the King and Queen and the whole royal household and I myself followed him on board the man-of-war. When we took the fortress of Kongsten there was such a lot of shooting and firing that I said to Papa, who was standing

next to me: "Papa, send an officer to the Norwegians and tell them that they could be independent for all you cared. Don't keep on shooting at them with your guns." And Papa said: "Of course not, Oscar, we are only shooting at them with dummy shells." "But in that case, Papa, it is not a real campaign, is it?" "No, Oscar, only an excursion."

Bernadotte said the Norwegians would retire behind their mountains, and when his son asked him if he could cross the mountains Papa said he had crossed the Alps once with an army, and when he said that he looked very sad. "In those days," he said, "I defended a young Republic's independence. Today I am taking it away from a small freedom-loving people. That shows you, Oscar, how one outlives oneself."

Oscar described a whole campaign that lasted only a fortnight. After the Swedish victory, the king and his son went back to Norway because Bernadotte had to appear in Oslo in person to confirm the Union. They rode there on horseback and slept in tents, Bernadotte not wanting to inconvenience the Norwegian peasants. As Selinko, imagining Oscar's words, writes: "this union is exclusively Papa's work. Papa at once started a weighty speech. Norway's new constitution defends the Rights of Man for which I have been campaigning in France ever since I was fifteen. This union is more than just a geographical necessity, it has been a deeply felt desire of my heart for a long time! I don't think it made any impression on the Norwegians. And I don't think either that they will ever forget that Papa beat them with dummy shells." Truth was stranger than fiction in the lives of the Bernadotte kings. Karl XIV Johan and Désirée remained Francophiles to the end. Their grandson lived to see another revolution that transformed Europe to no less an extent than the Napoleon adventure which brought the dynasty to the Swedish throne.

King Gustav V, like many Stockholmers, was shocked and frightened by the Russian Revolution. He visualized Stockholm in ruins. Towards the end of the First World War the possibility of revolution and war in Sweden was so great that King Gustaf V packed his bags to avoid a bullet in a cellar. In November 1918 the Swedish left-wing party published a manifesto declaring that a revolutionary wave was sweeping the world and it was "now the turn of Sweden, this backward land governed by a First Chamber with a representation reminiscent of the Middle Ages." The left demanded a republic, an eight-hour day, votes for women as well as men over twenty, workers' control of industry and the transfer of state-owned land to the working class. The king narrowly avoided precipitating the first civil war in the region. His support of the old power structures in society, the nobility, the army and navy, the majority of the middle class and all the farmers, provoked a demonstration of 50,000 workers and liberals who themselves marched on Stockholm to demand that the king inform the prime minister in advance of statements on political issues. The guns of August 1914 saved the Swedish monarchy from possible extinction but the growth of working-class power throughout the Nordic region led to constitutional changes that reduced the king to a powerless figurehead within a decade, leaving him free to polish his skills in tennis and embroidery. How did this happen?

On the eve of the First World War the king decided to openly interfere with the political process and threw his weight behind the conservatives. On 5 February 1914 around 30,000 farmers marched to Stockholm's Royal Palace to demand a more militaristic foreign policy. The king welcomed the farmers wearing the uniform of a general. His wife, Queen Victoria, who had been described by Bishop Billing as "the most masculine man in the Royal Family", personally wrote the king's draft speech, while resisting the temptation to be prominent herself. The king's speech was in direct contradiction to the policy of Prime Minister Karl Staaff and represented a challenge to the parliamentary system.

On March 1920 the first Swedish social democratic government was formed by Hjalmar Branting, and major constitutional reforms led to the establishment of the Swedish welfare state. One of its earliest products was the creation of Cinema City at Råsunde to entertain as well as inform the new and growing egalitarian society in which fairytale kings were expected to know their place and keep their mouths shut in public. Gustav V died at the age of 92 after a near record reign of 43 years during which he presided over a relatively small and inexpensive Royal Family with no political power or influence whatsoever. He served most of his time as a social democratic constitutional monarch trying to escape court ceremony and going hunting. He was a silent witness to Swedish neutrality during the Second World War and the slaughter on Sweden's borders with Norway and Finland.

Street in Gamla Stan

Chapter Nine

SLAUGHTER

STOCKHOLM'S TRAGIC PAST

The dancing kings and queens of Sweden had, until the twentieth century, ruled a country with blood on its hands. In showing films like *Winter Light, Shame, Ådalen 31* and *Persona*—films about nuclear holocaust, wartime collaboration in a Nazi setting and mental breakdown— Stockholm's cinemas have informed and entertained an audience hardened to killing. Conventional oil paintings and watercolours face and show a similarly grim reality. Sitting around their big Swedish stoves looking through their windows in the misty indistinct Baltic light, farmers' children were educated by pigs squealing and struggling as they were slaughtered. When the pigs died the snow was red with blood. Carl Larsson's watercolour of this common experience, *Butchers and a Butcher's Woman*, hangs on the wall of an art gallery in Djurgården.

THE STOCKHOLM BLOODBATH

Stockholm lives with a tragic past. The city promotes with lurid descriptions rather than hides such events as "The Stockholm Bloodbath". In 1520 the King of Denmark, Christian II, occupied Stockholm after a violent war and a long siege and had himself crowned King of Sweden. The rules of war laid down that if a city under siege surrendered and did not have to be taken by force, its citizens were spared rape and the sword. Christian II broke this rule and committed a war crime equivalent to Churchill's firebombing of Dresden or Cromwell's slaughter of the Irish at Drogheda. Christian's cruelty has never been forgotten. Engravings and woodcuts show exactly what happened. Christian II invaded Sweden with an army of Scottish, French and German mercenaries. The Swedish leader, Sten Sture the Younger, died of his wounds in a retreat to the security of Stockholm, where only the royal castle, held by his widow Christina Gyllenstierna, resisted. She capitulated in September and on 4 November 1520 Christian II had himself crowned and created, somewhat optimistically, hereditary King of Sweden. The coronation orgy lasted three days. King Christian and Archbishop Trolle enjoyed themselves like children at a birthday party, eating and dressing up. The spared Swedish combatants felt safe for a time under the military conventions of the day. But once the customary period of coronation celebrations was complete, Christian II reneged and in Stortorget, Gamla Stan's main square, set up his execution site. Derry explains what happened next in *A History of Scandinavia*. The king's enemies were arrested, taken to Stockholm Castle and tried by Archbishop Trolle for heresy and showing disregard for ecclesiastical rights and authority. The criminals were duly found guilty and handed over to the king. The ecclesiastical crime of heresy was not covered by the full temporal amnesty that Christian II had granted when Stockholm surrendered. The royal executioner set to work immediately, his 82 victims including two archbishops and noblemen from many of the great families.

As Derry records: "The marketplace ran with blood and resounded with the lamentations of onlookers. When the bodies were eventually burnt on a huge pyre the exhumed remains of Sten Sture and a child of his were added to crown the horrifying scene." The executions spread as far as Finland and were continued during the king's triumphant return journey to Copenhagen across southern Sweden, the total number of victims being estimated at 600, murdered as he passed by.

The Stockholm Bloodbath so radicalized the nobility, the clergy, the farmers and the peasants that they sank their differences for the time it took to replace Christian with a Swedish king. Sweden's period as a great European power followed the massacre and established the Vasa dynasty. This did not put an end to slaughter, however, as Gustav Vasa's granddaughter, Christina, turned out to be as mad a monster as Christian II. Christina's crimes, like Christian's, were carried out with the direct approval of God. As absolute monarch Christina made her own rules on earthly morality and was answerable only to one-way prayer traffic.

The Swedes are proud of their grisly history and the present tourist bureau cheerfully assigns high priority to death and mayhem as tourist attractions. Smiling guides explain that "Stortorget is intimately connected with the Stockholm Bloodbath." Detailed paintings are produced to show what happened. The Black Death had reached Stockholm in the autumn of 1350. Nowadays the City of Stockholm ranks the Black Death in cultural importance with the 1912 Olympic Games. In a matter of fact tone, *Stockholm Milestones* informs its visitors that witch hunts took place in Stockholm. "Those identified as witches [were] put on trial in the Southern City Hall, the current Stockholm City Museum, and then condemned to death. They [were] beheaded before being placed on bonfires."

CHRISTINA THE RIPPER

Regal violence inspired the Nobel literary laureate, Samuel Beckett. Beckett was among the most eminent and sensitive of the many outside observers to identify the connection between sex, violence and religion in Stockholm. For his first serious imaginative work, published by 1930 in Paris by Nancy Cunard at the Hours Press, Beckett chose Queen Christina as a subject. He then had his heart set on an academic career. The innovative form of his writing was in the style of an unconventional poem. The content matter—Stockholm, prostitution and slaughter—was savagely jumbled together in what he cleverly punned as "a whoreoscope". Beckett focused on the fate of Christina's ungrateful and unappreciated protégé, the French philosopher René Descartes, the cruel predispositions of the queen herself and the life of a mythical prostitute, Rahab, as "a shining whore who ended up in Dante's third heaven." Beckett described Christina as bisexual and promiscuous, and connected the story of Rahab's adventures to Descartes' Stockholm experience. Beckett saw the Swedish sovereign as "Rahab of the snows, the murdering matinal pope—confessed Amazon, Christina the Ripper."

Christina slaughtered her equerry Monaldeschi as a kookaburra kills a snake: a long process in front of a noisy, cheering coterie. Abdication and exile not having dimmed her perceived prerogative as an absolute monarch outside Stockholm, she summarily condemned one of her retinue, Marchese Monaldeschi to death for alleged treachery. At the time the Swedish queen was in the Galerie des Cerfs, staying at Fontainebleau en route to Rome, royally installed as a guest of the King of France in the early stages of her Catholic conversion.

When she had decided to kill him, the victim threw himself at the queen's feet, and her three bodyguards drew their swords. After conviction and sentence, judge and prisoner walked up and down the trial room for two hours while the queen listened patiently, without anger or emotion, to his excuses and pleas for mercy. Eventually the queen withdrew and one of the executioners explained to Monaldeschi that "Her Majesty had told him to carry out the execution quickly." The queen's chaplain repeatedly begged Christina to change her mind, at least about the time and place of execution.

Veronica Buckley best describes the actual killing:

> The unhappy priest returned to the gallery. In tears he embraced Monaldeschi, charging him to prepare for death, and to think of his eternal salvation. At this, Monaldeschi shrieked, then sank to the floor, and began his last confession. So distraught was he that his sins emerged in indiscriminate pieces of Latin, French, and Italian, and twice he got up, crying out in desperation. Père Le Bel nonetheless did his duty with care, and had just begun to question the Marchese "to clear up a doubtful point" when the Queen's own chaplain came in. Seeing him, Monaldeschi got up once again, "without waiting for absolution", and went over to him. Hand in hand, the two withdrew to a corner, where they spoke together at some length. The chaplain then left the room, taking Ludovico Santinelli with him, but Santinelli quickly returned. He raised his sword and said, "Pray for forgiveness, Marchese! You are about to die!"

Buckley tells how Santinelli pushed Monaldeschi to one end of the gallery, "right beneath a painting of the Château de Saint-Germain". Père Le Bel turned away, but not before he had seen Santinelli thrust his sword into Monaldeschi's stomach. Monaldeschi grabbed at the sword, but Santinelli pulled it back and, in doing so, cut off three of the Marchese's fingers. Santinelli saw that his sword had been bent and called to the two courtiers that the Marchese must be wearing chain mail under his clothing. After being struck in his face Monaldeschi cried out to Père Le Bel. Santinelli "considerately withdrew a pace or two," allowing the priest to go to him. The Marchese knelt down, and asked for absolution. It was granted, and as penance Père Le Bel instructed him to endure his death patiently and forgive all those who had caused it.

Marchese Monaldeschi gave up and threw himself onto his stomach on the floor, inviting the final blow. A courtier came forward and struck his head, knocking out a piece of skull. Still alive, Monaldeschi pointed to his neck, which was struck two or three times without doing much damage as the coat of mail had slipped up over it. Père Le Bel exhorted Monaldeschi to remember God and bear it all patiently. In a macabre interruption Santinelli then asked Père Le Bel whether or not he should continue the execution. The priest replied indignantly that he could not advise him and Santinelli apologized for having asked such a question. The wounded Marchese turned to see the chaplain standing at the end of the gallery. The chaplain did not move and Monaldeschi dragged himself along the panelled wall towards him. Père Le Bel approached but Monaldeschi seized the chaplain's two hands and began a second confession. The chaplain told him to ask God's forgiveness, then asked Père Le Bel if he might grant the Marchese a further absolution. At that point a long, narrow sword ran Monaldeschi through the throat. Monaldeschi fell towards Père Le Bel, and lay in final agony another fifteen minutes, while the priest exclaimed "Jesus! Mary!" and other holy words. At a quarter to four Monaldeschi breathed his last. Père Le Bel began to pray, while Santinelli seized the body and shook the dead man's arms and legs, unbuttoned his breeches and underpants, and felt in all his pockets. He found only a small knife, and a prayer book.

Christina was sorry but thought that justice had been done. She prayed that God would forgive Monaldeschi and promised to have many masses said for the repose of his soul. Père Le Bel was charged with disposal of the body. He sent for a bier and, though the corpse was heavy and the road bad, Monaldeschi was in his grave by a quarter to six. Buckley recorded that two days later, Christina sent a hundred pounds to a monastery to pay for thirty masses to be offered for Monaldeschi and she duly pocketed her receipt.

Perhaps Christina can be excused for her nonchalant approach to murder. Her family background had conditioned her to gore and grief. Christina lived in a bloody, as well as cold, environment. Her father, Gustav Adolf, was butchered after leading a cavalry charge. Fighting near Leipzig, he was shot in the arm, lost control of his horse and was dragged along the ground with one boot caught in a stirrup. When he fell free he was shot through the temple, through the side, again in the arm and in the back, then stabbed with a dagger. Soldiers found his body that night, naked except for his shirt, beneath a heap of other dead. The king's body was carried on a powder wagon to a village church near the battlefield. What was left of his blood was stored and his body was embalmed and escorted via Berlin to the Baltic coast. The newly-widowed Queen Eleanora met the cortège in mid-December, took the king's heart, which had been preserved, wrapped it in a linen kerchief and placed it in a golden casket. Queen Eleanora and the remains of the king did not reach Nyköping until mid-summer. Maria Eleonora refused to have the king buried, kept the open coffin in her bedroom and rejected criticism and pressure from the Riksdag that it was un-Christian to fondle the dead. The king was at last interred on 15 June 1634 in the Riddarholm Church, the body being accompanied on a silver bier by his bloodstained sword, just as it had been taken from the battlefield at Lützen. Alongside Gustav Vasa's helmet, the Armory of the Royal Palace displays Gustav II Adolf's stuffed horse, Streiff, and his blood- and mud-splattered underwear and boots.

The Vasa Disaster: The Lion Sinks

While the Vasa dynasty no longer rules, one of the family products, a warship named after them, still dominates the Stockholm landscape. Queen Christina's personal effects, even her coronation coach, were all sold off to pay debts. Little remains of her estate at Gripsholm Castle. By the grace of Swedish naval daring, engineering, expertise and persistence the Vasa family is now better known for its ill-fated venture into marine architecture than its effect on the Lutheran reformation or in building Sweden into a great power. You can choose to read about the *Vasa* on the museum website in Korean, Japanese, Latvian and about fifty other languages, and since the wreck was dredged up tourists from all these countries have turned up to see the world's only surviving seventeenth-century ship, one of the foremost tourist attractions in the world in the system-built, one-off Vasa Museum. It is a macabre memorial to a maritime disaster, and the presentation might arguably seem ghoulish to non-Stockholmers. One of the model cherubs decorating the ship remains lifelike in its moment of death, eyes bulging, unmistakably a Swedish baby, dead under water as if it had just been murdered by its mother in the family bath.

The Swedish King Gustav II ordered the *Vasa* to be built to intimidate Poland, which was at war with Sweden over control the Baltic Sea. The contract was given to a Dutch shipbuilder, Henrik Hybertsson, who was asked to build the world's biggest warship. Henrik died during the con-

struction phase but, in relatively gender-blind Stockholm, his wife was encouraged to take on the project management and under her the result was
a triumph. The *Vasa* appears small today, but sitting raised and reconstructed in Stockholm it still looks dangerous. Its total length, including
the bowsprit, was 226 feet. Its height from the keel to the top of the main-
mast was 170 feet. It displaced 1,210 tonnes and had a sail area of 13,725
square feet. Most impressive were the 700 sculptures and ornaments that
decorated the warship. One of the cherubs is the spitting image of what
Max von Sydow must have looked like as a toddler. The roaring lions'
heads at the gun-ports were savage symbols of Gustav Adolf as "the Lion
of the North". As you might expect in Stockholm, one of the woodcarvers
put Renaissance symbols, icons of Greek mythology and Swedish dynas-
tic glorification aside to carve what the Swedes have translated into English
as a "vulgar woman with large breasts licking her nose with her tongue."
If you see the real thing, you will need no explanation.

The maiden voyage on 10 August 1628 was the vessel's only sortie
under sail. Although the king was not able to be present, the official launch
went ahead. The king had over-ridden the shipwright's advice and added
an extra deck of guns, which caused the disaster on the day. In front of a
Sunday crowd of townsfolk, diplomats and foreign eminences the *Vasa*
fired a salute, a gust hit the ship, it heeled, water rushed into the open
gun-ports and within minutes Captain Söfring Hansson and all aboard
were in the water. Although it was summer and close to the beach, few
could swim in the seventeenth century, and about a third of those on the
maiden voyage drowned, perhaps fifty in all.

When the *Vasa* was salvaged in 1961 archaeologists found 25 skeletons. If the design and operating systems of the *Vasa* represented a failure,
the salvage was a triumph of Swedish know-how. Anders Franzén located
the wreck in a hundred feet of water in 1956. Looking for it had always
been his hobby. The *Vasa* does not appear in any histories of Sweden or
guidebooks before the wreck was found. Mistakes were left to lie in the
past. Successes, however, were trumpeted. After 333 years on the bottom
it was not easy to get the ship back, but the Swedish navy managed the job
over a two-year period and the *Vasa* was in a temporary museum by 1962,
in a permanent mist of polyethylene glycol, which stopped it from shrink-
ing. In 1990 the Vasa Museum was set up at Galärvavsvägen on
Djurgården. When I first saw the *Vasa*, early in the wreck's restoration, it

looked like a sunken warship; now it looks like it could sail to Helsinki or Tallin. What you will miss is the seventeenth-century post-mortem—none occurred. There were a few arrests, no-one was found guilty, all agreed on a general admission that design faults had contributed (no mention of the king) and life went on as normal until the next disaster.

THE CHERNOBYL DISASTER: TERROR FROM THE SKY
The devil took time off from playing chess with Max von Sydow to revisit Stockholm on 26 April 1986 when the Chernobyl nuclear power plant exploded, spreading radioactive contamination over Sweden. The Swedes had been worried about nuclear disaster from the time of Hiroshima and Nagasaki. Fear accelerated when the government and its electricity company engineers set up a local nuclear power industry. A repeat experience of the anguish of the Black Death had haunted Swedes since the energy crisis of the 1970s drove them closer to nuclear power dependence for electricity supplies as cheap oil was no longer available. They feared the maw of their industrial giants. Demonstrators were for a time on the streets of Stockholm, protesting against the nuclear fuel cycle, predicting

stench and doom when a local power plant failed. Stockholmers were predictably the sternest and most moralistic critics of the Three Mile Island disaster, but nothing had prepared them for Chernobyl.

Chernobyl was the world's worst civil nuclear disaster. The Swedes were among the first victims when a power surge blew the top off a primitive Soviet Union reactor in Ukraine. Initially the Swedes believed that an accident had happened at one of their own nuclear power stations on the Baltic coast. I was relatively close by, swimming happily in an indoor Finnish pool in Åbo, when Swedish scientists monitoring radioactivity in the atmosphere realized that Cesium 137 and Strontium 90 levels were so high that they decided to evacuate 600 workers from their own power sites. The Soviet Union took its time to acknowledge the disaster, and then only after furious protests from Sweden; Stockholm was only 600 miles away from the danger zone.

The Soviet Union eventually admitted gross human error. Prime Minister Ingvar Carlsson, who had accepted nuclear power on behalf of Sweden, agreed that the Soviet power station was run by the Marx Brothers—and he meant Harpo, not Karl. "Chernobyl," fumed Carlsson, "has spread radioactive iodine and cesium over Swedish fields, forests, marshes and lakes." The explosion ruined the food sources and threatened the livelihood of 15,000 Lapps. Stockholmers, like Lapps, ate fish and berries, even if they were not dependent on hunting for their daily food. The furious prime minister pledged that the twelve nuclear power plants in the country would be gone by 2010. Carlsson wanted Stockholm's city dwellers to continue to enjoy living close to the local woods, hunting fungi among the birches, fearing vipers, not cancer.

Within days of the catastrophe Swedes had monitored rainfall over their country. They found that Sweden had been polluted more than many neighbouring countries due to the weather at the time of the explosion, by chance sending large falls of radioactive rain to Stockholm and thus burdening the country with the risk of future cases of acute childhood leukaemia. Despite low population density, by 2004 medical studies statistically determined what all had feared: extra cancer cases had been triggered due to Sweden's exposure to about five per cent of the total radioactive emissions that drifted from the disaster site.

Ironically, the chain of events that led to the Chernobyl disaster followed a routine safety test. Plant operators bungled. They removed too many control rods and disabled a system that would have shut down the reactor when the power turbines stopped and reduced the coolant water. The resultant power surge burned down the building. The fire sent a plume of radioactive debris into the upper atmosphere as Soviet fire fighters in helicopters dumped lead and boron onto the reactor core. Chernobyl nevertheless survived the fall of the Soviet Union, was re-commissioned with a new plant and produced electricity for another fourteen years until international pressure forced its closure in 2000. The old plant is at the centre of one of the most radioactive spots on earth and the concrete sarcophagus, hastily built to cover the damaged reactor, is weakening.

THE *ESTONIA*: SUNK OFF UTÖ

Possibly equally radioactive, and also covered in a concrete sarcophagus, are the sunken hull and the corpses of some of the passengers and crew of the Stockholm-Tallin ferry *Estonia*. Before it sank, a cruise on the *Estonia* was a popular, cheap trip for Swedish senior citizens and an easy way out of the former Soviet Union for the Russian mafia in a conduit of traffic said to include superfluous nuclear weapons. At the Estline terminal on the Frihamnen Wharf there were cries and shock when the news broke that many more Swedes had drowned when the *Estonia* foundered off Utö than went down with the *Vasa*.

After the dissolution of the former Soviet Union and the independence of the Baltic States, Stockholm became the vital western entry port for a daily service between Sweden and Estonia, established to help Sweden's Baltic neighbours achieve a peaceful transition to prosperous democracy when the Soviet Union collapsed. When it sank, flying the Estonian flag, the *Estonia* was, like the *Vasa*, a proud symbol of national sovereignty. The vessel was delivered on 15 January 1993 to the Estline Marine Company Ltd., which was owned equally by the Estonian state and a Luxembourg subsidiary of a Swedish public joint stock company, Nordström and Thulin. The *Estonia* made its first voyage on 1 February 1993 and traffic continued every second day from Stockholm and Tallin respectively.

A mariner's superstition is that it is bad luck to rename a ship. If so, the *Estonia* was in for very bad luck. For thirteen years the ship flew the Finnish flag, starting life as the *Viking Sally* in a daily operation between Stockholm and its former colonial outposts in Åbo and Mariehamn. The Viking Line was a marketing consortium operating ferries between Finland

and Sweden. In 1986 owners of the competing Silja Line took over ownership of the vessel, operating it as part of the Viking fleet until April 1990 when the Silja Line took over completely, renamed *Sally* the *Silja Star* and kept up the Stockholm-Åbo run. In less than a year it was transferred to another company subsidiary to operate in the Gulf of Bothnia between Vasa in Finland and Umeå and Sundsvall in Sweden. For this the ship was renamed *Wasa King* and operated that route until sold to the Estline company. It was registered in Cyprus and marked for doom.

The *Estonia*, although of an old design and with a retrospectively obvious technical fault in its front loading visor design, had safely spent fourteen years in the Baltic and Gulf of Bothnia and almost 20,000 hours on the open sea where the worst conditions exceeded wave heights of fifteen feet. The Stockholm-Tallin route was the roughest by far, four times stormier than the Sea of Åland, heavy breakers on the beam or bow being almost certain when conditions were bad.

About midnight on 27-28 September 1994, an engineer on the *Estonia* found that water was coming onto the vehicle deck. The ship was two hours out from the Estonian coast, just off the remote Finnish island of Utö. It was returning to Stockholm harbour in a south-westerly gale, with waves in the Baltic over thirty feet high. Most of the passengers were seasick, exhausted from the battering and clinging to their cabin bunks. As usual, many of them were drunk.

The crew's cabins were at the top of the ship, just above the ten 76-person capacity lifeboats, about seven flights of stairs above the keel level. On the bottom deck of the ferry were 28 trucks and two buses. The ship's engineer reported that the passengers' cars were up to their axles in sea water, unexpectedly coming through the hydraulically operated bow door. Baltic waves had breached the waterproof seals. Land-based marine engineers later gloomily calculated that 1,500 tonne-per-minute wave forces overwhelmed the bilge pumps. Below the waterline trucks broke their holding chains in the storm. Unchained vehicles shifted from their parking positions and crashed about on the truck deck. The ship soon began to roll, the weight of water and runaway trucks eventually toppling the *Estonia* to its port side. It sank at about two in the morning. Although elements of the Finnish defence forces were nearby on Utö, only about one in ten of the passengers and crew were found alive in the lifeboats by Finnish rescuers at dawn. All of them were young and fit, overwhelmingly male.

When the instruments on the bridge first alerted the master that his vessel was in danger he did not face the truth that the ship had not merely developed a stubborn list, but was sinking. Asked to slow down by worried subordinates, the master berated them and responded that schedules had to be maintained. As the night drew on, the waters of the Baltic became more and more open, the waves higher and higher, and the consumption of alcohol increased in the tacky, pole-dancing entertainment section where young Estonian women were trying to build a career that did not involve prostitution in a new, capitalist world. Passengers began to worry. Families consulted each other. A few decided to forget the idea of sleep for the night and take up prudent escape positions on the upper decks—very few. The first most of the passengers knew of their fate was when they saw the crew abandoning ship and heading for the lifeboats. A coded message in Estonian had told the crew—but not the passengers—that the ship was sinking. The last minutes were brutal. The young and fit struck out at the old, the weak and the women as they climbed over each other to escape up stairs that were no longer going upwards as the ship had turned on its side and was about to roll over and sink.

The official figures declared that, of the 1,049 people on board, only 136 survived. But who knows? The actual death toll will never be precise because the Estonian shipping and port authorities were not particularly fussy about the numbers of passengers recorded as carried on the *Estonia*. Most of the survivors were crew. The immediate response was an inquiry which, in the tradition of Swedish inquiries, blamed no-one but made disconcerting observations. While trucks broke their chains and careered about on the vehicle deck, the major warning of the end was an enormous noise that stopped the pole-dancers and drinkers and woke snoring sleepers as the fifty-seven tonne bow door parted from the ferry. It was found in 225 feet of water about a mile and a half from where the ferry sank. The bow door was brought to the surface by Finnish engineers on the icebreaker *Nordica*. Studies on land focused on the hydraulic locks: were they closed at the time of the accident? Broken pins were found in the hinges. Puzzled Stockholm maritime trade unionists muttered that the *Estonia* crew was incompetent, ill trained and inexperienced.

Ten years later the relatives of the dead still complained that while the bow door had been retrieved and pored over, the *Estonia* itself had not been raised. In Stockholm the *Dagens Nyheter* tried to put a brave face on the tragedy. Certainly, it said, the sinking was Europe's worst post-war maritime disaster but, it chirped, Estonia itself had grown into a country with self-confidence, and ferries to Sweden were now just one alternative for Estonians who wished to go abroad. The BBC showed photographs of the victims' relatives lighting candles at a memorial service and pointed out how political pressure remained in the Swedish parliament from members who were sceptical about the sinking. King Carl XVI Gustaf laid a wreath by a granite wall bearing the names of all those who had definitely been killed.

As I set off to work at the Vitterhets Academi on the freezing autumn morning after the disaster, I read "*Estonia* Sunk" in the newspaper headlines. With my poor appreciation of newspaper Swedish, literal minded and confused by the unimaginable, I wondered, "How could a country sink?" Just as the spirit of New York was dented by the terrorist destruction of the twin towers, Stockholm's natural melancholy was lifted a notch by its worst shipping loss since the Second World War. The official inquiry into the disaster by the Finns (who rescued the survivors) the Estonians (who ran the ship) and the Swedes (whose idea the shipping line was) blamed the Germans, (who constructed the vessel) for bad design of the hinges on the bow doors. The Germans complained that everyone in the north blamed them for everything and rumours continued that the *Estonia* was being used to smuggle fissile material from the former Soviet Union and that the ferry had been sunk to prevent detection after a tip-off to the Swedish police.

FLIGHT 686: THE MILAN APOCALYPSE

Stockholmers' unreciprocated enthusiasm for frontier Finland, or at least for the Åland skerries, is only matched by their fondness for the warmth of Italy. Naturally, regular, well patronized flights connect Stockholm with Rome and Milan. By coincidence, I flew out of Milan airport a few weeks after a Scandinavian Airlines System passenger aircraft crashed on take-off. The MD80 jet hit a Cessna, piloted by a distracted German who strayed onto the runway after taking a wrong turn. Looking out of my window on a BMI Boeing 737, I could see the remains of the accident. Burn scorches disfigured the ground; the airport infrastructure which the SAS aircraft had crashed into still looked like a bomb had recently hit it.

The first airport in Milan was built in 1934 as part of the triumph of Italian fascism. The present airport, Linate, opened in 1960. By 2001 each day saw about 300 aircraft movements transporting eight million passengers a year. Those who died were extremely unlucky, but statistically this is always the case where air crashes are concerned. What made Linate different was the acceptance by the airport authorities, and the rest of Italy, of a high rate of near misses, which elsewhere in the world would have triggered some sort of remedial action. Aircraft from carriers such as Austrian Airlines, Air France and Lufthansa had all, at one time or another, either finished off the Linate runway, had to abort take-offs because there had been other aircraft on the runway, or had experienced near collisions. The Catholic Italians had an almost Buddhist detachment where air safety was concerned. When the SAS plane hit the other aircraft on the runway, it was only a few feet from the ground. But travelling at V2, the chances of an aborted take-off and a successful deceleration— which Air France had managed on 10 November 1987, Lufthansa on 13 September 1995 and Austrian Airlines on 28 August 1997—were slim indeed.

Many observers present at the time do not recall the SAS crash impacting on the Swedish psyche at all. Why would it? The Swedes are masters at concealing emotion. Stockholmers did not question the inevitability of air crashes any more than they were astonished at first sight by ships sinking or a tsunami tidal wave. What bothered them was that fate, or the devil, seemed to have singled their country out for harsher treatment than was usual when major disasters hit citizens of a major capital city. The *Estonia* was not the only roll-on-roll-off ferry to sink. Before the design specifications of this particular sort of vessel were abandoned almost a quarter of them sank. But only the *Estonia* matched the *Titanic*. In 2001 there were seventeen major air crashes in the world, but the one involving SAS was Italy's worst ever airliner disaster.

The SAS jet was heading for the airline's hub in Copenhagen when it crashed. Four airport baggage handlers died on the ground. The roof of the central storage hangar collapsed. After the disaster, a long section of the aircraft lay on the ground where it had fallen. About twenty rows of seating were still intact, as was the whole of the rear tail and engine section. The SAS logo still proudly recalled Viking navigation and Swedish engineering triumphs.

The baggage handlers in the central store hangar where the wreck finally came to a stop thought a bomb had gone off in their warehouse. Many of the ground staff were lucky to be alive. They could see nothing because of smoke and flames. The smell of burning kerosene choked them. More than one testified to experiencing an apocalyptic moment. While a Scania truck carted off the wreckage, the surviving baggage handlers were taken to hospital, called their wives, reassured them that they were still alive and wondered why they were chosen to live through a catastrophe that had killed their workmates. The arrival of first aid at an aircraft crash on takeoff or landing is always instant. Five hundred *carabinieri*, police, firemen and Red Cross workers risked their lives in the smoking and burning hangar to try to find and save passengers who might have survived. Vincenzo Fusco, the airport director, went into shock and could not bring himself to appear for three hours. The Red Cross called in an extra two hundred workers, while the fire brigade had the task of taking the bodies of passengers to the morgue for identification by their families.

The Italian response to the disaster was to hold a church service, which was attended by the President Ciampi and the Prime Minister Berlusconi. The two cultures, Nordic and Latin, met to mourn in Milan Cathedral. The Stockholmers did not expect a quick answer to what had happened, what went wrong, who was guilty and who should pay. They remembered the fire at the Fenice Building, Venice's opera house, which mysteriously burned to the ground on a Monday evening, 29 January 1996. The artist Anders Zorn, and Swedish highnesses, royal if not serene, were as often in the Palazzo Barbaro as the Drottningholm Court Theatre. For their part, the Milanese preferred to leave the catastrophe to those best equipped to handle it—the Church fathers—while at the same time daydreaming in church and admiring the blonde hair and blue eyes of the ecclesiastic representative sent by the Vikings.

President Ciampi presided at the ceremony with Cardinal Martini. Prime Minister Berlusconi wept openly, mopping his eyes and face with a large white handkerchief. The Stockholmers did not like what they saw. Forgetting their own response to the *Vasa* and *Estonia*, they were disgusted by the incapacity and indifference of the Italians, and said that what had happened was unacceptable. Wives and mothers from Sweden, standing out in the cathedral with their strikingly different hair and eye colour, cried out that they had lost their sons; their husbands; that they had been killed by stupidity, by meanness, by financial parsimony, by indifference and how these things could happen they could not imagine.

A cardinal could be relied on to have the last word. Cardinal Martini said, "Linate, it is your fault." While understandably not resiling from accepting the inevitability of God's mysterious ways, Martini said that the deaths were the result of a tragic series of errors and were caused by negligence. Faced with the tears, the anger and the pain of the relatives, and their moments of near-mad unhappiness, the cardinal confronted those responsible from the eminence of his marble pulpit. As he addressed a congregation of 1,200 (the Church and laity alike had expected only 300 to turn up), the Scandinavians and Italians wept in the silence of the great building. Martini attacked the guilty and said that not a month from the disasters in New York, those in Milan had seen a tranquil airport turned into a bloodbath.

With characteristic sexist accuracy, the *Nazione* pointed out that the priestess who assisted at the ceremony as representative of the Lutheran Nordic area in *un lutto europeo* (European bereavement) had *capelli biondi*, or blond hair. Hanna Hagen, *sacerdotessa*, found this remark strange, coming as she did from a region of Europe where gender, ethnic identity and appearance had been ruled out as status and personality markers for many generations by social democracy.

It was a relief for the Swedish mourners in Milan to return to SAS after the ceremony, even if the Stockholmers were likely met by grim-visaged Norwegian or Danish stewardesses who refused to speak to them in Swedish, switching to English to avoid any suspicion of sovereign subordination.

Stockholm may not be the capital of Scandinavia but the owners of the SAS Group are Stockholm-based and in 2007 the company's shares fell 27 per cent in six weeks, the time it took to address three SAS crash landings. SAS were not at fault when the unfortunately named "Bombardier" turbo prop Q400s crashed when landing gear failed but the system worked to the extent that all such aircraft were withdrawn from service before a single passenger was killed.

Chapter Ten

THE NOBEL PRIZES

DOING IT FOR ME

THE SCIENCE OF WINNING

Alfred Nobel's death on 10 December 1896 is celebrated more glamorously than his life. Only he felt the sting of his death. His astonishing achievement in creating a money-generating foundation has brought happiness and benefits to many and put Stockholm on the world map for inventors, intellectuals and geniuses. Aware of the paradox that the armaments industry was the cause of human misery as well as providing national security, Alfred bequeathed to the world, as one of his priorities, the Nobel Peace Prize. The peace prize was awarded in Oslo, a fitting tribute to Swedish know-how in finessing the end of the union with Norway without bloodshed, unlike its inception.

Nobel was not unusual in having several wills. In his second will he bequeathed money to the Swedish Club in Paris, the University of Stockholm and the Karolinska Institute for medical research to create a fund whose amassed interest every third year, according to a decision by the management, would be awarded as a prize for the most important pioneering discovery or invention in the field of physiology and the medical arts. Proceeds from his estate were to be given as a reward for the most important pioneering discoveries or works in specified fields of knowledge and progress:

> Without thereof making an absolute condition, it is my wish that those
> who through writing and action have managed to fight the strange prejudices still harboured both by nations and by governments against the
> establishment of a European peace tribunal would especially be considered. It is my express wish that every prize designated in this will be
> given to the most deserving person, without the slightest consideration
> if the person is a Swede or a foreigner, a man or a woman.

The Town Hall, scene of Nobel Prize ceremonies

The Royal Swedish Academy of Science, Physics and Chemistry and the Royal Karolinska Medical-Surgical Institute were responsible for selecting the scientific prize-winners. The first prizes were given in 1901, when Wilhelm Röntgen was honoured with the Nobel Prize for Physics and Chemistry for the discovery of x-rays. His award, and the award for medicine to fellow German Emil von Behring for serum therapy, began a marathon race between individual scientists determined to get the prize for themselves. A century after the first winners travelled to Stockholm, a Darwinian jungle was well established in which scholars fought tooth and claw for the spoils. Ideas were cannibalized, reputations were murdered by colleagues in the name of ambition and an Australian laureate, Peter Doherty, published a do it yourself instruction manual on how to beat the competition, *The Beginners Guide to Winning the Nobel Prize*.

Doherty gave avuncular advice so useless that it might have encouraged would-be Nobel Prize winners in science to think that if Doherty could do it, anyone could. Among his tips was: "Avoid prestigious administrative roles. Don't become a dean, a director or a president." This was not easy if you were Niels Bohr, Lawrence Bragg, Sir Macfarlane Burnett, Francis Crick, Pierre and Marie Curie, Albert Einstein or a Jim Watson. Doherty ordered: "take care of yourself and live a long time." That ruled out Louis Pasteur, who died in 1895, a year before Nobel, but included Ivan Pavlov who lived to be 87 and was unusual for a Russian critical of communism in dying of natural causes. One piece of advice would have been useful if it had not applied to hundreds of thousands of men and women. Doherty recommended: "Be selective about where you work." He should have added: "and choose Cambridge University." A Cambridge oar takes a central place in the Nobel Museum, and its totemic visual impact cries that science is not a boat race but that victory goes nevertheless, more often than not, to the Fens.

Enrico Fermi conformed to none of Doherty's criteria. He died young at 53 and combined supreme ability as a theoretical physicist with equal genius as an experimenter. Fermi's pasta recipe was as important to him as his textbooks on atomic physics, molecules and thermodynamics. His inclusion of anchovies in a simple blend of ingredients available in Pisa, where he studied for his doctorate (or Rome where he was professor until 1938), was a pasta discovery as significant to him as his contribution to the development of the atomic bomb. He did not choose where to work. He eventually was forced from Italy by the mortal danger he faced from fascists and took to bomb-making at Los Alamos as second choice to cooking. High energy nuclear physics was of lasting interest to boffins but Fermi's wider gift to mankind can still be tasted with surprise and relish throughout the pasta-eating world, surprisingly often cooked on the top of an Aga stove designed by his fellow laureate Gustav Dalén, who was also down to earth in applying his talents. Perhaps the Australian's tips should have included advice to avoid dangerous experiments. Dalén was blinded by a laboratory explosion.

Sweden has been remarkable in its efforts to make the world a peaceful planet. Nobel's peace prizes, awarded from 1901, were the offspring of his unrequited, mistimed love for Baroness von Suttner. She drew his mind to practical means of stopping the destruction of the human race, helped distract him from the troll and was given the peace prize herself in 1905. The significance of the year and the institution that awarded it, a Nobel committee appointed by the Norwegian parliament, was striking as Norway was, that year, the country imperial Sweden relinquished, despite Norwegian provocation and sabre rattling. The Nobel Peace Prize is now debased, being used as an instrument of foreign policy by its awarders. It did not take long for the Norwegian and Swedish governments to realize that the press spotlight on Nobel laureates provided both governments and recipients with a platform so large it could influence world public opinion. The example of the four residents of South Africa who have won the prize, Albert Luthuli, Desmond Tutu, F. W. de Klerk and Nelson Mandela, is instructive. De Klerk jailed political prisoners by the tens of thousands, while Mandela considered Nobel's dynamite to be the terrorists' weapon of choice and used it in an armed struggle which embraced violence. He joked about the flexible Swedish ethical standards that gave him an enormous amount of cash in the hand and a Nobel Peace Prize. Only Albert Luthuli and Desmond Tutu, who had never been urban guerrillas or politicians who killed people, qualified as men of peace.

COLOSSAL IMAGINATION

While scientific prizes (including one for the dismal science of economics added in 1939) were given to experts in office politics, the literature prize was the award for colossal imagination. Many winners of the Nobel Prize for Literature are now all but unknown, but in their day even the most obscure of them was instantly transformed by Swedish benevolence into a literary lion. The Frenchman Sully Prudhomme was given the first prize in recognition of a rare poetic combination of heart and intellect, qualities that might be taken for granted as prime characteristics not only of Prudhomme's works, but of the city of Stockholm itself. Prudhomme was followed by Christian Mommsen, the greatest historian of his time; the Norwegian poet Bjørnstjerne Bjørnson; a Provençal philologist and poet Frédéric Mistral and a Spanish dramatist, José Eizaguirre; an epic writer, Henryk Sienkiewicz; a poet, Giosuè Carducci and, in 1907, Rudyard Kipling. Given his career, Kipling was not likely to line up in Oslo for the peace prize. The Nobel committee closed their eyes to Kipling's racist jingoism, and gave him the prize for "virile ideas" and a "talent for narration". ("Virile ideas" could be taken as a self-referencing phrase describing a quality necessary to survive in Gamla Stan. It might also be admitted to the general list of qualities to be found in Stockholm to an extent unknown elsewhere.)

A philosopher, Rudolf Eucken, was followed by a Swedish literary genius, Selma Lagerlöf; the poet Paul Heyse; Count Maurice Maeterlinck (known for his fairytales); Gerhart Hauptmann, a theatre producer and, on the eve of the First World War, the first non-European to gain the Nobel Prize for Literature, Rabindranath Tagore. During that conflict, while the cannons roared, four writers—Romain Rolland, Carl Gustav Von Heidenstam, Henrik Pontoppidan and Karl Gjellerup—were made famous and treated briefly like royalty as they collected the money in Stockholm. However, no prize was awarded in 1914. That year, the Kings of Sweden, Norway and Denmark met in Malmö, not Stockholm, to declare Scandinavian neutrality for the duration. The Nobel committees were not particularly distressed by the war, but at its beginning communication was cut between referees for the potential prize winners and the award-processing bureaucracy. After the Bolshevik revolution and the victory of Britain and France in the war against Germany, two writers were singled out for single works of genius: Carl Spitteler for *Olympian Spring* and Knut Hamsun for *Growth of the Soil*. The preoccupation with establishing a new world order, in which the themes of rebirth, organic growth and pacifist progress were the watchwords, was over by 1921 when Anatole France picked up the prize. In the years before the Stockholm Nobel committees had their lives again disturbed by world war, a "happy Spanish dramatist", Jacinto Benavente, was chosen. After came W. B. Yeats for expressing the Irish national spirit, and the Pole Wladyslaw Reymont was rewarded for his national epic, *The Peasants.*

From 1923 winners were given their prizes in the Stockholm Town Hall. Ragnar Östberg, a Swedish architect who had restored the state hall in Uppsala Castle, won a competition to design this secular cathedral. Peter Davey, editor of the *Architectural Review* in *Arts and Craft Architecture*, commented that the process of building this magnificent monument would have delighted William Morris. In Östberg's words:

> Studios and workshops for sculpture, painting, iron and copper work, woodcarving, the designing of textiles, furniture patterns, decorative work and models of the building all were fitted up with the interior of the building. As all these various workers, architects, sculptors, painters, art workers in copper and iron, designers of textiles, carpenters and stonemasons were working in close contact with the building under erection and its various premises, their co-operation yielded the most happy results.

Einar Forseth's stiff mosaic of the Queen of Lake Mälaren was the glory of the Swedish Town Hall. Davey's own view was that Östberg had made possibly the finest public building that arts and craft thinking ever produced; a fusion of all the visual arts in which individual craftsmen had their freedom; a re-interpretation for the twentieth century of Swedish myth and tradition enriched by a deep understanding of materials and their proper expression. Davey also understood that it was "ironic that many of the glories of the Stockholm Town Hall were made possible by businessmen who had been enriched by the First World War, which finally killed the Arts and Craft movement in Britain."

The Prize committee must have found 1925 a difficult year. Strindberg was never on the list, but his suitor George Bernard Shaw was eventually awarded the prize for a "stimulating satire". The 1920s ended with Grazia Deledda being honoured for what was called "plastic" clarity, plastic being all the rage at the time in the city. Henri Bergson received the next prize "for his ideas" (as the committee said somewhat lamely), Sigrid Undset for her medieval history descriptions and Thomas Mann "principally for *Buddenbrooks*".

PRIZES AMONG WARS

As the fight between communism and fascism intensified in the 1930s and after the bloody disaster at Ådalen, Stockholmers invented their own middle way of solving disputes at Saltsjöbaden. A similar middle way was clear in the literary tone of the writers selected in Stockholm to star for posterity. Sinclair Lewis was given the prize for "wit and humour", not thick on the ground during that decade. The poet Erik Karlfeldt was chosen, as were John Galsworthy for *The Forsyth Saga*, Ivan Bunin for classical Russian prose and Luigi Pirandello for bold scenic art. Later, Eugene O'Neill's "original concept of tragedy" won the award for him and Roger Martin du Gard was honoured for his cycle of novels, *Les Thibault*. After Pearl Buck was invited to Stockholm for her description of peasant life in China, and Frans Sillanpää was given the prize for his writing on the Finnish peasants' relationship with nature, the Academy closed its doors to the financial and public relations promotion of literary imagination as the Second World War threatened to destroy Stockholm itself.

Finnish writers found it hard to lay down the sword for the pen. The Finns fought two wars against the Russians, the Winter War and the Continuation War. After a trumped-up *casus belli*, the Soviet Union crossed the border into Finland in November 1939 and prepared to put their malcontent enemies in Russia's former model Grand Duchy to the sword. This began the Winter War. Finns wondered where they were going to find space to bury all the Russians they were going to kill. The prolonged battle on Finnish soil involved the Finns accepting Germans as brothers in the fight against the Soviet Union. This produced a crisis of conscience for Stockholmers. Many supported Germany. Families were torn apart when some members wished to fight on the Finnish side for old time's sake. In the end the Swedes did for Finland what they did for Norway—almost nothing. They facilitated the passage of German troops through T-Centralen en route to either crush Norwegian resistance heroes or kill Bolsheviks and eventually destroy Finnish infrastructure and devastate towns north of the Arctic Circle. When the Germans retreated to Stockholm on the Finnish railway track, an ingenious hook on the back of the last German locomotive, ripped up railway sleepers as the train headed out of Helsinki. By the time the final German train reached the safety of Stockholm, Rovaniemi was burnt to the ground and unusable steel rails stretched for hundreds of miles along the unusable railway route.

Some Stockholmers even imagined a Hiroshima-Nagasaki end to the capital of Sweden itself if the United States became sufficiently irritated with Sweden supplying war material to Germany and decide to bomb Stockholm. By the end of the Continuation War in 1944 many Finnish war heroes were, like Gustav Mannerheim, Swedish speakers who, like the Ango-Irish in another context, were relics of Swedish imperialism in the era when the Vasa dynasty was supreme in the Baltic.

When it was clear that the Germans were going to lose and a regular postal system was re-established, the prize assessors and the Nobel Foundation chequebooks were relocated. In 1944 Johannes Jensen received the prize for intellectual curiosity. A Chilean author, Gabriela Mistral, won the prize in 1945 as the committee in Stockholm decided to open its eyes as well as its bank accounts and became more multi-cultural. The prize was awarded to T. S. Eliot, "a pioneer poet", and to William Faulkner for "the Modern American Novel" before humanitarianism resurfaced in 1950, when the winner was Bertrand Russell, champion of "freedom of thought". (Of course, not everyone benefits from freedom of thought: Bertrand Russell's wife didn't when he cycled off to leave her.)

In the darkest days of the Cold War, Pär Lagerkvist, who was singled out for his poetry, made a familiar trip to Stockholm where, unlike most of the laureates, he understood everything that was being said by everyone he met. The Frenchman François Mauriac's country was delighted when he was selected in 1952. By then the Nobel laureate brought tourists and export income not just to Stockholm, but to the booksellers, hotels and restaurants of the lucky countries whose nationals were honoured. There were so many of them that in Stockholm "laureate spotting" rivalled ice hockey in popularity in December each year. Winston Churchill was given the prize in 1953—an appropriate choice for he had produced huge income for Nobel's defence industries in a lifetime devoted to waging war. No reference was made at the ceremony to Churchill's role in encouraging fighting on the beaches. The Stockholm publicity spotlight was rather shifted onto Churchill's "brilliant oratory" and mastery of history. (If Adolf Hitler had won the Battle of Britain and rearranged Europe's borders like Napoleon, there is no doubt the Nobel Committee would have singled out his achievements in writing *Mein Kampf* and awarded him the prize for literature too.) Hitler's attempts to master history failed. But the extent of Swedish sympathy for German values has never been a secret.

Some Swedish authors are destined never to win a prize as they write on issues that are embarrassing, unresolved and left to moulder. Henning Mankell, in *Depths*, describes how during the First World War the Swedish navy had charted Scarpa Flow, Pentland Firth and the British naval bases in the Orkney Islands. They regarded the English as arrogant and less well-equipped than the German navy. Were Sweden to be drawn into the war, according to Mankell's fictitious naval officer, Captain Hans Rake, Master of the *Svea*, "there should be no doubt as to where the sympathy of the Swedish military lay." It was long into the twentieth century before a Swedish prime minister could conduct a conversation in decent English.

Ernest Hemingway was a popular choice for his *The Old Man and the Sea*, but his successor, Halldór Laxness from Iceland, was virtually unknown. Juan Jiménez had the virtue of writing typical poetry in a much-spoken language, and Albert Camus' clear-sighted illumination of the problems of the human conscience brought the prize back to France.

POLITICAL MUSCLE, ARTISTIC TEMPERAMENT, THE EXOTIC AND OBSCURE

The rulers of the Soviet Union, the next country to be honoured, searched their flexible consciences and decided that the Nobel Prize was a devilish instrument of western propaganda that glorified sabre-rattling reactionaries. Boris Pasternak, the Nobel committee's choice for the 1958 prize, was described rather weakly in Stockholm as "important", and being important he was delighted to accept. But not content with working towards the day when the last capitalist had been hanged by the gut of the last imperialist, Sweden's old enemies in Moscow ordered Pasternak to decline. It does not take much imagination to guess what his reaction was when his Russian comrades prevented Pasternak from getting his hands on the money. The committee returned to arcane choices for the next three years. Three poets—Salvatore Quasimodo, St.-John Perse and Ivo Andrić—were largely unknown to English speakers when chosen and remained so thereafter. Not so John Steinbeck, honoured for his humour. Giorgos Seferis travelled north from the Mediterranean world to accept the prize for the Hellenic world of culture, but Jean-Paul Sartre, singled out for being rich in ideas and filled with the spirit of freedom and the quest for truth, flexed his mind muscles and demonstrated his free spirit by turning it down. From the 1960s the Muscovites released the handbrake, and both Michail

Sholokhov and Aleksander Solzhenitsyn were permitted to accept the Nobel Prize for Literature.

Samuel Beckett accepted the prize, not as an expert on Queen Christina, but as an advertisement for the power of the Irish imagination. The award then developed into a predictable Cook's tour of exotic, undiscovered locations of the mind, with thinly-veiled foreign policy connotations from the aggressively independent Swedes of the era. Jewish writers were honoured as war in Israel and Palestine put the Middle East into view in Stockholm. Nelly Sachs and Samuel Agnon shared the money. Miguel Asturias, writing about the indigenous people of Latin America, was pointed out to the literary world in 1967 as the man of the moment.

The Japanese were represented by Yasunari Kawabata in 1968, and the educational and consciousness-raising mission of the Swedish Academy was spelt out in clear prose in 1973, when the Australian writer Patrick White was given the prize and particularly praised for "introducing a new continent to literature", a somewhat patronizing error. White had difficulty finding a publisher and his first editions sold only a few copies. He nevertheless had the benefit of knowing Stockholm, having had his first glass of red wine on the quays as a sixteen-year-old while on an adventurous tour of Scandinavia with his parents. White was a defiant homosexual whose experience distanced him from the gay cause because he was unusually morose. A language graduate of Cambridge University, he came from a family so fabulously wealthy that he could have ridden from Sydney to Brisbane, stabling his horse each night on a family property. White was not a typical Australian, yet *Voss* touched the Stockholm imagination as few laureates' work had, as Australia, like Sweden, was a huge country with all the existential problems imposed by distance.

Stockholmers who could read English on the underground trains seldom read the works of the 1971 and 1972 winners, Pablo Neruda and Heinrich Böll, but almost everyone poked their noses into White's *The Aunt's Story*. From that time Australian low culture began to colonize the vacuous empty space of Stockholm television, with *Skippy the Bush Kangaroo* and *Neighbours* bringing to Norsborg, Österskär and Märsta the healthy, wholesome, uplifting animal-friendly ethos of a similar society half the world away in Australia. In a post-television career change, the boyish human hero of *Skippy* took up exporting kangaroo meat to Germany, a move that would no doubt have delighted Alfred Nobel.

After Patrick White's victory, men with beards at the Academy gave the prize to Harry Martinson for writings that "catch the dew drop and reflect the cosmos." Martinson shared it with Eyvind Johnson, who "served freedom", or so it was said. Serving freedom was a big idea in Stockholm in the 1970s, and Stockholmers believed human values to be under threat worldwide. The Academy duly stood up for those who confronted the illusion of the good life: writers such as Eugenio Montale, a poet who, like Elias Canetti, Czeslaw Milosz, Odysseus Elytis and Vicente Aleixandre, illuminated "present day society". In the 1970s the Academy abandoned antiquarianism in favour of the hip and current. Both Saul Bellow and Isaac Bashevis Singer qualified for the passion of their narrative art. No doubt when Saul Bellow picked up his cheque he was gratified to find that Stockholm was not as he had described another fictitious world capital in *Herzog*:

> A city. In a century. In transition. In a mess. Under organized power. Subject to tremendous controls. In a condition caused by mechanization. After the late failure of radical hopes. In a society that has no Community and devalues the person. Owing to the multiplied power of numbers which made the self negligible. Which spent military billions against foreign enemies but would not pay for order at home. Which permitted savagery and barbarism in its own great cities.

In fact, Stockholm was the polar opposite. In the 1980s Gabriel García Márquez, William Golding, Jaroslav Seifert, Claude Simon, Wole Soyinka, Joseph Brodsky, Naguib Mahfouz and Camilo Cela joined the ranks of the rich beneficiaries of Alfred Nobel's decision to set up an explosive factory in a Stockholm harbour. By the 1990s the income from the prize was so large that it relieved writers of the need to write. (Prizegiving on such a majestic scale is not my idea of the way to produce literacy excellence as quality drops off. Far better a spell of serious deprivation in prison, preferably under British, Soviet, South African or the US penal system.) After being awarded the Nobel Prize royalty income was guaranteed and frequent flyer points to literary festivals could be banked on forever. A change in the Swedish tax law, which greatly benefited non-profit organizations, and the relentless growth in the value of the Nobel investments over a hundred years turned Octavio Paz, Nardine Gordimer,

Announcing the winner

Derek Walcott, Toni Morrison, Kenzaburo Oe, Seamus Heaney, Wislawa Szymborska, Dario Fo, José Saramago, Günter Grass, Gao Xingjian, V. S. Naipaul, Imre Kertész, John Coetzee and Jean-Marie Gustave Le Clézio into the equivalent of major lottery winners.

When Nadine Gardiner travelled to Stockholm, Nobel's guiding impulse to be of great benefit to humanity was spelt out to her at the ceremony, in case she and the rest of the world had forgotten. One thing the Nobel literary prize winners had in common was their wish to have the right of complete freedom of expression. The audience at the prize giving could be sure they were hearing from artists who pulled no punches. Harold Pinter was typical with his gritty attack on George Bush and Tony Blair for their adhesion to the nonsensical concept of a war on terror. Prize winners made headlines.

Not all Stockholmers were pleased with Nobel's generosity. In February 1898, unhappy with Nobel's will, King Oscar summoned Alfred's nephew Emanuel (who was then a Russian citizen), ticking him off because the will was unpatriotic in not exclusively rewarding Swedish citizens. Referring to Baroness von Suttner, the king complained that Nobel had been influenced by women and declared his ideas to be fantastic. In Stockholm this was not a compliment. Branting, editor of the *Social Demokraten* and from 1896 a member of the Stockholm City Council, assessed Nobel's will as demonstrating both magnificent intentions and a magnificent blunder. The blunder lay in choosing the Swedish Academy to award the prize, for the Academy was intrinsically conservative and could be relied upon to give the award only to senile foreigners. Despite the pivotal position of the sovereign at that time in shaping public opinion and government policy, the major Stockholm newspapers approved of Nobel's generosity and dismissed the views of the philanthropist's critics. The *Dagens Nyheter* commented that the will was "a major event in our cultural history". The *Svenska Dagbladet* was equally positive, concluding that there "exists only one noteworthy action comparable for promoting spiritual growth in Sweden... When Gustav II Adolf transferred his privately inherited state fortune to Uppsala University."

CITY OF THE SHADOWLESS: PATRICK WHITE AND THE FEAR OF REJECTION

Over the years the observance of many of the rules came to be honoured only in the breach. The experience of Patrick White, the first Australian victor, illustrates how matters might be arranged. David Marr's biographical *Patrick White* explains it this way:

> The critics of Stockholm tend to see their city as the Rome of World literature, and they stake out territories for themselves keeping an eye on trends in India, pinpointing a new talent in Central America—as if responsible for these provinces to mother church.

Ingmar Björksten, midwife to the touchy business of bringing two irascible non-conformists together in order to achieve a first for the Antipodes, was the most important scholar to pencil in Patrick White on his form card as a possible winner. Björksten believed White's turn had come after Beckett won the prize. Patrick White had only unconventionality in common with Artur Lundkvist, the Swede who was to change his life. Lundkvist never threw off his southern accent, which grated in the capital. Stockholm colleagues thought him coarse, which he was. As much a Stockholm outsider as the founder of IKEA, Lundkvist had avoided university but still managed to write eighty books against the wind in the structured society of Swedish publishing. Although out of place in the world of tails and starched waistcoats, at sixty-two Lundkvist was finally offered a place in the Swedish Academy. Being an iconoclast and with a non-conformist style, he immediately liked Patrick White's work. The Stockholm publisher Bonniers first signalled White's importance when Lundkvist praised White's early novel, *Happy Valley*; White was put on the same level as Steinbeck, Eliot and Auden in a lengthy review.

While the terms of Nobel's will indeed excluded any applicant for a prize, some subsequent laureates, if not actually lobbying for the honour, were in early contact with those in—or on the fringes of—the Swedish Academy, actively promoting or obstructing their interests. Patrick White and Graham Greene were cases in point, Greene being blackballed, White being feted. In both cases the struggle to obtain a positive result or learn the worst took years. By the time White was tapped on the shoulder by the Swedish ambassador in Australia to hear the good news, he was fed up and exhausted by the whole affair to such an extent that he cried off visiting Stockholm to accept his prize personally and gave away all the money.

White complained that the Nobel Prize for Literature ruined his life but it did not dampen his enthusiasm for Stockholm. On the midsummer before the award, White and his partner Manoly Lascaris visited Artur Lundkvist. White insisted that the Swedish press was not to learn of his visit until he had left the country. White found Stockholm delightful at the time, remarking that everybody was most agreeable and hospitable. Scandinavians, he added, seemed almost incapable of the rudeness and bad temper that prevailed in other countries in the 1970s. He added, "architecturally it is a dream, especially in those long summer nights of pale green light."

Marr reveals that in Sydney Björksten had persuaded White to receive Lundkvist in his home prior to White making his secret dash from Australia to Sweden to visit Lundkvist's summer house. All three knew this meeting was to be about the Nobel Prize for Literature. Marr stresses that White's attitude was deeply ambivalent. For over a decade he had refused every award and decoration offered to him, but he wanted the Nobel, as none of the praise heaped on him over the years could equal the absolute vindication it offered. Yet he could not allow himself to be seen to want it. From 1969, when his name was first rumoured to be on the shortlist, he forbade his publishers to mention that he was a contender, deflected any questions about his chances of winning and, for fear of being thought to be courting the Swedes, refused to visit Sweden. Marr explains:

> White had to guard himself from the pain of being a contender who misses out and from the old spectre of destruction by fame should he win. He wondered about Swedes—"very well-behaved, well-spoken, clean, rational… but shadowless"—and outlaid a little pre-emptive spite, observing from time to time that it would "only be humiliating" to have what was not given to Tolstoy, Henry James, Proust and Joyce.

Marr recounts that:

> Lundkvist came to dinner at Martin Road with his wife, the poet Maria Wine, in late March 1970. Everyone was stiff. White knew he was under scrutiny and Lundkvist found himself awkward in the presence of the writer he admired so much. They skirted the subject of the Prize for some time. When Lundkvist mentioned it, White burst out, "I'm so damned tired of this. Over and over I figure as a likely candidate and nothing comes of it." Lundkvist replied, "Many would offer their lives to be considered likely candidates." White fell silent and the Nobel was not mentioned again that night. In letters to friends afterwards, White remarked that he found the Lundkvists polite, earnest and Swedish. "I don't think we made much contact."

Each year the appropriate members of the Academy agree on a shortlist and then disperse to their summer cottages to read. White was in a strong position in 1970, further strengthened during that summer when the new Swedish edition of *The Tree of Man* became available. But much of his support came from those academicians who were nervous about awarding the prize to Alexander Solzhenitsyn, the other principal contender. By autumn the Academy found the courage to brave Soviet hostility and gave the prize to the Russian. "Reservations don't occur in the Swedish Academy," Lundkvist told the Stockholm paper *Expressen*. "You either say that the Academy made a good choice, or you refuse to comment. I choose the second alternative."

Karl Ragnar Gierow, secretary to the Academy, was implacably hostile to Patrick White and proved to be a formidable enemy, delaying White's preferment and sulking. White himself did not feel he created Australian literature:

> I feel what I am, and I don't feel particularly Australian. I live here and work here. A Londoner is what I think I am at heart but my blood is Australian and that's what gets me going.
>
> I'm not for nationalism at all—nor for flag-wagging and drum thumping. There have been plenty of authentic voices before mine and many Australians will say that mine is not authentic.

The occasion when Patrick White was absent at the Nobel ceremony (represented by the artist Sidney Nolan) is beautifully described by Marr:

> The scene in the grand auditorium of the Concert Hall might have come from the pages of one of the great Russians who never won the prize. The King's party faced a line of laureates in black across a stage bare but for a large N on the pale blue carpet. Nolan, who had taken advantage of his visit to Stockholm to clinch a major exhibition of paintings at the Moderna Museet, wore the rose pink and pearl grey ribbon of a Commander of the British Empire. Carl Gustav in evening dress and decorations stood in a little knot of Swedish nobility. Diamonds in swags on pale silk and bare throats drew fire from the arc lights. The royal party spilled over the stage into the first rows of the auditorium, a scene of confused hand-kissing and bowing. Across the back of the stage, academicians sat in tiers like schoolboys about to be photographed around the bust of Alfred Nobel. The inventor of dynamite was bathed in a pool of pale blue light. Wreaths of spring flowers lay at his feet.
>
> Lundkvist came forward to read the official discourse on Patrick White. Traditionally this was the task of the secretary of the Swedish Academy, but Gierow was still so angry about the award that he refused. Lundkvist took over the role, quoting Gierow the old Swedish maxim: "He who lets the Devil in the boat should row him ashore." Lundkvist spoke for a few minutes in Swedish and then English. Nolan crossed the stage, shook the King's hand, and took the box containing the medal. To mark each award the Stockholm Philharmonic in a gallery above the stage played an interlude of appropriate music. To honour Patrick White

for introducing "a new continent to literature" the band played Percy Grainger's *In an English Country Garden*.

Patrick White's ambivalent response to the honour was exceptional. Toni Morrison spoke for most when she explained in a radio interview in Edinburgh that the speech she gave in the Stockholm Town Hall was window dressing. Morrison had a Pulitzer scalp on her belt for her master work, *Beloved*. When she was awarded the Nobel Prize for Literature she became the first African-American woman ever to win it. Morrison revealed that in Stockholm, before the king, she had tactfully eschewed self-interest, declaring gracefully that she accepted the prize on behalf of women, on behalf of black women, on behalf of the ill-used victims of racist patriarchy, and on behalf of black American women. She subsequently confessed that as a literature laureate she gave the Swedish sovereign and the other dinner guests the speech they wanted to hear. However straight-shooting the laureates were in their imaginative works and declaiming their views on the world, at the prize ceremony they were conscious that conformity to protocol and good manners were required. Away from Stockholm in the less squeamish setting of the Edinburgh Festival, Morrison confessed what motivated the prize winners. In her interview with Ramona Koval, in which Koval disingenuously asked what Morrison felt when she received the cheque, Morrison cheerfully confessed with undisguised, almost hysterical elation, that most of all, "I accepted the Prize FOR ME!"

House at Järntorget

Chapter Eleven

NORTHERN NECROPOLIS

DEATH AND DYING

READING THEMSELVES TO DEATH

Brought up in a city with a blood-stained history and popular culture reflecting the grisly experiences of Viking rape and murder, European wars, sinking ships, aircraft crashing, even a tsunami tidal wave and a nuclear power plant meltdown as part of their life, Stockholmers are at home with death and like to read about it. Along with their tracksuit and a shroud they usually have a half-finished book in their bedside cupboards. When they are not scheming new systems, devising strategies to market their ideas and inventions or worrying about problems outside Sweden in countries they can locate precisely on an atlas, Stockholmers read books.

What their favourite books have been over recent years illuminates the city's current interests and preoccupations. As the millennium approached one new writer, Mare Kandre, wrote a gothic novel, *Bestiarium*. Bestiaries have always been popular in the city of the occult. Per Odensten's *En lampa som gör mörker* (*A Lamp Which Grew Darker*), a tale of hate, hypocrisy and inhumanity, suggested that the second millennium would not usher in a period of happiness and good governance. Reviewers took this to be a summary of the twentieth century, and Stockholmers felt a collective sense of loss, natural at the end of a century. Reminiscences were published about Sweden in the 1950s, while past youth, ageing and death were themes in a short story collection *Is* by Ulf Eriksson. The present century brought with it novels about travel in time and space. Science fiction was popular. Lars Jacobson wrote a piece, *Berattelser om djur och andra* (Tales About Animals Among Other Things), which critics noted approvingly "provoked horror." History was not forgotten, with a bookshop bestseller on Bela Bartok's flight from the Nazis. By 2005 the arrival of the twenty-first century was already taken as past and shoppers returned to stories of gender estrangement from the female point of view.

Skogkyrkogården, a Stockholm cemetery

Stockholmers are bookworms with a particular taste for the politically correct and gravitate to the literary output of a hippy success story, Ordfronts Förlag. The first members of what began as a publishing commune decided in the late 1960s to print books while they raised sheep and grew potatoes, hatching their dreams of self-sufficiency in an old smokehouse in southern Stockholm. Publishing proved more profitable than peasant farming and Ordfronts Förlag developed its marketable determination to the fight for freedom, independence and human rights all over the world. Its list grew to specialize in issues important to Stockholmers: the consequences of US foreign policy for the Third World, globalization, refugees in Sweden, the critical state of the world's oil supplies and the problems facing modern families in the age of divorces. Ordfronts Förlag moved from being marginal to become a viable publisher on the back of Henning Mankell's genius as a crime writer. The publisher is global in its author net and publishes a large number of foreign authors from Noam Chomsky to Ian McEwan.

Ordfronts Förlag has flourished in a vibrant market. Long winter nights and terrible television lead to high national book sales. A perceptive freelance literary critic, Immi Lundin, put current Swedish reading interests in their social context. Swedish readers prefer authors to write about everyday events with detailed care, but to underpin them with a feeling of threat. This has been a recurrent characteristic of many recent Swedish novels. "Reasons to reflect on Swedish society from an estranged point of view," wrote Lundin, "were often presented in novels concerned with illness and crime."

One of the most popular works of fiction in twenty-first century Stockholm is set on a particular late summer day, 13 August 2002. Strange electrical storms infect the whole town with a communal headache. Stockholm's normally reliable machines break down, electric lights flicker and, in a shocking and gruesome development, the newly dead come back to life in the cemeteries and churchyards. John Ajvide Lindqvist's neo-gothic horror novel, *Hanteringen av odöd* (which might be translated as "Handling Zombies"), taps into a preoccupation with the undead. The plausibility of Lindqvist's zombies was praised by Pia Bergström in the *Aftonbladet*, and Maria Küchen in *Expressen* congratulated the author for moving on from vampires. The novel offers a 336- page account of a weird collective experience. A retired journalist with the only unimaginative touch in the novel—his name is Gustav Mahler—is first to spot what is going on, having rushed to his local cemetery to investigate. He accepts the evidence before his eyes; after all, resurrection of the dead is routinely promised by the state Church and should it occur, it will naturally be in graveyards.

Contrary to what Lindqvist imagined, the recent dead have not actually been resurrected, but the obituaries of those who have just died command attention for what they indicate about current Stockholm social trends. Stockholm has always been a town where necrology is more important than chronology; who was who always had a greater subliminal priority than who is who. It is a tricky balancing act. Swedes have a clinical view of death but are very interested in the subject. These days funerals are usually held three days from the date of death, not, as one diplomat has observed, to allow respite for emotional acceptance, but to provide order and allow family and friends to schedule the event, "as everything they do in their ubiquitous agendas".

The feats of the dead have been celebrated since Viking times with obsessive attention to the detail of their lives. Ingmar Bergman, who died in 2007, was a notable exception and was quickly laid to rest by Swedish public opinion. His cinematographer Sven Nykvist died in Stockholm the year before on 20 December. This left very few of a generation of Swedish internationalists who, like Nykvist, worked for Woody Allen, Lassse Hallström, Roman Polanski, Louis Malle and Peter Weir. Nykvist received Oscars for best cinematography on Ingmar Bergman's *Cries and Whispers* and *Fanny and Alexander*. He was credited with conjuring up luminous camera work, and his technical mastery sustained and supported Bergman while leaving Nykvist himself in the flickering shadows of world acclaim's back row. Nykvist obtained his life's inspiration and focus in Rome's Cinecittà film studios, where he spent twelve months with the Italian new wave leaders. It is not possible to see movies where he was "the light master" without being conscious of Nykvist's singular presence transforming Bergman's vision. Nor can one underestimate the importance of Nykvist's exposure to Italian sunshine in forming his sensitivity to life and death, light and darkness.

Lars Gyllensten also died in 2006. Born in Stockholm, like Nykvist he was in his mid-eighties and personified the openness and the random nature of interests and influences that shape and characterize the

Stockholm savant. During his life he published forty scientific monographs on embryology and wrote thirty novels. He was a professor of histology for almost twenty years at the Karolinksa Institute. The Karolinska nurtured him as a young medical student and did not stand in his way when he pursued absorbing philosophical investigations in a life that juggled science and literature. Gyllensten was awarded the Nobel Prize for Literature, not histology. Because he was so fascinated by literature as well as pathology, he spent a term as permanent secretary of the Swedish Academy. In an action that was as intensely discussed as his Nobel award, Gyllensten chose to become an inactive member of the Academy. He deplored the Academy when it failed to condemn extremist Muslim attacks on free speech. The Ayatollah's call for the death of Salman Rushdie when his novel, *The Satanic Verses*, was denounced as blasphemous by some Muslims smoked Gyllensten out and he left his Academy life behind without hesitation, furious that the Swedes had not stood up for Rushdie. Gyllensten spent his life exploring the relative and subjective nature of truth and reached the conclusion that absolute scepticism was the necessary basis for experience and knowledge.

Gyllensten's principles were to some extent vindicated when the Swedish Academy turned its eyes to the Muslim world after 9-11 and in a bridge-building exercise gave the 2006 Nobel Prize for Literature to Orhan Pamuk, a Turkish novelist from a country that had grown in international importance as it bridged both Europe and Asia. The Swedes were impressed with Pamuk's Bergmanesque expression of his attachment to Istanbul: "My imagination requires that I stay in the same city on the same street in the same house, gazing at the same view. Istanbul's fate is my fate. I am attached to this city because it made me who I am." When the Swedish Academy praised Pamuk for discovering the "melancholic soul of his native city" they understood the term, as Stockholm too was a melancholic city. Pamuk was a sure winner in Stockholm. His masterpiece, *Snow*, revolved around a plot involving beaten and depressed women driven to suicide in a patriarchal society against a background of swirling snow.

MACABRE MONARCHS
Queen Christina was not the first to complain that Stockholmers took death too seriously. "There is no country in the world where they mourn

their dead as long as they do in Sweden," she said gloomily: "they take three or four years to bury them and then, when they do, all the relatives, especially the women, weep all over again as if the person had just died."

Queen Christina's experience illustrates how long reverence and respect for the dead has counted in Stockholm. Death changed Christina's life. As a six-year-old, she was taken from one castle to another as battles raged in the Nordic region. Her disrupted, uncertain childhood only stabilized when her heroic father died in battle. She left her Polish playmate in Stockholm and German cousin, to be locked up by her mother at Nyköping Castle. Christina complained that "it would have been a lovely court if it hadn't been spoilt by the Queen Mother's mourning." Nyköping, on the east coast, had once been Sweden's capital and the site of Queen Maria Eleonora's private residence. Maria Eleanora had nostalgic affection for it as it was there that Gustav Adolf had been proclaimed king. Fifteen national parliaments were held in Nyköping between the seventeenth and eighteenth centuries. But after her father was killed, Nyköping Castle was a prison, not a home, for Christina. She admitted that Maria Eleonora "played the role of grieving widow marvellously well," and that her mother's grief was sincere. Veronica Buckley explains how Christina responded: "I was even more desperate than she was, because of those long dreary ceremonies and all the sad and sorry people about me. I could hardly stand it. It was far worse for me than the King's death itself. I had been quite consoled about that for a long time, because I didn't realize what a misfortune it was. Children who expect to inherit a throne are easily consoled for the loss of their father."

The founder of the current dynasty, ex-French Marshal Jean-Baptiste Bernadotte, who died in 1844, was buried with his more famous wife Désirée in the Riddarholmskyrkan, his life summed up thus by the official *aide-mémoire* to Stockholm's tombs and cemeteries:

> Once one of Napoleon's most trusted generals, Bernadotte was adopted by the childless Charles XII of Sweden and elected Crown Prince in 1810. Crowned in 1818, he married Désirée Clary, Napoleon's first love. The dynasty he founded still reigns in Sweden today.

The electronic obituary note for Désirée Bernadotte does not waste words and runs:

Désirée Clary "Desideria".
Queen of Sweden and Norway. The former fiancée of Napoleon, she
married General Jean-Baptiste Bernadotte in 1798. She travelled to
Sweden with him in 1811, but returned to France shortly afterwards
because she didn't like the cold. Became Queen of Sweden and Norway
when her husband was crowned in 1818, but did not return to Sweden
until 1823. Crowned in 1829. Mother of Oscar.

THE DEMOCRACY OF DEATH

Queen Christina was buried in the Vatican. In death, as in life, the best real
estate was reserved for kings and queens. But the town planners did not
neglect the needs of Stockholm's ordinary citizens. There are two styles of
cemeteries in Stockholm where zombies might one day be found, like trolls
in the underground. *Kyrkogård*, churchyard, and *begravningsplats*, burial
place, have different shades of meaning, although they both amount to
the same thing. Churchyards largely contain the graves of dead parishioners. Although burial places have purpose-built chapels, they do not
serve the same bureaucratic ecclesiastical function. In Strindberg's era, *begravningsplats* was used in a common saying, then more literally appropriate in Stockholm, to "smell a rat." In popular consciousness, where
kykogård were associated with marriages and baptism, *begravningsplats*
brought to mind funeral funds and burial expenses.

To supplement the city's ancient churchyards, a new graveyard site
was planned in 1815 for all Stockholm's inhabitants who did not have a
plot ready near a church. The north grave-digging place, Norra
Begravningsplatsen became overcrowded by the 1870s when the population grew beyond the expectations of the architects. Their plan was to use
a French model with half circles of plots and alleys to allow mourners and
respect-payers to promenade between the tombstones. Death spares no-
one, and a variety of final solutions was provided. In 1887 Norra
Begravningsplatsen planned the Nordic area's first high-tech crematorium
to add to the standard nineteenth-century columbaria and mausoleums.
It was hoped that the cemetery would be an inspiring place for meditation
and an easy area to find sought-after grave sites. But the filling in of the
semi-circular areas with their connecting alleys resulted in a maze where
it was impossible to find a specific site, unless one was searching for a small
minority of the buried dead, the Jewish and Roman Catholic clients.

All bodies laid to rest were subject to a system in death as in life but without the straightforward logic of the *tunnelbana*. For example, ten entrances led mourners from site 18B to 20B at the north, which merged with the sinuous collection of graves on the north-east to run into about a hundred different areas. Despite its Arcadian location near Haga Park, the north grave-digging place remains gloomy, depressing, usually avoided, uninhabited, and its chapel and crematorium are unwelcoming and forbidding.

Taking the dead seriously, like excessive drinking, is a Viking tradition. It is thanks to them that customs surrounding being drunk, dead and buried are celebrated now in the pre-Christian tradition nowhere more heartily than in Stockholm. The drinking horn, the burial mound, the welcome of oblivion and the atavistic care of the sacred interment sites have survived unchanged. The smaller graveyards attached to the many smaller Stockholm churches are spiritually refreshing in their orderliness. Calm cultivation of the burial landscape produces a healthy social context which fulfills the need to be able to mourn in a soothing and pleasant environment. Only in Swedish Finland, in the Åland Islands and in parts of Latvia, still smelling of long-lost Swedish influence, do graveyards exist as calm and perfect.

Stockholm may not be the capital of Scandinavia, but it is the major Necropolis of the North. Burial systems have been at the heart of cultural life from the Iron Age and Viking Age to the Modern Age. A natural priority of early Christian missionaries to Sweden was to stamp out pagan burials and to downgrade the importance of the plentiful pagan burial sites. Cemeteries are prime sources in understanding the secrets of Stockholm's past. Graveyards with burial mounds can still be recognized in the Swedish countryside, many as yet unexcavated. Stone Age and Iron Age graveyards are often to be found in the immediate vicinity of present-day churchyards.

Electronic grave finders on the worldwide web make tomb spotting easier than train spotting. The dead are arranged alphabetically and, as in the Stockholm telephone directory, so many have the same name that they are identified by occupation. In the Stockholm e-catalogue of the dead there are some strange combinations, reflecting the egalitarian spirit of Swedes, which applies especially in death. To say Stockholmers have a morbid interest in death is an understatement. Citizens usually make an early decision on their style of grave marker, including the colour of granite. This is taken seriously as a major marker of identity and style, as important as the choice of ring-tone on a mobile phone. After death no distinction is made between Nobel Prize winners for medicine, gladiator fitness champions and some of the most effective administrators employed by the United Nations. Every single dead person is identified, catalogued and their remains retrievable. Hymn writers and football commentators may not have much in common, but in the Swedish lists of the departed, an ice hockey player is given equal rights with the sculptor Carl Milles, who has distanced himself in death, as in life, by being buried at his own fine home, Millesgården on Lindingö Island.

For reasons of space and because Stockholm is an inclusive society where no-one misses out on anything, some occupational categories tagged onto the dead in the multifarious guidebooks used to locate graves do not do justice to their subject. While swimmers, prime ministers, trade union bosses and ice hockey players are obviously celebrities who need no further puffing, there was only one, Paul U. Bergström. Simply to describe him as "shopman" is hardly enough for the entrepreneur who founded PUB. To make matters more complex, some headstones commemorate non-existent people: one is dedicated to the fictional character Pippi Longstocking, and all the children on Bullerby Island and Saltkråken Island.

Swedish liberalism has been championed by its writers and artists whose contribution to social improvement was innovative and outstanding. Naturally, the cemeteries are full of those who have not only changed the direction of European intellectual life, but have also been part of the process to pool Swedish resources for general higher purposes and to benefit the wider world. Most important of these is the grave of August Strindberg, which has an appropriately complex designation: Section Ku 13A, grave 101-9136 is in the Norra Kyrkogården. Even King Gustav sent a wreath to lie on the republican's coffin at the burial. Tributes were paid in parliament. Prince Eugene represented the Royal Family at the grave itself. Workers marched in a crowd of ten thousand to the graveside under one hundred red banners. Strindberg's humble request for a quiet send-off was ignored. Strindberg asked that no death mask be taken, no photographs, and ordered: "I wish to be carried to the grave at eight in the morning to avoid a gathering of the curious... I will lie in the new cemetery, but not in the rich people's part, the market of vanity. At the grave-side there shall be no music, songs or speeches."

He was buried on 19 May 1912, no notice being taken of his last requests. Many other artists lie with Strindberg. Victor Sjöström, the director of one of Sweden's most delicious films, *Wild Strawberries* (1957), has his plot in the Norra Kyrkogården close to Mauritz Stiller, his friend in life. Stiller, who will always be remembered as Garbo's director, is in the Jewish cemetery plot, Section F. The Lutherans have kept a tight rein on who is buried where since their victory in the Reformation.

The upside of enthusiasm for mourning is that the contents of Stockholm's several cemeteries now provide a who's who of Swedish civilization and an index of national priorities. In a country where *system* and *bolaget* are revered, the inventive geniuses of Stockholm take pride of place and most are buried in the city's cemeteries. Top of the pantheon of inventors who changed the world was Alfred Nobel, buried in the Norra Kyrkogården. Another buried here is Gustav de Laval, tagged over-simply as "inventor". Stockholm has always been well supplied with adventurous politicians and explorers, careers which inevitably overlap.

There was, and is, cachet in being buried in Stockholm's collection of graveyards. Spots are waiting, pre-booked. Judging from what he writes about Sweden, Henning Mankell, who was born in Stockholm in 1948, may well prefer to be buried in Africa. Yet even those who prefer, for tax reasons, not to be seen to live in Stockholm demand to be buried there. No-one illustrates this better than the woman who was born Greta Louisa Gustavsson and died Greta Garbo. She was buried in 1990 in the Skogskyrkogården cemetery. For most of her eighty-five years she was retired and lived outside Sweden, but her heart belonged to Stockholm and there it will forever be. Skogskyrkogården is another UNESCO World Heritage site, four miles south of Stockholm with its own tunnelbana stop. It was designed after a competition victory in 1914 by Gunnar Asplund and Sigurd Lewerentz. Opened in 1920, its setting among pinewoods is distinctly sombre.

Some coffins and urns contain the remains of names so international that visitors wonder, "Were they Swedish?" Ingrid Bergman made films in and out of Sweden, but it was her non-Swedish performances that placed her in the incomparable star class: *Casablanca*, *For Whom the Bell Tolls* and *Anastasia*. Early work, like *Intermezzo*, was made in both

Swedish and English. Her fantastic life with Roberto Rossellini came in for moral censure. Even at her burial there were some doubts about her. Were her remains really in the urn? The Stockholm bureaucracy ruled that as the urn was not empty, the Norra Kyrkogården was officially declared her burial site.

The most tragic collection of corpses belongs to a small unloved group of the famous dead. Many of them, even in death, had supporters who apparently could not wait to remove their coffins and contents from Stockholm. Chief representative of these is René Descartes, unique in his lifetime among philosophers for agreeing with the teachings of natural sciences—with Galileo's views, for instance—but not thinking it necessary to break with the Roman Church. Descartes' day job was as a military engineer, while philosophy was more a hobby pursuit. Christina recognized Descartes as an outstanding philosopher, saw him as a humanist rather than a Christian, was delighted with his philosophy, and in September 1649 invited him to Stockholm. He hated the cold, saying that in Stockholm "here a man's mind seems to freeze in winter, just as the water freezes." His reception matched the frosty weather. Christina did not have serious meetings with him until December 1649, and by 1650 Descartes had only managed a handful of conversation with her. Having concluded that Christina was a dilettante, he planned his escape from the frozen north, only to collapse on 22 January, 1650 and drop dead ten days later— "Sweden's one contribution to the history of international philosophy," as Sven Stolpe remarked in his *Christina of Sweden*. Descartes had loathed Stockholm and felt he had been fooled by Christina; for one of the world's greatest philosophers to end up in Adolf Frederik Kyrkogård was thus too much for his disciples to bear. When they could afford it, they moved Descartes' body from its Stockholm church to a more receptive nook in Paris.

The graveyards also accommodate those who personify Swedish specialties: philanthropist administrators ready to die for a high cause. The Stockholm graves accordingly hold a higher proportion than might be expected of those whose cause of death is "murdered". The diplomat Folke Bernadotte was murdered by the Stern Gang in Jerusalem during a UN mission in Palestine. His body also lies in the Norra Kyrkogården.

Stockholm's cemeteries are very popular on certain days. At some times of the year they almost need the ubiquitous ticket machine, so useful in the *systembolaget*. Relatives and executors would be well served if they could take a numbered white slip to prevent unpleasantness and queue jumping on the cemetery paths at peak demand, day and night. Sven Hedin, the last Swede to be knighted (in 1902), spent his life mapping and exploring Central Asia. He lies in Adolf Frederik Kyrkogård. Prime Minister Per Albin Hansson, one of Sweden's longest serving social democrat leaders and architect of the welfare state, is in the Norra Begravningsplatsen.

As they lie beneath Stockholm soil, many of the famous dead have their lives re-written by revisionist progressives. Olof Palme, murdered in 1986 while I slept a hundred yards away in Vasagatan, after some time had his cause of death re-badged from "murdered" to "assassinated" by the cemetery electronic guide book. "Assassinated" implies political interest, murder, random killing; but whatever the verb Palme lies unwillingly in Adolf Frederik Kyrkogård. Erik Höglund, who designed for Boda glassworks, lies in Maria Magdalena Kyrkogård.

The cemeteries are subterranean clubs for eminent professionals. Gunnar Asplund, architect of the Stockholm City Library, is in the Skogskyrkogården. Johan Sergel, who died around the time of the Swedish-Norwegian Union, would no doubt turn in his grave if he could have seen his name perpetuated in one of Stockholm's least felicitous public spaces, Sergelstorget. Gösta Ekman, who co-starred with Ingrid Bergman in the original Swedish version of *Intermezzo* in 1936, was buried in the Norra Kyrkogården two years after the movie opened. Vilhelm Moberg, author of the emigrant novels, also has his grave in Norra Kyrkogården. It is visited frequently by the relatives of the millions of Swedes who settled in America.

Earlier national icons, like Carl Bellman, revered as Sweden's national poet, lie in the Klara Kyrkogård. Bellman's ballads reflected poverty, debt and hardship, his lot until patronized by King Gustav III. There are books yet to be written about Karin Goering, buried in Stockholm. Countess Karin Fock was the daughter of a Swedish baron and his Anglo-Irish wife. As a young married woman, Karin fell in love at first sight with the former commander of Baron von Richthofen's Flying Circus—the ex-First World War German fighter ace, Herman Goering. Goering was a pilot on the mail and passenger run between Berlin and Stockholm but his life reached take-off speed when he gave up his job with Svenska Luftraffik after being inspired by Hitler at a public meeting. Hitler hired Goering on the spot to command the Sturmabteilung or "brownshirts". Karin died in 1931, well before her husband became infamous and carried a jewelled marshal's baton. Herman lived long enough to be expelled from the Nazi Party by Hitler, captured by US forces and tried at Nuremberg, only to commit suicide with a phial of hidden poison the night before he was due to be executed as a war criminal.

Some of the residents of the Stockholm cemeteries achieved wider popularity dead than alive. Gunnar and Alvar Myrdal are buried together in the Garden of Remembrance in the Norra Begravningsplatsen. These social democrat apparatchiks, chiefly remembered for their ill-judged policy of population control through sterilization, tasted early fame and fortune when their economic theories were used as one of the platforms of the early welfare state. Their popularity waxes and wanes.

The most tragic grave in Stockholm is that of Anna Lindh. She is buried in the Katarina churchyard. Lindh should have been Sweden's first female prime minister. It is incredible that Sweden, the nation that is the world's foremost exponent of practical women's liberation, has yet to break

through the gender barrier where the rank of prime minister, is the prize. Lindh is commemorated by a simple granite rectangle with her birth and death dates: 19 June 1957-11 September 2003. There is a sculpture of a tiny tree with a bird resting in the crook of its branches, one of which has spring growth showing. The cemetery provides a high-tech e-note for those with palm computers or superior mobile phone connections that informs them that the Swedish foreign minister: "was stabbed in the chest, arm and stomach by an unknown assailant while out shopping in Stockholm. She died after undergoing surgery. She was 46 years old, and had been touted as the next Prime Minister of Sweden."

One Stockholm grave I avoid is the one which might have been my plot. There the bell might have tolled for me. It is a memorial to the victims of the *Estonia* disaster, dated 28 September 1994, and for the people who drowned in the Baltic Sea when the ship sank. I was pencilled in for that crossing but pulled out when my wife came down with a bad cold and didn't wish to make it worse with an overnight ferry journey to the Baltic States. What happened that night will never be known. Becky Ohlsen, in her guidebook *Stockholm* (2004), visited the site and wrote: "The monument at Gälär Kyrkogården in Stockholm has been vandalized with text saying that the sinking wasn't an accident and the Swedish Government is lying."

Chapter Twelve

LUST

HOW STOCKHOLMERS ENJOY THEMSELVES

JOY, PLEASURE AND DELIGHT

There is a semantic difference between the English word lust and *lust* in the Swedish language, which is an everyday word. Stockholm is a city whose citizens, while waiting for death's knock, seek joy, pleasure and delight. In the first edition of their Swedish-English dictionary Wenström and Harlock defined *lust* in so many contexts that it overwhelmed every other noun or verb. There was hardly any activity that did not call for lust. It was commonly used to describe joy, pleasure and delight, all so abundant in Stockholm. Lust covered the simple inclination to do something, for example "to have a bent" for making Darlarna wooden horses. It extended to the disposition to drink beer and to be garrulous thereafter. Using the word lust, Stockholmers could ask whether a partner would like a game of chess, or to go out to supper that night. An individual might have a lust for painting, for athletics or for learning French. One could be a merry dog, a boon companion, and describe this in a matter of fact way as lust.

The word "lust" sits oddly in many English contexts where it elides in Swedish and in the Stockholm consciousness. A summer house is a *lusthus*, and almost every Stockholmer has one of these. There, in the skerries or by a lake or wherever, they can be lusty, expressing lust through merry parties, singing, being jolly or even by being odd, comical or droll. A special sort of lust is experienced by lighting a bonfire—a *lusteld*. Up-to-date dentists in the years before the First World War could give their patients *lustgas*, laughing gas. When cured of their toothache, the smiling fortunate could take a *lustfärd*, pleasure trip, to a *lustpark* or public park. A special holiday trip in a steamer was called a *lustresa*, and in the plural it indicated a cheap excursion. The very rich would retire to their country seat or to a *lustslott*. Those remaining Swedish counts usually had a *lustlager*, an encampment for the diversion of a prince, but the woods be-

Fun in the *lustpark*

longed to all Stockholmers, and camping was a privilege shared by every citizen. For hundreds of years it has been legal to walk, ski, ride, cycle or jog cross private property. Using the term "everyman's right", *allemansrätt*, Stockholmers could moor their boats, swim and fish, but not net, going ashore where there were no nearby houses, and enjoy their lust for picking wildflowers. *Lusttur*, a lust turn, describes taking a stroll on the Strandvägen, a Nordic *passegiata*. If one does not have a taste for the *lusttåg*, lust train, or the outdoor life trekking away from Stockholm, eggheads can *lustvandra*, wander in the realms of learning.

Many Stockholmers like shooting, hunting and fishing. One can say with a straight face that the present King of Sweden has an entirely appropriate lust for hunting: *hans lust ar at jaga*, his lust is to hunt. If you cannot find fun, jollity, drollery and oddity in Stockholm, all summarized as lust, there is no hope for you.

The structured lust found during plentiful public holidays exists to a large extent because Stockholmers have surplus income to spend on pleasure. Despite famous fiscal fugitives, systematic and fair tax laws have redistributed wealth since the Social Democratic Party became the country's driving political force for change. During the long post-war boom Sweden became prosperous with a balance of payments surplus generated by the dominance of Swedish industry in world niche markets. The importance of making public holidays was stressed by a media compliant with government expectations. All Saints' Day is an example. It was abolished in 1772 as part of a sweep to rid Sweden of vestiges of distasteful aspects of Catholicism, as saints were no longer permitted and saint worship was considered abominable. In 1952, during the Cold War, a public relations campaign put 1 November back on the calendar as a public holiday. For a time, the government tried to redefine All Saints' Day as a time to remember war victims. But it made no sense to focus on Swedish war dead, and Stockholmers prefer to celebrate All Saints' Day as if it were Halloween, not Remembrance Day. They take a weekend break, visit their parents and spring clean their cottages. Norwegians are not in their sights. Instead, they hunt specified amounts of elk or deer and fill their Electrolux freezers with food to provide quick snacks in summer and warm memories in winter.

Stockholmers can enjoy regular scheduled lust-filled holidays throughout the year: Advent, Walpurgis Night, Lucia, Annunciation Day, Mothers' Day, Fathers' Day, All Saints' Day, Easter, Lent, Twentieth Day Knut, the Feast of Mårten's Goose, Midsummer, Whitsuntide and the August crayfish season are all cobbled together from lusts ancient and modern. St. Knut's Day is on 13 January, twenty days after Christmas Eve. St. Mårten's Goose is a goose eaten on 10 November, the eve of St. Martin's Day.

THE THRILL OF COMPETITION

When Stockholmers take a stronger than usual liking for something they add the word for strong, *stark*, before *lust*. In 1912 a strong lust was felt for athletics, which was then the rage. Count Pierre de Coubertin's vision that nothing but good could come if the athletes of all the countries of the world could be brought together on friendly fields of amateur sport brought to life the moribund ancient Olympic Games. The idea that the ideals of classical Greece could be resurrected was particularly appealing to the Swedes. The Stockholm Olympics were only preceded by modern Olympics in Athens, Paris, St. Louis and London. Stockholm's rage for

1912 Olympic Games

egalitarian Olympian athletics was equalled by the town's hostility to destructive national rivalries, jealousies and to malevolent differences of all kinds. The Social Democrats were not the first Swedes to try to eliminate considerations of wealth, political attitude, social status, race and religion.

More Olympians participated in Stockholm than ever before: a total of 2,400. A greater number of women athletes hurdled and ran, high jumped, broad jumped and hopped, skipped and jumped. Swedes won the high diving, the javelin, the cross country team race, the running, hop, step and jump and the tug o' war. They did well, as did their Finnish neighbour, despite their status then as Russian being unresolved to Finnish satisfaction. While in its short history the hitherto most acrimonious modern Olympic Games was recorded as being held in London in 1908, the first Stockholm Olympics were remembered not only by their systematic organization and peaceful sportsmanship, but because a Swede was given the gold medal for the decathlon after it was taken from an American Indian who was disqualified for non-professionalism. In 1912 Sweden won the ten-metre yachting class in a boat named *Kitty*, the team cycling road race, the high diving and gymnastics in a competition where they had an advantage, insofar as it was held under the "Swedish system". Swedes took gold medals for shooting, including areas where they were specialists—moving wild boars and running deer.

Swedes continued to derive so much pleasure from sport that by 1948 and the London Olympics in Wembley Stadium their athletes were considered by the English to be excessively prominent at the games. Although annoyed by sneers about "neutral Sweden", Swedes were at the top of the medal table (depending how one calculates top). The racist jibes about Swedes and sport resurfaced once more a couple of generations later when a Swede, Sven-Göran Eriksson, was appointed, and more or less failed, to coach England's World Cup football team to success. What would a Swede know about football? Predictably and incorrectly, the coach was panned for his perceived interest in girls, not goals, reinforcing a stubborn national stereotype.

Lusteld, getting a fancy for lighting fires, was, and is, often experienced by capital city dwellers. Stockholmers like to experience the therapeutic discomfort of peasant living on agreed set days, which allows them to keep in touch with their primal ancestral instincts. Midsummer Night has been celebrated for centuries by Swedes dancing round and jumping through huge bonfires, providing *lusteld* in abundance. Traditionally, on the morning of midsummer houses were cleaned and decorated with birch branches and leaves. A leaf market was usually set up at Riddarholm so the unfortunate few who had to stay in town over the holidays could have their twigs. Generally speaking, the raising of a maypole in a protracted and sometimes dangerous ceremony taking longer than necessary signals the onset of summer. The pagan symbolism of the midsummer maypole is obvious. Folk dances to Olof Palme's least favourite musical instrument used to accompany the maypole raising. But the general sight of pale old men with silver flowing beards and flint knives in their hands staggering about the higher ground on consecrated hills in the afterglow of pyres lit on a Midsummer Eve is over. Midsummer poles and bonfires have their roots in the heathen festival in honour of Balder. Most Swedes do not now run through the embers but there are always a few drunks with burnt toes who have retained their athletic heathenism.

Swedes often have a lust for flying the national flag, and flag frisson is deeply felt in Stockholm. Raising the Swedish flag, although done year round, has a special day set for it in the calendar. Flying the flag began in earnest in 1893 when the Swedes decided that more than the usual level of nationalism was in order. Norwegians had begun to struggle for independence from the union with Sweden from the moment they were forced to be a subject nation. Like the Irish, Norwegian nationalists had made significant progress throughout the nineteenth century, stressing the importance of language and the flag. As in Dublin, most in Oslo hoped that their union would be severed without violence. Edvard Grieg contrasted the possessive conservatism of the Swedish king and nobility with the democratic temper of the Norwegians.

The union has been over for a century, but all in Stockholm are expected to share a united glow when on 6 June the Swedish flag is flown in Skansen, as tradition has it, in the presence of the king. Free flags are distributed to national organizations, while foreign diplomats stand by and applaud. Yet it was not until the late nineteenth century that any foreign ambassador was able to fly his country's own national flag so acute were Swedish sensibilities to the symbolism involved in hanging out the national colours. It was a United States ambassador who solved the diplomatic impasse without disturbing protocol by flying the Stars and Stripes discreetly alongside the Swedish flag. Flag flying is like kite flying in Southeast Asia. Many Stockholmers have a lust to fly the flag from their flagpole as often as they can, and to chop off someone's flagpole at the base is the worst insult a neighbour can inflict in town or at a summer house. The flag question is not just Freudian, it is a signal statement of national identity and sovereignty.

Mothers' Day is altogether different. A foreign import, it was introduced to Stockholm in 1919. The government instruction booklet printed to set minimum standards for public holidays specified: "raise the Swedish flag, bring mother coffee in bed and, if possible, a *prinsesstorta*" (a pale green marzipan-coated cake filled with vanilla flavoured egg-cream). Mothers having breakfast in bed were all expected to experience pleasure, if not lust, in seeing the Swedish flag raised.

Pleasure in Stockholm is widespread and accessible because enjoyment is not class-based. Sweden is famously an egalitarian society, with every citizen formally valued and more often than not given a title. Titles comprehend the whole population, and in a way that seems not quite real to foreigners all occupational or identity designations cause the individual to visibly swell whether introduced by his or her title in a conversation in the street or, at another extreme, when announced at a reception. Anachronistic although their examples are, titles remain important in Stockholm, and visitors can still be startled by elderly gentlemen jumping to attention on first meeting, clicking their heels and asking: "Forsberg, engineer from Malmö, perhaps I can introduce myself?"

NAME DAYS

Unless they are determined hedonists, foreigners are uneasy enjoying simple lust in Stockholm. Most of it seems reserved for the locals. Stockholmers are luckier than most insofar as they can celebrate as individuals twice a year—once on their name day and once on their birth day. In Stockholm the day of the year one is born is celebrated as a name day, and the hundreds of thousands born on that day of the year with the same name always experience many different sorts of lust. Swedish Flag Day, 6 June, is also the name day of all Gustavs, celebrated in the poem by the nineteenth-century poet, Esaias Tegnér:

A sheen there was on Gustav's day,
fantastic, foreign, frivolous, you say?
Complain as we will, the sun shone then;
where were we now had it never been?
All culture stands on unfree soil;
Native barbarism was our all.
But sense, once planted, broke its iron tongue;
The singer found his note, and life was young,
Gustavian all Swedish things became.

This special name day, with its regal connotations, has been celebrated since 1772, when King Gustav III added it to the canon. But the 365 days of the year cover most eventualities, and the calendar is scrupulous in being as fair and inclusive as possible. Only Christmas Day has no name day attached. During the rest of the month, boys and girls—Oskar and Ossian, Beata and Beatrice, Lydia, Sven, Nikolaus, Angela, Virginia, Malin, Daniel, Alexander, Sten, Sixten, Gottfrid, Tomas, Stefan and Johan—can all be "merry dogs" on their name days. Being around Christmas, Adam and Eva's name days lead up to 25 December. Jewish Stockholmers are not forgotten, with Benjamin, Abraham, Isak, Israel and Moses lifting a glass to their own special twenty-four hours. All appreciate how important it is to conform to social expectation and display the sentiment of *lust* when it is applied to being jovial in this traditional celebratory context.

Although Stockholm has a large immigrant community of recent refugees who are not Christian, Muslim forenames do not yet trip easily off the tongue. While the Carl Larsson industry puts out an annual calendar that has Dick, Doris, Tony, Bert, Iris and Sylvester, along with Knut, Karl, Svea, Henrik, Tore, Bror and Nils and a couple of hundred approved other Swedish forenames, Muslim residents have not made their presence felt at the deepest level of social and community integration—the celebration of an individual's personal name day. The *Weekly Standard* investigated the paradox, and Johan Norberg suggested that the root of the problem was immigration and the country's bent towards charity. "In a fit of absent-mindedness, Sweden has suddenly become as heavily populated by minorities as any country in Europe," said the Washington-based weekly. Its third largest city, Malmö, had a population of forty per cent foreign-born, mainly from Somalia, Morocco, Iraq, Lebanon and the Kurdish areas of Turkey, while in a country of nine million about 1,080,000 were immigrants. Linguists were even detecting changes to the language with the "sing-songy, heep-de-deep-de-doo intonations" of Swedish "purged" by the "urban newcomers". "Not all of these things are necessarily threatening," said the *Weekly Standard*. The newspaper stressed that it was "important to distinguish between, on the one hand, cultural shifts (like the presence of a mammoth mosque that stands across from the ice-skating rink in Medborgar Square, smack in the middle of southern Stockholm) and internecine murders on the other." Included in the latter was the rise of honour killings. "These have generally involved girls executed by their brothers or fathers for wearing short skirts or dating Swedish men." This unfortunate trend, the paper remarked, had led to the establishment of safe houses containing mostly Muslim women on the run from irate relatives.

The Smörgåsbord
The simplicity of a bread and butter table and concern for how it looks grew from the background of poverty, when the pleasures of life were restricted to fish, potatoes, beets, cucumbers, dill, apples, cream, lingonber-

ries and mushrooms. Cooking and eating are as reassuring as mother's milk, express historical continuity and conserve a mythical, happy past in Stockholm. Those who believed in Valhalla thought of it as place where one could live forever on roast pork. Mostly Viking chopping boards were privileged if they contained a salted herring. In the Greta Garbo era Hollywood housed sufficient Swedes to annually import 800 tins of sour herring, *surströmming*, which *Time Life* described in *The Cooking of Scandinavia* as one of the world's strangest dishes and a potent expression of the saying that one man's meat is another man's poison.

Surströmming is delicious with dill, boiled potatoes and beer. Caught in May and June, the fish are placed in brine, decapitated, cleaned, left in the sun for a day, and fermented in barrels before being tinned. *Time Life* observed: "the tin will have begun to swell, and at its puffiest must be opened gingerly, like a bottle of champagne."

Not that there is much champagne served at a normal *smörgåsbord*. Like sex, the smörgåsbord has been misunderstood by foreigners who take it to be a gigantic feast, a symbol of gluttony rather than familial reassurance, a time to gorge rather than share simple domestic peace and contentment. The smörgåsbord and gluttony do come together, admittedly on the ferries from Stockholm to Finland, where travellers are inclined to ignore smörgåsbord protocol and pile their plates so full of ill chosen assortments of colonic spasm generators that they can hardly carry them to their tables. I do not doubt that the world's best smörgåsbord is served at Stockholm's Opera Cellar Restaurant. A 25-foot long table offers more than sixty selections, from herring at the cold end to anchovy and potato pie at the other. During the austerity years of the Second World War the table was reduced from ten to five dishes.

The best basic rules for a rational approach to a smörgåsbord which will not put the gastronome in an intensive care unit are straightforward. The ritual begins with herring, dill and boiled potatoes. This poses a selection problem as there are over twenty different herring treatments: marinated, smoked, with sour cream, fried and so on. A favourite is simple herring, taken by serious eaters with aquavit. Although many tourists have not worked it out, at the next course it is customary to change plates for the fish dish. The salmon is centrepiece. So much salmon is continually brought to the table by waiting staff that for some novices it seems a challenge to eat gravlax until they burst.

If you have not eaten by mistake too much liver paste, cheese, rye bread, crisp bread, raw egg yolk with parsley, onions and anchovies, sliced cucumber or hardboiled eggs with caviar, it is a mistake to stick to the gravlax and mustard sauce. Try the sliced smoked mackerel or eel, or if you are lucky the Baltic pike. The third step to take is to head for the meat, cold at first: jellied veal, roast beef, ham or tongue. The smörgåsbord is traditionally finished off with hot dishes. Meatballs are meatballs, and you can get them at any IKEA restaurant in the world; they are just as good as if a Stockholm restaurant had browned them for the unappreciative Alfred Nobel. The tastiest dish on the smörgåsbord is Jansson's Temptation, named after Erik Jansson and a baked dish of potatoes and anchovy fillets. Erik Jansson is not always spelt the same way as the recipe, but variations in spelling were common in the nineteenth century when Jansson immigrated to the United States. There he founded a colony called Bishop Hill in Illinois, and the rest of the story runs like *Babette's Feast*. The Jansson who left Sweden was a zealot and puritan, but one evening he was caught by a parishioner tucking into an anchovy and julienne potato casserole, baked with cream and onions. Jansson was disgraced and denounced, but ate happily ever after, ignoring jokes about Mrs. Jansson.

THE BISHOPS INVITE YOU IN

The bishops who did not emigrate and remained behind ate like princes of the Church. It was hard and thirsty work Christianizing Swedes. The task began in Uppsala, where an early Christian missionary found a temple dedicated to Odin in which dangled eighty-one bodies: men, horses and dogs. Animal and human blood was splashed around the temple walls. Looking for converts developed the appetite of the missionaries and bishops alike.

Stockholm has always fallen well behind the glamour appointments in the Swedish Church for those who seek the crook and mitre: Lindköping, Skara Strängnäs, Västerås, Växjö, Lund, Gothenburg, Karlstad, Härnösunds, Luleå and Visby. Swedish bishops take seriously the injunction to feed their sheep and, in passing, continue to live as if in the prosperous Middle Ages, setting the tone for high society gastronomy. According to their own coffee-table book *The Bishops Invite You In*, Swedish bishops show that they leave their daily bread and simple food to their parishioners.

The food and favourite recipes now favoured by the bishops make heady reading. Stomachs rumble, and one looks around for a bottle of wine. If you are invited to dine by the Bishop of Uppsala, expect anchovy pie and a special dessert of fresh strawberries and whipped cream. In Lindköping marinated pork steak is on the menu. In the oldest bishopric, Skara, with records reaching back to the eleventh century, the bishop prefers pancakes. In Strängnas guava cake is served. In Västerås the bishop usually invites his guests to eat layered sponge cake. Swedish bishops have a sweet tooth, as well as fast track facilities for importing tropical fruit. In Lund they drink punch parfait; in Gothenburg the Dean's Delight describes a meal comprising giant brandy snaps eaten after English-looking roast beef.

In Stockholm things are more modest, as befits the capital of a nation known for its attachment to the middle way rather than the middle-aged spread. The Bishop of Stockholm, Henrik Svenungsson, lives simply not in a palace, but an apartment, at 30 Artillerigatan. When entertaining, he usually sits six down to dine on a lace table cloth with green candles. If fourteen are invited Birgitta Svenungsson, like Henrik, prefers simple food—avocado and smoked salmon, orange and fish balls in *crème fraîche*, gravlax in a salt bath, chicken fillets with green pepper sauce and a chocolate cake for dessert.

THE FELLINI FACTOR

One does not need to be a Muslim uninvited to a bishop's palace, or dislike chocolate cake, to be unimpressed by the variety of pleasure possible in Stockholm. Stockholmers are peripatetic and when they are not abroad on business or holiday they are in their summer cottages. The vacuum is filled by foreigners now, so common in summer that Swedes complain they hardly ever hear Swedish spoken in Stockholm. Many visitors are indifferent or repelled by the local *lust*. Ernie Dingo, a television travel journalist, lost his heart to the ever present possibility of crossing a bridge and seeing water while he walked about in connection with his calling. He found Stockholm novel and exciting. His fellow Australian, Colin Simpson, did not like the sweet bread served at Swedish breakfast or the shortage of nightclubs. He described Stockholm positively as a northern Venice with a Grand Canal as wide as Sydney Harbour. He was surprised by mellow brick baroque façades with scrolled gables, describing them as "olde worlde"—picturesque to a degree he had not expected would exist in Sweden, such a "modern land". Although he had been to Stockholm many times, Simpson felt he knew it less well than cities in which he had spent less time. Perhaps, he mused, this was because it was a many sided place with so many water-divided segments.

Film director and screen writer Woody Allen lusted not only for Stockholm, but wanted to be Ingmar Bergman. Other visitors have been churlish and dismissive. Sir David Frost, for instance, imagined hell to be a place where the language was Dutch, the cooking English, the police German, the politicians Russian and the television programmes Swedish. More serious commentators have belittled Swedish social democratic achievements by labelling them Nazi and totalitarian.

The most perceptive of the group critical of Stockholm is Polar historian Roland Huntford, whose 1972 work *The New Totalitarians* became a bestseller. Huntford claimed that personality had been suppressed in Stockholm and that the collective was worshipped at the expense of the individual. He argued that Sweden was always a supplier of materials for European wars. In the age of sail Sweden provided maritime nations with pine and spruce. Copper was immediately recognized as a strategic necessity for a successful army, and Sweden had mountains of copper and iron. In his long denunciation Huntford identified only skill in engineering innovation and bureaucratic expertise as positive Swedish attributes. His final complaint was that not only was Sweden totalitarian, but it remained medieval in spirit. He concluded by damning *The Seventh Seal* as a typical example of Swedish cinema insofar as individual values and spontaneity were overshadowed by a dark, oppressive sense of destiny in a land untouched by Shakespeare, Boccaccio, Cervantes and Pushkin.

Europe's finest and not so fine minds cheerfully travelled to China or Australia but avoided the Nordic area. Charles Dickens, Lewis Carroll and H. G. Wells all made it to Moscow but not, as far as I know, to Stockholm. However, the English biographer Michael Holroyd, whose mother and grandmother were Swedish, made frequent trips to Stockholm but said that he never liked it nor fitted in. Holroyd spoke for many who shared the same reaction, both listless and lustless. He found his mother excruciatingly embarrassing when she was out of Stockholm, but, as he described in *Basil Street Blues* (1999):

When she was surrounded by family in Sweden, my mother was obliged to behave more formally. I was reminded of our large family gatherings at Easter and Christmas or on Saint Lucia's Day when I saw Ingmar Bergman's film *Fanny and Alexander* in the mid-nineteen-eighties. We preserved something of the same strict protocol of hospitality, the correct toasts and then the growing merriment and finally a soaring into surreal entertainment. It was all fantastical to me, for although everyone addressed me in English, they spoke fast incomprehensible Swedish among themselves. And then, though they were all introduced to me, my mind had somehow wandered and I did not know who most of them were anymore.

It was a relief to get back to London...

For all its beauty, Stockholm can be resisted. The Stockholmers' love of the warmth of southern Europe is not always reciprocated. Love especially often has a one-way ticket. In Fellini's autobiographical masterpiece *Amacord* (1974), which won an Academy Award for the Best Foreign Film of its time, two Italians standing outside a cinema discuss the message they have just got from a girlfriend in Stockholm. The dialogue ran:

Here is a telegram.
Lollo, read Silver Streak's telegram from Stockholm!
COME IMMEDIATELY I CAN'T LIVE WITHOUT YOU INGE.
Is she the horsey one?
So will you go?
It's cold up there now.

Fellini's gigolo decided to stay at home, anticipating that his love would grow cold in the chilly weather. Many others have the same fears, and worry about getting a frosty reception. Stockholmers are known for taking themselves and everything else seriously, which sometimes makes them heavy going. There is no evading the sense of purpose that drives the Swedish community. A perspicacious poet writing in *Punch's Almanac* in the 1930s produced a full-page poem illustrated by sixteen cartoons and given the title "Reforming the Butterfly". The verse showed how far Stockholmers would go, using their will power and intelligence, to improve things, to build a better roller bearing, longer-lasting steel, a more powerful explosive and a superior system of political organization, to achieve the impossible. The light-hearted lines captured the pervasive urge to improve things. Not even butterflies were safe from attention in such an ambivalent city.

Reforming the Butterfly

Clarissa was chaste, Clarissa was careful,
Clarissa could promise, Clarissa "forgot,"
Clarissa was dressed on her triumphs when tearful,
But could she cook Breakfast? Clarissa could NOT.

Clarissa was chic, Clarissa was charming,
Clarissa could prattle, Clarissa could plot,
Clarissa the Cat could be, oh! so disarming,
But could she cook Luncheon? Clarissa could NOT.

Clarissa could criticise Polo or Poker,
Clarissa could handle a horse or a yacht,
Clarissa could browbeat her Banker or Broker,
But could she cook Dinner? Clarissa could NOT.

Clarissa was cute, Clarissa was clever,
Clarissa once chiselled Chanel from a Scot,
Clarissa succeeded in every endeavour,
But could she cook supper? Clarissa could NOT.

Dyspeptic and Bankrupt poor Carlos grew gaga,
Till one day "Eureka! I've got it," he cried
"Clarissa, mon chou, I will buy you an Aga—
The Cooker which Generates Culinary Pride."

Her Aga cooks food till it tastes like Ambrosia,
Her Aga's so simple, sweet-tempered and smart,
Her Aga's so cool her cheeks never grow rosier,
Clarissa finds cooking an Elegant Art.

Clarissa now caters and cooks to perfection,
Clarissa's found joy in a Wifely Career,
While Carlos again has his Banker's Affection,
For fuel for his Aga costs £4 a year.

Further Reading

Anderson, I. A., *History of Sweden*. Oxford: Oxford University Press, 1968.

Austin, P. B., *On Being Swedish: Reflections Towards a Better Understanding of the Swedish Character*. London: Secker & Warburg, 1968.

Baedeker, K., *Norway, Sweden and Denmark: Handbook for Travellers*. London: Dalau & Co., 1903.

Berg, J. and Lagercrantz, B., *Scots in Sweden*. Stockholm: P. A. Nordsted & Sons, 1962.

Bergman, I. and Burgess, A., *Ingrid Bergman: My Story*. London: Sphere, 1980.

Bloch, M., *The Duke of Windsor's War*. London: Weidenfeld & Nicolson, 2003.

Brown, D., *The Cooking of Scandinavia*. Amsterdam: Time Inc, 1969.

Buckley, V., *Christina Queen of Sweden*. London: Harper Perennial, 2005.

Carlgren, W. M., *Swedish Foreign Policy during the Second World War*. London: Benn, 1977.

Childs, M. W., *Sweden: The Middle Way on Trial*. New Haven: Yale University Press, 1980.

Constantini, C., *Fellini on Fellini*. London: Faber & Faber, 1994.

Cornwallis, G., *Sweden*. London: Lonely Planet, 2000.

Davey, P., *Arts and Crafts Architecture*. London: Phaidon, 1995.

De Botton, A., *The Architecture of Happiness*. London: Hamish Hamilton, 2006.

Derry, T. K., *A History of Scandinavia*. London: George Allen & Unwin, 1979.

Doherty, P., *A Beginner's Guide to Winning the Nobel Prize*. Melbourne: The Miegunyah Press, 2005.

Elder, N. C., *Government in Sweden: The Executive at Work*. Elkins Park: Franklin Book Co., 1970.

Fant, K., *Alfred Nobel: A Biography*. New York: Arcade Publishing, 1993.

Fox, A. B., *The Power of Small States: Diplomacy in World War II*. Chicago: University of Chicago Press, 1959.

Friis, Henning K., ed., *Scandinavia between East and West*. New York: Cornell University Press, 1950.

Fry, J., *Limits of the Welfare State: Critical Views on Post-War Sweden*. Farnborough: Saxon House, 1978.

Futrell, M., *Northern Underground*. London: Faber & Faber, 1963.

Griffiths, T., *Scandinavia: At War with Trolls*. London: Hurst, 2004.

Hallendorff, C. and Shuck, A., *History of Sweden*. New York: AMS Press, 1929.

Harvey, L. E., *Samuel Beckett: Poet and Critic*. New Jersey: Princeton University Press, 1970.

Heckscher, E. F., *An Economic History of Sweden*. Cambridge, Mass: Harvard University Press, 1968.

Helgeson, S., *New Design in Sweden*. Helsingborg: Swedish Institute, 2007.

Hovde, B. J., *The Scandinavian Countries, 1720-1865: The Rise of the Middle Classes*. Boston: Chapman and Grimes, 1972.

Huntford, R., *The New Totalitarians*. New York: Stein & Day, 1972.

Jones, M. and Olwig, K. R., *Nordic Landscapes: Region and Belonging on the Northern Edge of Europe*. Minneapolis: University of Minnesota Press, 2008.

Jutikkala, E. and Pirinen, K., *A History of Finland*. New York: Praeger, 1974.

Lamm, M., *August Strindberg*. New York: Benjamin Blom, 1971.

Langmead, J., ed, *Wallpaper City Guide to Stockholm*. London: Phaidon, 2006.

Larsson, C., *A Farm*. New York: G.P. Putnam's Sons, 1976.

Larsson, C., *Our Family*. London: Methuen, 1980.

Larsson, C., *Our Home*. London: Methuen, 1976.

Larsson, S., *The Girl with the Dragon Tattoo*. London: MacLehose Press, 2008.

Leitenberg, M., *Soviet Submarine Operations in Swedish Waters, 1980-1986*. New York: Praeger, 1987.

Lindqvist, H., *A History of Sweden: From Ice Age to Our Age*. Stockholm: Norstedts Forlag, 2002.

Mankell, H., *Firewall*. New York: The New Press, 1977.

Mankell, H., *The Dogs of Riga*. London: Vintage, 2002.

Marr, D., *Patrick White: A Life*. Sydney: Vintage, 1992.

Marr, D., ed, *Patrick White: Letters.* Sydney: Random House, 1994.

Morris, J., *Over Europe.* London: Faber and Faber, 2006.

Mosey, C., *Cruel Awakening: Sweden and the Killing of Olof Palme.* New York: Palgrave Macmillan, 1991.

Myer, M., *Strindberg: A Biography.* Oxford: Oxford University Press, 1987.

Nemirovsky, I., *Suite Française.* London: Chatto & Windus, 2006.

Ohlsen, B., *Stockholm.* London: Lonely Planet, 2004.

Pauli, H. E., *Alfred Nobel: Dynamite King, Architect of Peace.* London: Nicholson & Watson, 1947.

Pearson, M. P., Sharples, N. and Symonds, J., *South Uist Archaeology.* London: Tempus, 2004.

Proctor, J. and Roland, N., *Sweden.* London: Rough Guides, 2003.

Runblom, H. and Norman, H., *From Sweden to America.* Minneapolis: University of Minnesota Press, 1976.

Samuelsson, K., *From Great Power to Welfare State: 300 Years of Swedish Social Development.* London: Allen and Unwin, 1968.

Scase, R., *Social Democracy in Capitalist Society: Working Class Politics in Britain and Sweden.* London: Croom Helm, 1977.

Scobbie, I., *Sweden.* London: Benn, 1977.

Selinko, A., *Désirée.* London: William Heinemann, 1954.

Simpson, C., *The Viking Circle.* Sydney: Angus and Robertson, 1966.

Stolpe, S., *Christina of Sweden.* New York: Macmillan, 1966.

Strindberg, A., *Confessions of a Fool.* London: S. Swift, 1912.

Strindberg, A., *The Plays.* Translated by Michael Meyer. London: Secker & Warburg, 1964.

Sundberg, I., *Sweden: Its People and Its Industry.* Stockholm: P. Norstedt, 1904.

Walker, A., *Garbo: A Portrait.* New York: Macmillan, 1980.

Weibull, J., *Swedish History in Outline.* Stockholm: Swedish Institute, 1993.

Wenström, O. E. and Harlock, W. E., *A Swedish English Dictionary.* Stockholm: P. Norsted and Sons, 1912.

Wikander, U., *Kreuger's Match Monopolies, 1925-1930: Case Studies in Market Control through Public Monopolies.* Stockholm: LiberFörlag, 1979.

Index of Literary & Historical Names

Index of Places & Landmarks